Customer Care
Excellence

How to Create
an Effective
Customer Focus

4th Edition

Sarah Cook

RECOMMENDED BY
INSTITUTE OF DIRECTORS

KOGAN
PAGE

First published by Kogan Page Limited in 1992 as *Customer Care*
Fourth edition 2002
Reprinted 2003

120 Pentonville Road
London N1 9JN
United Kingdom

22883 Quicksilver Drive
Sterling VA 20166-2012
USA

www.kogan-page.co.uk

This book has been endorsed by the Institute of Directors.

The endorsement is given to selected Kogan Page books which the IoD recognises as being of specific interest to its members and providing them with up-to-date, informative and practical resources for creating business success. Kogan Page books endorsed by the IoD represent the most authoritative guidance available on a wide range of subjects including management, finance, marketing, training and HR.

The views expressed in this book are those of the author and are not necessarily the same as those of the Institute of Directors.

British Library Cataloguing in Publication Data

A CIP record for this book is available from the British Library.

ISBN 0 7494 3792 8

Typeset by Saxon Graphics Ltd, Derby
Printed and bound in Great Britain by Clays Ltd, St Ives plc

Contents

Preface

In today's competitive, fast-paced and global economy, the growing demand from service-driven organisations for practical guidelines in developing a customer focus has given me the impetus to write this book.

The contents are based on my own hands-on experience of helping many organisations, both big and small, become customer orientated.

This book is intended to be practical. It is designed to be used as a reference and source of ideas for managers of businesses who wish to implement service quality as a means of competitive advantage, as well as for those managers in organisations who may already have developed a strategy and wish to implement this further.

The book outlines how to plan, introduce and sustain a programme designed to increase customer satisfaction and retention.

Technology can help create a customer orientation, yet in essence, service is a 'people' issue. How well individuals are inspired, enabled, motivated and recognised by their leaders and managers counts most towards creating a company-wide customer orientation.

I believe strongly in the ownership of service initiatives by service providers in order for customer service to become a way of organisation life.

Experience shows that the success of a service philosophy depends on continuous commitment to service improvements.

I hope you will use this book to measure how customer focused your organisation is. I recommend that you regularly review what you have achieved, discuss openly how you could do better and develop a plan of action so that improvements in service quality can be made on a continuous basis.

Sarah Cook
The Stairway Consultancy
e-mail: sarah@thestairway.co.uk

Acknowledgements

Many thanks to all the businesses whose quest for service excellence and customer satisfaction have enabled me to utilise them as examples of best practice in this book.

My special thanks also to Joyce and Sue for all their hard work in typing this manuscript.

1

An Introduction to Customer Care

We have become a service economy. Yet few organisations are truly delighting their customers.

This chapter introduces the concept of service quality and defines what this means to the customer.

At the end of this and subsequent chapters, a checklist is provided to allow you to take *practical* steps to develop and sustain a customer focus within your organisation.

SERVICE IN A COMPETITIVE ENVIRONMENT

Over recent years organisations have placed increasing emphasis on customer service as a means of gaining competitive advantage.

Who would have imagined 15 years ago, for example, that organisations such as Amazon.com could capture market share from the high street by offering the customer a wide selection of value-for-money products backed by a quality service? Or that companies such as First Direct could fundamentally challenge the traditional way customers do business with their bank by offering a friendly, efficient service 24 hours a day, 365 days a year?

In 1954 Peter Drucker wrote in *The Practice of Management*: 'There is only one valid definition of business purpose: to create a customer.' He said that an organisation's ability to remain in business is a function of its competitiveness and its ability to win customers from the competition. The customer is the foundation of the business and keeps it in existence.

As competition has become more global and more intense, many organisations have realised that they cannot compete on price alone. It is in these marketplaces that many companies have developed a strategy of providing superior customer care to differentiate their products and services. Surveys suggest that service-driven companies can charge up to 9 per cent more for the products and services they provide. They grow twice as fast as the average company and have the potential to gain up to 6 per cent market share.

Through undertaking a major change programme which was intended to focus on the customer, The Royal Bank of Scotland went from near to making a loss to a £200 million incremental profit within two years. Through focusing on the customer, retailer Tesco managed to increase its profitability and market share, becoming the market leader in a highly competitive and cost-conscious marketplace.

Financial services is typical of many sectors in its change of focus towards customer service. The nature and number of competitors and the ability of retailers, banks, building societies, insurance brokers, estate agents and other financial service companies to offer similar products at similar prices has led to increasing emphasis being placed on personal service as a means of adding value to customers. However, like very many other market sectors, few organisations succeed in leading the way.

Benefits of a customer-centred organisation

In increasingly competitive marketplaces, best-practice organisations have demonstrated clear benefits of focusing on the customer. Excellent service enable a business to:

- differentiate itself from the competition;
- improve its image in the eyes of the customer;
- minimise price sensitivity;
- improve profitability;
- increase customer satisfaction and retention;
- achieve a maximum number of advocates for the company;
- enhance its reputation;
- ensure products and services are delivered 'right first time';
- improve staff morale;
- increase employee satisfaction and retention;
- increase productivity;
- reduce costs;
- encourage employee participation;
- create a reputation for being a caring, customer-oriented company;
- foster internal customer/supplier relationships;
- bring about continuous improvements to the operation of the company.

THE CHANGING NATURE OF CUSTOMER SERVICE

Recent years have seen enormous pressure on service organisations to improve the way they do business with their customers. A lack of good service even risks public humiliation as the Passport Office found to its cost when its Service Charter mark was withdrawn for inefficient delays in issuing passports during a busy summer period. The challenge for a business today is to 'inject' innovation into its life-blood so that it becomes part of its very being.

Successful service organisations constantly strive for higher levels of customer service. When online bookseller Amazon was established, its founder recognised that it could not offer comfy sofas or coffee to those who browse through its virtual bookstore, so it set about finding innovative ways to enhance the customer experience.

Only a few organisations have been able to do this successfully, but their success is noteworthy. First Direct revolutionised the retail banking sector with its introduction of a telephone banking service. Its focus on speed, convenience, quality and service resulted in 38 per cent of new customers being referred from existing ones. Sandwich chain, Pret à Manger, which started in one store in Victoria, now owns over 500 outlets. It puts it success down to a 'relationship of trust' with its customers, attention to detail and constant innovation.

CHANGING CUSTOMER BEHAVIOUR AND EXPECTATION

Today's consumers are increasingly sophisticated, educated, confident and informed. They have high expectations of the service they want to receive. They want greater choice and will not be 'sold to' or manipulated.

Value for time

Already, the 24-hour society is here. A report by Future Foundation predicts that, by 2007, over 2 million people in the UK will be working between 9 pm and 11 pm and around a million will work between 2 am and 5 am. In a survey commissioned jointly by BT and First Direct, over 50 per cent of respondents wanted pharmacies and public transport accessible 24 hours a day. A third of those surveyed also wanted 24-hour access to a wide range of other retail outlets and sports, leisure and entertainment facilities.

Supermarkets are leading the way in 24-hour shopping. Asda opened the first 24-hour stores in 1994. Tesco had 81 round-the-clock stores in 1999, and in addition offered home shopping from over 100 stores. The home shopping service allows people to order goods over the Internet; the Web page displays each customer's most frequently purchased items at the beginning of the list to aid selection and the order is relayed to a computerised trolley where on-board computers guide an order-picking assistant on the most efficient route round the store to collect the groceries.

Consumers are increasingly mobile and are looking for value for time. MORI carried out research for mobile phone operators Orange and found that a third of small companies and 40 per cent of medium companies have employees who are consistently mobile. They are reliant upon technology to keep in touch with their office and the customer. For example, Veeder-Root is a company that manufactures, installs and services 8,000 instruments that measure petrol levels in the underground tanks below many of the UK's petrol stations. Field engineers are supplied with a laptop computer linked to an Orange handset so that they always have access to the latest customer information. They can call for the latest customer report in advance of each visit and diagnose problems on site without having to travel back to the head office. This process has resulted in increased levels of productivity and customer and employee satisfaction.

Consumer rights

Today's customers know their rights and are more likely to make their opinions known if they feel that these have been violated. Research by the Henley Centre found that 35 per cent of adults in the UK agree that they love to complain every now and then. The survey also showed that 45 per cent of adults had complained in person about poor service (up from 39 per cent in 1997) and 42 per cent on the telephone (up from 27 per cent in 1997).

A MORI poll shows that a clear majority of customers claim that social responsibility influences their choice of products and services. Consumer concern over human-rights violation and environmental abuse has endangered sales of brands as diverse as Nike, Coca-Cola and Shell. The debate over genetically modified food has brought together a wide range of consumer interest groups to stop the development of such foods.

What is emerging is a 'pull' scenario in which the customer is becoming empowered. This is facilitated by new media, where Internet 'infomediaries' (information intermediaries who search for the right trading partner, making comparisons and completing transactions) offer the consumer greater choice, and Web sites have the chance to receive opinions from customers which can be expressed to a far-ranging audience. Working on the basis that most airlines fly at 65–70 per cent capacity, Priceline.com allows the consumer to name the price that they are prepared to pay for airline travel. It then contacts the customer within the hour with the option of a non-refundable ticket at the price the customer has stipulated. According to an Oftel survey of July 2001, 45 per cent of UK homes had access to the Internet. This equates to 10 million homes and 33 million people. E-mail too has been widely adopted, substantially replacing both the fax and the phone as a means of both global and local communication.

One-to-one service

It is no longer financially viable for many companies to 'mass market' their products or services. A DTI and CBI survey found that the real differentiators in marketing are innovative and customised products and customer support. Customisation and individualisation are key. Online bookseller Amazon knows the purchase histories of individuals, and can offer a bespoke service to the customer. Levi's offers a customised section in-store where you can make a product personal and unique.

Smart competition

The advent of increasing globalisation allows organisations to compete on a regional, national and pan-continental basis. Amazon.com has broken traditional consumer purchasing patterns on a global scale via the use of technology. Today, its market share is threatened by cyber competitors. The message is clear: nobody can rest on their laurels. Competition is global, not local.

Technology

One of the greatest drivers of change is the range of possibilities opened up by the increased use of technology. From buying products or services online to using the Internet to pay bills via a mobile phone, the use of technology can potentially revolutionise organisations' interface with customers.

Chubb Insurance Group processes its claims on the spot; Chubb representatives visit a customer's premises, input data via a laptop computer and print out a cheque there and then. US home delivery retailer, Peabody, uses its customer database to remind individuals in advance when they are likely to be running out of household provisions.

Cisco, the US manufacturer of networking equipment, has empowered its customers to serve themselves using its Web site in real time. Customers can instantly access their purchasing information on the Web site. The company estimates that, in one year, this way of working saved Cisco $268 million, of which $125 million was saved on customer support (customers supported themselves using the Web), $8 million on recruitment and training (as this was transferred to the Web), $85 million on software distribution costs (as software was downloaded over the Web) and $50 million by moving to paperless information distribution.

CUSTOMER RETENTION

As customers begin to experience a better service their expectations rise. Furthermore, the service experienced is transferable in the mind of the customer. The customer makes conscious and unconscious comparisons between different service experiences – irrespective of industry sector. Customers' expectation, for example, of the service experience they will receive from a car rental service may be based not only on their expectation and experience of the service itself but also experiences they may have had in the high street or on the Internet, with other car rental companies and other leisure and travel organisations.

A company's ability to attract and retain new customers therefore is a function not only of its product or product offering but also the way it services its existing customers and the reputation it creates within and across marketplaces.

Many organisations, however, overlook the potential of *existing* customers to develop their business.

Caring for existing customers

Statistics underline just how crucial retaining customers can be:

- Reducing customer defections can boost profits by 25–85 per cent (Harvard Business School).
- The price of acquiring new customers can be five times greater than the cost of keeping current ones (US Office of Consumer Affairs).

- The return on investment to marketing for existing customers can be up to seven times more than to prospective customers (Ogilvy & Mather Direct).

Yet, while most companies regard the acquisition of new customers as a crucial element in their sales strategy, very few of them record customer retention rates and even fewer analyse the reasons why previously satisfied customers become dissatisfied and go. Frederick Reichheld states statistics for the average attrition rates in US companies:

- 50 per cent of customers are lost in a five-year period;
- 50 per cent of employees are lost in four years;
- replacement customers will not contribute to profit unless they are retained for at least three years.

Only best-practice organisations, such as Toyota, have customer retention levels higher than 70 per cent. Put another way, most organisations lose significantly more than 30 per cent of their customers before, or at the time of a repurchase decision, mainly through poor service. The only reason market shares do not drop is because competitors are usually in the same position and are losing customers to their competitors! The result is a constant churn of dissatisfied customers looking for a company in which they can put their faith.

Research conducted by the Tarp Organization in the US demonstrates that service is a key determinant in choice of product. Its importance increases however when consumers are asked why they *change* products:

Reason for choice of product –
7 per cent technical specifications
50 per cent manufacturers' response and liability.

Reason for changing product –
8 per cent quality or cost
40 per cent dissatisfied with service.

A customer's reasons for initial purchase decisions, therefore, can be based on both tangible and intangible factors, the service features relating to both performance and a sense of caring:

Tangible	**Intangible**
Performance	Sense of caring
Quality	Courtesy
Reliability	Willingness to help
Cost	Ability to problem solve.

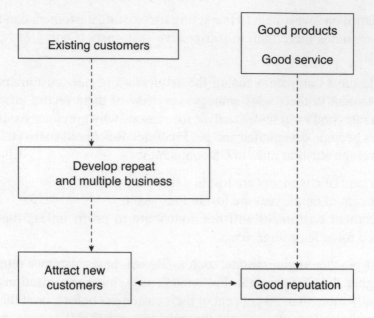

Figure 1.1 The power of existing customers

In the car market, where the value of items is high and purchase frequency low, research shows that it can cost up to 17 times as much to attract a new customer as it does to keep an old one.

If the company can develop repeat and multiple business relationships with existing customers, it is more able to maximise both its sales overheads and resources, as Figure 1.1. shows.

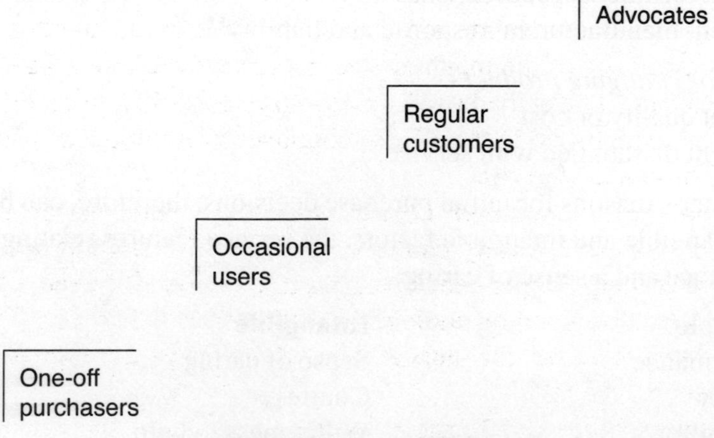

Figure 1.2 Loyalty ladder

The loyalty ladder

Most service organisations' customer bases consist of those people who use products or services on a more or less frequent basis. Some customers for example may only have a relationship once with the company at one extreme; at the other, customers will use the organisation's products or services on a regular basis.

Customers' relationships with the business can be depicted in terms of a loyalty ladder, shown in Figure 1.2. The more advocates you have, the better your retention rates and long-term profitability.

Reasons for developing long-term relationships with customers

On average it is estimated to cost five times as much to attract a new customer as it does to keep an old one. Long-term relationships with customers are therefore more profitable because:

- The cost of acquiring new customers can be high.
- Loyal customers tend to spend more and cost less to serve.
- Satisfied customers are likely to recommend your products and services.
- Advocates of a company are more likely to pay premium prices to a supplier they know and trust.
- Retaining existing customers prevents competitors from gaining market share.

Loyalty programmes

In recent years competitive markets have been flooded with customer loyalty programmes. Some of the best-known schemes are the frequent-flier programmes of the major airlines and loyalty schemes introduced by food retailers. During the last 10 years, more than 150 loyalty programmes have been established in the UK, issuing over 50 million cards and costing over £3 billion in rewards.

According to *Customer Loyalty Today*, 51 per cent of all British shoppers possess a loyalty card and of those who shop at supermarkets which offer them, 70 per cent have a card. Everyone it seems is launching loyalty schemes, sending individually addressed letters and customised promotions to offer the appearance of building a relationship with customers.

However, observed data and predicted norms show that few buyers are 100 per cent loyal in a year and those who are tend to be light buyers of the product or service. In reality customer loyalty may be divided among a number of brands. Customers will regularly buy from a repertoire of goods and services within a given field. Therefore customer loyalty programmes may engender behavioural loyalty but they may not guarantee attitudinal loyalty when a competitive brand develops its own loyalty schemes or the customer cashes in his or her rewards: they may be as susceptible to changing products or services as ever. Furthermore, reward schemes may change the way customers think about the product but not necessarily in a positive way. For example, they may come to expect rewards on an ongoing basis.

Frederick Reichheld, director of US company Bain, writing in the *Harvard Business Review*, says,

> Creating a loyalty base system requires a radical departure from traditional business thinking. It puts creating customer value rather than maximising profits and shareholder value at the centre of business strategy and demands significant changes in business practice.

Reichheld says this means recognising that companies have to target the right customers – those whose loyalty can be developed, and not those who are easier to attract by cutting prices. Smart organisations such as Tesco target increased purchase and repeat visits by analysing usage and buying patterns.

Customer lifetime value

Customer lifetime values enable an organisation to calculate the net present value of the profit the business will realise on a customer over a given period of time. It is an immensely powerful tool because it allows companies to work out how many transactions it will take to recoup the initial investment in attracting and servicing each new customer and generate a worthwhile return.

When companies invest in programmes to strengthen customer loyalty they can therefore do so knowing whether the resulting changes in purchase behaviour will increase the profit derived from each customer. Customer lifetime value is calculated by working out the customer retention value and average annual revenue to arrive at a total revenue figure from which cost can be detracted to arrive at a gross profit – or lifetime value for each customer.

Customer lifetime values have become a cornerstone in the transformation of ScotRail's marketing strategy which has reversed the long-term decline in passenger numbers. Using a new customer database and a lifetime framework model the company has been able to quantify the cause and effect relationship between service performance and retention rates. This in turn has enabled it to calculate likely changes to lifetime values in a broad range of scenarios and shape its customer service strategies accordingly.

Using calculations of lifetime values, US car insurers discovered that with certain segments of young drivers it took 10 years to break even, but only 10–15 per cent would stay that long, and it takes at least 4 years before most US insurance companies break even on the average customer. But one company's bad customer can be another's money-spinner. American Car Insurance Company, USA, enjoys a remarkable 98 per cent retention rate in car insurance for US military officers. The reason for this success is the company's responsiveness to its market and the development of a system tailored to its customers' needs.

It is generally accepted that mobile populations are inherently disloyal. Analysis of demographics and previous buying history gives some indication of a customer's inherent loyalty. People who buy because of personal referral tend to be more loyal than those who buy because of an ad. Those who buy at the standard price are more loyal than those who buy on price promotion. Research also shows that home owners, middle-aged people and rural populations tend to be more loyal customers than other sectors of the population.

Creating goodwill

The relationship an organisation creates with its existing customers determines the 'goodwill' customers feel towards the company and hence the quality of its reputation.

Research conducted by British Airways indicated that experiences passengers have with staff play a major part in generating goodwill. The survey showed that human relations with passengers are twice as important as operational factors. It also demonstrated that bad experiences can destroy goodwill more than positives add to it. Although the main service arena which passengers experience is in flight, cabin crew, ground staff and others can also upset goodwill by unhelpful behaviour.

Research indicated that the main sources of gaining positive goodwill were:

- *Making the best of the occasional and inevitable bad experiences* – eg delays, bad weather, running out of food, drink or duty-free items, empathising with problems and turning them to advantage. The study also indicated that the airline could generate more goodwill by dealing effectively with the mishaps such as lost baggage, than it could if nothing had gone wrong in the first place.
- *Showing and demonstrating concern for others* – children, old people, the disabled and anxious. There is a vicarious satisfaction in seeing the quality of caring which is available even if not required personally. It is an unspoken reassurance to every passenger.

  Virtually without exception passengers interviewed in depth indicated heightened levels of anxiety concerning flying. It was the 'hardbitten' businessmen more than any others who described greater satisfaction in seeing children being taken care of, given presents, etc.
- *Encouraging, reinforcing, wishing customers a 'good trip' or a 'good holiday'* – even if it was recognised as 'automatic' like the Americanstyle 'Have a nice day'. There appears to be an almost magical value in a good wish quite out of proportion to its face value. When the staff are there and visible, giving a touch of personal contact (for example by using their names), the experience is lifted out of the machine- and system-dominated routine and the passenger is less likely to feel submerged in a faceless, mindless crush.
- *Unsolicited 'giving'* by the staff reinforces this further, through, for example, spontaneous talking, sitting next to a passenger and sharing conversation, unscheduled pilot comments, the appearance of the captain and visits to the flight deck. These are recognised as rare 'treats' but need to be seen to happen from time to time 'if not to me, then at least available'.
- *The closed confinement of the aircraft* and the total lack of control of the passenger to affect what is happening plays heavily on major areas of human anxiety. This kind of atmosphere is a 'hot-bed' whereby small experiences, which in other contexts would be shrugged off, can blow up out of proportion. Difficulty in putting hand luggage in a locker, spillage of drinks or the way in which trays are handed out can all become foci for anxiety, a bad omen for the trip or a way to relieve feeling.
- *Problem-solving by staff* is important, particularly asking about the problem and showing empathy and understanding (which can be all that's needed to reassure taut feelings).

● *Giving factual information* – actually offering solutions about connections, services, check-in queries, drinks available, seats, feeling unwell, etc, has a dual benefit: the rational content and the emotional message: 'your problems count – you are an individual not simply another bit of cargo whose transport from A to B is organised by the airlines'.

This research demonstrated that the way customers are handled by members of staff creates a lasting impression of the organisation.

For airlines, therefore, personal service is a determining factor in creating goodwill among customers.

Product/service continuum

Traditionally, the importance an organisation places on providing a good service to its customers increases as the product it sells becomes less tangible. So, for example, when a customer chooses to purchase a dishwasher, after-sales service is only one of the deciding factors. However, when a customer is choosing an accountant or a doctor, personal service is a very important factor in his or her choice (Figure 1.3).

WHAT IS EXCELLENT SERVICE?

We have seen that the ability to provide an excellent service is a prerequisite of both attracting and retaining customers. But what constitutes good service?

Most people's definitions will be based on personal experience. The garage which unexpectedly provides complimentary umbrellas to its customers when they come to collect their cars and it's raining, the newsagent who gives the customer a free sweet when they come to pay their newspaper bill – these would be seen by many as good service.

Ask anyone for their opinions and you will find that, even when discussing the service received from one organisation alone, customers'

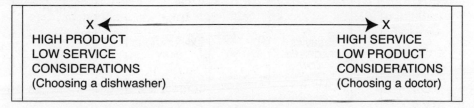

Figure 1.3 Product/service continuum

expectations and experiences can vary. One person's shining example of the treatment he or she has received can be another person's horror story. Yet it is the perception of each customer that counts. The customers' perception is their reality. Customer service is about *perceptions*: it is often a subjective and intangible experience.

As Professor Levitt points out: 'The customer is aware only of failure, of dissatisfaction, not of success and satisfaction.'

The perception of the service which customers receive is dependent upon their *expectations*. If the treatment which the customer receives is *better* than his or her expectations, this is excellent service. If the treatment which the customer receives is *less* than his or her expectations, this constitutes bad service (Figure 1.4).

Under-promise, over-deliver

To provide excellent service, therefore, an organisation needs to *exceed* customer expectations. Numerous studies demonstrate that customers' expectations can often be conditioned by the service providers themselves.

If a company tells a customer that its service engineer will call between 9 am and 1 pm and the service engineer turns up at 1.15 pm, this is seen as bad service. The company has conditioned the customer's expectations and these have been disappointed. It is rumoured that when customers wait in queues in Disney attractions, the published waiting time is always five minutes more than the actual waiting time, so customers' expectations are exceeded.

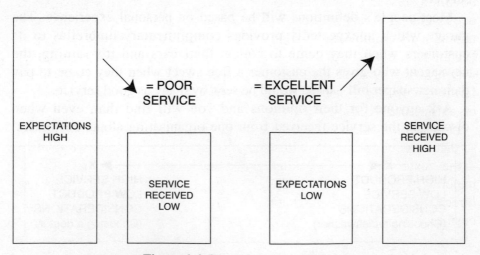

Figure 1.4 Exceeding expectations

An important factor in providing a good service therefore is always keep to promises and not to guarantee things which you cannot deliver. To provide excellent service an organisation needs to *under-promise, over-deliver*. As Tom Peters says, 'We can no longer afford to merely satisfy the customer. To win today, you have to delight and astound your customers with products and services that exceed their expectations.'

PERSONAL VERSUS MATERIAL SERVICE

Further research shows that customers want to deal with people they can trust – people who are knowledgeable and technically able and at the same time friendly and polite to the customer.

In providing training to staff to improve customer service, organisations often focus on the 'hard' skills – product knowledge, technical skills and administration, without bringing about a change in attitude in the way staff deal with customers personally.

Research also shows that what is memorable to the customer in terms of service experience is the personal touch rather than the material aspect of the service – for example the physical environment in which a customer may buy a piece of equipment is less memorable than the way in which the member of staff dealt with the customer's concerns.

To provide excellent service a balance is needed between both personal and technical or material needs.

Often a service provider cannot be separated from the service. When buying a service customers are buying the whole person. The number one challenge in any service organisation is to win both the hearts and minds of its employees. Problems occur when an organisation's service becomes so 'automated' that there is no human or personal element to the way in which customers are treated. Encouraging staff to go that one bit further for the customer is one of the greatest difficulties facing service organisations.

Organisations such as Disney train their staff to 'live' the Disney role so that the ethic is brought to life by their staff, the 'cast' as they are known – the customers are the audience. Gallup carried out a study in six major business sectors in the United States. It found that employees were three times more powerful than any other factor in influencing repeat business.

Developing a relationship

The social interchange between the customer and the service provider and the way this process is managed is pivotal to achieving excellent customer service (Figure 1.5).

Theodore Levitt of the Harvard Business School equates giving a good service with building a long-term relationship, or relationship marketing. He says:

> . . . The sale – merely consummates the courtship, at which point the marriage begins. How good the marriage is, depends on how well the seller manages the relationship. The quality of the marriage, determines whether there will be continued and expanded business or troubles and divorce.

Troubles and divorce occur, for example, when customers switch suppliers or changes their account. Customers, therefore, must be treated as individuals. They want to be valued and to feel their custom is important. When organisations provide a uniform standard of service, irrespective of customers' needs, there is a danger that customers may form the impression that they are just another account number, rather than a valued individual. This impression is often compounded when contacting call centres where the first thing the service advisor asks is the customer's account number, not name. As the head of training of a well-known service organisation said: 'You can train monkeys to smile and establish eye contact, but what happens when there is a non-standard requirement?'

EMBRACING CHANGE

In her book, *Customer Capitalism*, Sandra Vandermerwe, Professor of Economics at Imperial College, London, argues that today's successful companies will sustain competitive advantage through fundamentally

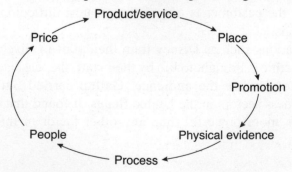

Figure 1.5 Developing customer relationships

transforming their businesses rather than maintaining the status quo. This will involve finding new ways of doing things both for and with customers.

Companies are awakening to the need for total change – IBM has moved from hardware into services in response to consumer demand, while British Telecom has moved from fixed voice telephone calls to data communication.

Autoglass, the replacement vehicle-glass company, is an example of an organisation that has used customer service to drive its business performance. When the company first started operating in the UK, a customer with a broken windscreen had to get three quotations from different windscreen companies before their glass was repaired. These needed to be approved by the motorist's insurance company before the work could proceed. Even then, it was the motorist who paid the windscreen-replacement company. Invariably, the repairers only worked from 9 am to 5 pm and only on weekdays.

Autoglass created a 24-hour centralised call centre, using only the second 0800 number to be issued in the UK (the first was to British Airways), which provided a round-the-clock replacement-glass service. This was followed by an agreement with insurers to directly recommend their policyholders to use Autoglass. From the customer's perspective, this cut out the need to obtain separate quotes, and also the need to pay for the window replacement. In addition, Autoglass introduced a mobile replacement service which enabled the work to be carried out at the motorist's home or place of work with guaranteed appointment times. These and other innovations were introduced as a result of reviews of service levels which were carried out, taking the form of independent surveys conducted on a regular basis, using 12,000 customers.

CONTACT CENTRES

What started as an experiment in the financial services sector has now spread to most major industries; the standard practice of using call centres (more recently called contact centres as they frequently deal with e-mail, written as well as telephone requests) in retailing, telecommunications, entertainment, utilities and travel is rapidly spreading to the public sector. Ease of contact, convenience and speed of service are the main benefits to the customer of using a contact centre.

The value of expenditure on telephone contact in sales, marketing and customer service in 1999 was estimated at £15.4 billion, up from £10.4

billion in 1994 and representing 2.5 per cent of the UK's gross domestic product. KPMG estimates that up to 39 per cent of UK organisations currently have a contact centre. This is predicted to rise to 45 per cent in five years' time.

Today there are estimated to be around 5,000 contact centres in the UK employing approximately 350,000 people. By the end of 2002, it is predicted that there will be around 1,000 more contact centres meaning that a total of 550,000 people will be working in them. The call-centre industry is now the fastest-growing job category in the UK. It is estimated that 50 per cent of contact centres offer a 24-hour service (this has risen from 20 per cent in 1997).

However, contact centres are not yet seen as the perfect answer to delivering excellent service. In a recent BT survey, some 92 per cent of people said they liked the notion of conducting business by phone, but further research states that 80 to 85 per cent of customers were dissatisfied by their experiences of conducting business on the phone. Only 10 per cent were happy with the service.

In addition, an Incomes Data Services survey of 150 contact centres employing more than 50,000 indicated that 40 per cent of the firms featured experienced problems with high staff turnover. The average attrition rate of contact centres that reported problems in the survey was 24 per cent. The most common reasons cited for people leaving was the 'work intensity of the contact centre environment', followed by competition for staff, poor pay, lack of career opportunities, unsocial hours and the use of short-term contracts. There appears to be three approaches to managing contact centres:

- low commitment to employees, little empowerment;
- some commitment to employees, some empowerment;
- high commitment to employees, high empowerment.

When contact centre employees were asked to comment on the factors which encouraged loyalty, the responses were:

- a caring company culture;
- team spirit;
- a competitive salary;
- a supportive and effective team leader;
- training and development.

Glasgow-based Newstel Information found that one of the biggest challenges was finding and retaining good people: 'It helps if the work is varied and people rarely do the same thing for long.'

Capital Bank (part of the Bank of Scotland) is one of the winners of the BT-sponsored 'Call Centre of the Year' award. Its centre is open 16 hours a day, seven days a week. The bank's policy is to keep pay rates and bonuses within the top quartile. The emphasis on its recruitment drives is to hire people who are self-motivated.

Capital Bank has 35 trainers working in its three contact centres. New recruits receive two weeks' induction training and a further four weeks' development before starting work. Once they finish the induction period and start in the contact centre, new recruits are classified as 'trainees' for a further six months. They then qualify for a pay increase and a car. Bonuses are paid for continuing good performance, as well as one-off incentives. The company also employs 'mystery shoppers' to listen to the quality of its calls. The result is that staff turnover rate is said to be 'virtually nil' compared to the 24 per cent industry average for 1998.

Employers at Thomas Cook's Global Traveller Services contact centre in Peterborough have found that they can offset the intensity of working by offering staff benefits including the use of a jacuzzi, pool, gym, restaurant and bar. Other contact centres offer coaching in stress management, as 54 per cent of centres in a recent survey reported symptoms of stress.

As the number of contact centres grows, there is increasing debate about the merits of cost and volume compared to those of value and quality when handling customer transactions. Hewlett-Packard, for example, have said: 'the priority is the customer, not having a call duration of five minutes. The key is resolving the problem and satisfying the customer.'

Some contact centres are offering added value to the customer via the use of sophisticated technology. At credit card company Capital One in the United States, intelligent call-routing instantly identifies who is calling and at the same time calls up data about the customer. It then reviews 50 options offered about how to route the call and, using its knowledge of the customer, picks the one it considers to be most appropriate. At the same time, the relevant data is routed to the customer service rep. Computers predict the reason for a customer's call correctly 50 per cent of the time.

At satellite broadcasting company BSkyB, once an account has been set up, the contact-centre technology recognises home numbers on all subsequent calls and knows which programme the customer wants to watch by the phone number dialled. Increasingly, contact centres are being outsourced. India is a growth area for this type of business. India has the largest English-speaking population outside of the United States.

With outsourcing comes the advantage of cost reduction but the need to ensure consistency of standards and alignment to brand values.

THE INTERNET

Rapid changes in consumer behaviour have been prompted by the introduction of new technology: e-business on the Internet. This offers customers greater speed and choice, 24 hours a day. For organisations, there are the advantages of being able to market more quickly and gather direct customer feedback to develop better products and customer loyalty. In 2000, easyJet reported selling 60 per cent of its tickets over the Net. It hopes to double that proportion in 2000.

Having a successful Internet-based product transformed Prudential. For its online banking service, Egg, e-business is fundamental to everything it does. Within days of its launch in 1998, Egg had received 1.75 million Internet hits. Egg is now firmly established as the UK's leading Internet financial brand.

According to Forresters, by the year 2004 half the people in Europe will be connected to the Internet and 65 per cent of people online will be making purchases. Contact centres, Internet banking and advances in automatic cash-machine technology have revolutionised traditional banking. Companies early to adopt the new technology, such as First Direct, Egg, Virgin Direct and Tesco, are rapidly accumulating customers. 'The idea that banks are no longer on the customers' side was one of the strongest impressions to come out of the surveys we did before setting up our operations,' said Andy Dewhurst, Tesco's Personal Finance Marketing Director.

IBM sold between $22 and $24 billion of product in 2000. IBM customer service activity is now firmly Web based – 28 million service calls in 1999 were entered into and solved on the Net by downloading fixes and advice to the customer, or by remote diagnostics and fixing for those on the IBM Network.

Retailing on the Internet is already giving customers a sense of being in control. For example, the delivery company DHL offers customers online access to the status and progress of their order. This shows that, unlike traditional media, the services on the Internet are controlled by the *user*, not the publisher of a Web page. It has made organisations rethink how they communicate with customers, what they understand markets to be, how they segment and how they plan and advertise their products and services as well as the level of service they provide.

As a spokesperson from Amazon said: 'The old adage is that a happy customer will tell one person, an unhappy customer will tell 10. On the Internet a happy customer will tell one person, an unhappy customer will tell 10,000.'

Having a Web site is one thing, but it needs to communicate key messages to customers, act as a shop window and accurately reflect the image of the company. An organisation's Web site needs to be integrated with the rest of the customer strategy in order to maintain brand synergy. Internet customers are very focused; they know what they want, often in one visit to the site. The question is, why should a consumer bother visiting a Web site twice? A lost consumer can be lost forever unless this is addressed.

WH Smith Online clearly identified differences between marketing books on the Web and on the high street, noting that:

* price is fundamental to consumer choice, not a promotional feature;
* the customer has instant access 24 hours a day;
* editorial content is essential to add value and differentiate service;
* customer service must be excellent, e-mail is the easiest way to complain;
* there is no neutral turf, a competitor is one click away.

Many organisations are muddled in their strategy for online services. In the first phase of corporate use, Web sites were purely for communication. As security for online transactions has increased, Web sites are rapidly becoming service and sales vehicles.

Flower Farm Direct is a Web-based flower business that sources fresh flowers directly from the growers at prices up to 50 per cent less than other Web sites. The US-based firm uses a system that automatically routes information from the Web site to growers and fulfilment centres, as well as managing shipping, delivery, billing, payment processing and financial reporting.

The Web offers organisations an opportunity to personalise and tailor the service provided to individual customers. The Heineken Web site, for example, features a virtual bar on the Internet. The 'bartender' chooses a topic of conversation, customers drop in for a chat. Customers have to give information about themselves to enter the bar. This information is then subsequently used to target the consumer with relevant offers. At Famous Moe's Pizzas, the home-delivery service shows a picture of a pizza with the relevant toppings added as the customer places his or her order, while

Odeon cinemas offer customers the opportunity to select a film according to their mood.

As the cost advantages of using the Web increase (it can cost between £1 and £3 to bill a customer by mail, whereas presenting the bill electronically costs a fraction of that), it is predicted that the Internet will help break down traditional trading barriers. SMEs may find themselves on a more level playing field with larger organisations. New 'born-on-the-Web' companies have a very low-cost base and can benefit from high speed of movement with no inherited baggage or infrastructure to hold them back.

Trends in the United States show that the middle man is likely to be squeezed. Brands including Timex, Clinique, Sony, General Electric and Ford are plotting direct sales using the Net. Some manufacturers are inventing lines exclusively for the Net, others compete directly.

Industry sources predict that the presence of infomediaries, searching for the best deals and trading partners on the Net, will increase. For example, eXchange is used by around 87 per cent of independent financial advisers to obtain over 45 million life and pensions quotations each year from providers.

In the United States, similar services such as Expedia and Carpoint offer the best deals in shopping for travel tickets and cars, respectively. Instead of trying to add value by making or selling products, they offer the customer a better way to buy and sell. The quality of their product is the quality of the match they can achieve in terms of the needs of the seller and the needs of the buyer.

As the Web becomes accessible via mobile phones and television sets, and the roles of TVs and PCs continue to converge, online companies will be able to reach more consumers 24 hours a day. It is clear that to be customer focused when using the Web, an organisation needs to:

- research and give customers what they want, not what the organisation wants to tell them;
- tailor their Web sites to individual customer needs;
- make the Web site interactive;
- test the market and be prepared to change and learn as it goes;
- integrate it into other customer activity.

Many first-generation call centres were implemented to reduce costs in the distribution chain. The Internet now offers an even lower cost base, putting pressure on call centres, many of which are now converting to 'contact centres' to meet the demands of e-business.

Although there is increasing integration between Web sites and contact centres, spoken, person-to-person contact will still be needed. It is predicted that more people will do their *research* on the Web site before clicking on a screen icon to be put through to an agent if they are confused or want to progress to make a transaction. At 1-800-flowers.com, a nationwide florist in the United States, customers are offered the options of making a freephone call, sending an e-mail or visiting the Web site to place their orders.

Contact centres are increasingly taking on the job of providing responses to e-mails. Yet, of 150 major UK companies who promote their Web sites on TV and in the national press, only 14 per cent responded to an urgent Web request from a potential customer within 24 hours – 39 per cent did not respond at all. A further survey commissioned by Motive Communications, found that 87 per cent of business users abandon sites during transactions due to difficulties in navigation. When US toy retailer, Toys 'Я' Us launched a Christmas promotion on the Web, the company was forced to send consumers a $100 voucher in recognition that the goods would not be dispatched in time for Christmas.

By 2003, it is predicted that 25 per cent of customer contact will be via e-mail. The danger of the Internet is that if they do not receive a reply, disgruntled customers and employees can use it for anti-corporate messages. Already there are 'parody' sites of many organisations set up by their dissatisfied customers. Many organisations are turning to artificial intelligence technology which reads and replies automatically to e-mails. When the server is unsure of what reply to make, it will forward the message to the appropriate person for them to reply.

CUSTOMER RELATIONSHIP MANAGEMENT (CRM)

The increasing power of the customer and the fierceness of competition mean that many organisations are seeing their traditional marketplaces and profit margins eroded. The challenge for business today is to move from product orientation to customer focus. The process of setting up a customer service infrastructure using contact centres and Web-enabled technology is a good start to becoming customer orientated. Currently, 75 per cent of technology investment is funnelled into basic contact-centre applications. However, organisations with the best practices are going much further by introducing the concept of Customer Relationship Management (CRM).

In a recent survey by KPMG Consulting, 89 per cent of companies said that they consider customer information to be extremely important to the success of their business. Yet only 16 per cent of respondents thought that their customers were fully exploiting the customer information provided; 12 per cent were unable to say how many customers they have.

In the late 1990s, 'third way' business culture called for a more holistic approach in order to bring a number of business disciplines together: direct marketing, database marketing, loyalty schemes and data mining. Strong investment in advanced database technology enables this process to take place. Statistics from US-based consultancy AMR Research show that projected sales of CRM systems will rise to $10.5 billion by 2003.

The principle of CRM is that the more information a company has about its customers, the better. According to Professor Adrian Payne of Cranfield University, CRM is 'the strategic process of identifying desirable customer segments, micro-segments or individual customers on a one-to-one basis and developing integrated programmes that maximise both value to the customer and the lifetime value of customers to the organisation through targeted customer acquisition, profit enhancing activities and retention'.

A report by KPMG shows that 43 per cent of companies could not identify the principle causes of unsatisfied customers and almost half were unable to identify customers on the point of defection. The current trend is towards focusing on customer *retention* as a corporate strategy rather than prospecting or winning new business. Research by Bain & Co shows that a 5 per cent increase in customer retention yields a profit in Net Present Value of between 20 and 125 per cent.

CRM involves managing the customer relationship across all its interfaces with the company as one entire process. Rather than seeing customer transactions on an *ad hoc* basis as, say, a contact from marketing or a request for customer service, it breaks down the 'silo' mentality of traditional businesses and shares information about the customer. One of the problems that many businesses have is that data has been traditionally stored across various parts of the company. So, for example, one department in a bank may know whether a customer has a current account, but may not know whether he or she has a mortgage.

A CRM system can help to identify sales prospects from existing or potential customer databases. It can assist with all aspects of the sale, eg offering online access to order status and a single view of the customer status when the sale is complete. It can collect information about the customer and the queries that he or she made. It can also be integrated with relevant databases and supply-chain management applications to help allocate resources, eg ensuring the highest level of service is given to the customers who produce most profit. It can also monitor customer-usage patterns, so abnormal patterns or a reduction in use can be identified. Financial services organisation, Capital One, for example, practises 'predictive service and selling'. Intelligent technology prompts an agent to contact the customer at key points in the life cycle.

IT company Ernst and Young Cap Gemini defines four elements in a CRM framework:

- **Know your markets and your customers** Knowledge of the customer can be obtained via IT systems which carry out customer-value management, data warehousing and data mining. At these points, companies are able to extract information about their customers from across the business, segment their customer base and predict individual customers' behaviour. This information can be shared across the organisation and updated automatically every time the customer contacts any part of the organisation: at point of sale, by using loyalty cards, using contact centres or visiting the Web site.

- **Target segments and individuals** Examining the flow of information between an organisation's front and back office helps to determine specific customer needs and requirements, and how best to target the most profitable customers. Information from third-party sources, such as 'lifestyle' data, can be used to help refine customer segments and a company's knowledge of the customers' individual needs. Segmentation means placing customers in groups that respond to and interact with a business in similar ways. Volvo, for example, actively targets its products at the growing family by understanding relevant lifestyle issues. It created a company-wide customer database which allowed customers to be tracked and targeted.

- **Sell** This involves moving from a *reactive* to *proactive* involvement with customers. In the United States, supermarket chain Wal-Mart discovered that sales of beer rose on Fridays if the stock was positioned next to disposable nappies. This was because fathers tended to do more shopping on Fridays than any other day of the week.

- **Service** Providing an after-sales service which is tailored to individual needs. Electronics distributor RS Components has developed a site, for example, where each customer has his or her own welcome page displaying tailored editorial content, advertising and new product alerts relevant to each customer.

Customer knowledge and insight is the linchpin of successful CRM. However, without this knowledge being shared and used throughout the organisation, businesses will fail to meet constantly changing customer needs. The implementation of a CRM strategy involves sales, marketing, IT, customer service, and finance, integrating systems across all these different departments to centralise information. Its potentially high failure rate is attributed to cultural obstacles such as internal departments being reluctant to share information.

Accenture Consulting CRM research says a typical $1 billion company with an increase of 10 per cent in CRM capabilities would see profits rise by $40 million. The latest development is e-CRM where Web technology provides further opportunities to enhance customer loyalty. However, businesses would be wrong to put all their faith in CRM as a means to achieving a customer focus. In John McKean's book, *The Information Masters*, he suggests that companies typically put 80 per cent of their investment in technology when ideally it should be 10 per cent (Table 1.1).

Table 1.1 Historical investment versus Ideal investment

Elements	Historical investment	Ideal investment
People	2%	20%
Processes	2%	15%
Organisation	2%	10%
Culture	1%	20%
Leadership	1%	10%
Information	10%	15%
Technology	82%	10%

Adapted from John McKean's book, The Information Masters.

A spokesperson for Shell Europe which has introduced CRM in a number of European contact centres, reports a tenfold differential in those centres where staff are behind the concept and those which are not. Research shows that 60–80 per cent of CRM projects fail. Those that are successful appear to have the following characteristics:

- strong commitment from the top;
- clearly defined and measurable goals;
- involvement of the customer;
- a business-focused rather than technology approach;
- the right team to design and implement the project;
- an incremental approach rather than step change.

The organisation and the customer

Customers perceive service quality through every aspect of their contact with the company.

In improving the quality of its service therefore an organisation needs to develop *all* aspects of its *relationship* with customers.

Customers often do not perceive the service they receive from an organisation as a complete entity. It is the fine detail of the organisation's relationship with the customer such as an incorrectly addressed letter, a lengthy delay in receiving an e-mail response, a service which turns out to be different to how it was originally advertised, which forms customers' impressions.

The dangers of a fragmented approach to customer orientation

Lessons can be learnt from the experience of companies which have instigated programmes to improve service quality in their organisations.

Many businesses have concentrated their efforts to improve quality on those members of staff who have direct contact with the customer. They fail to include support, head office and other employees in a quality improvement cycle. Instigating improvements in customer care at front-line level within a company is like treating a head wound when the poison has already escaped via the bloodstream into the rest of the body.

Research shows that a service company has no walls. That is, for the customer it is a transparent factory. Customers do not blame individual staff members for poor standards but the company as a whole. If a customer turns up at a hotel for a pre-arranged booking to discover that he or she has no room for the night, it is ultimately the management's responsibility to ensure that a system is in place to handle bookings efficiently and effectively, that members of staff have been properly trained and that good lines of communication exist between all parts of the organisation and the customer.

Many businesses discover that a campaign to tackle service quality improvements from the bottom by enhancing team members' skills, does not go far enough because it does not alter the prevailing attitudes among managers of the business. The reaction of team members to such initiatives can often be one of scepticism as managers are seen to say one thing and do another, and underlying problems prevalent throughout the organisation are not addressed.

The internal customer

When we talk of customers it is important to remember that everyone within an organisation provides a service. There are 'internal' as well as 'external' customers.

In too many organisations the value of the internal customer is overlooked. To supply a product or service to a customer to an agreed specification on a specific date can involve a whole chain of people – in product development, buying, manufacturing, warehousing, delivery and so on – each having to satisfy the needs of their colleagues down the line. Their internal relationship is of supplier and customer (Figure 1.6). Treating people with respect, passing on defect-free work and so on is absolutely crucial if the customer is to receive excellent service, right first time.

The quality of the service which reaches the customer is often determined by 'silent service' – the quality of the service that members of the organisation provide each other. Employees will not care for their customers if they do not believe their company cares about them.

Managers should think of the people who report to them not as their employees but as customers for whom they have a commitment to provide

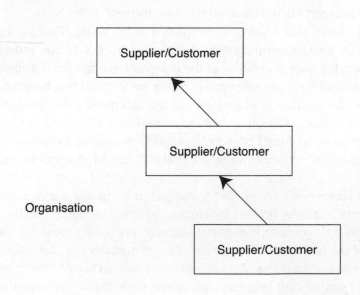

Figure 1.6 The internal customer

a first-class service. The external customer is much more likely to receive a good service if the provider of that service within the company has in turn received excellent service from his or her internal supplier.

The suppliers of service to front-line staff, for example, may be not only their managers but the personnel department, the training department and payroll, and so it works throughout the organisation.

THE SERVICE/PROFIT CHAIN

Work by Heskett *et al* at Harvard Business School has demonstrated a clear link between how employees are treated within the organisation, employee and customer retention, and profit (Figure 1.7).

Stew Leonard is head of Stew Leonard's Dairies and holder of the *Guinness Book of Records* for being the store with the highest sales per square foot in the world. A well-known service champion, Stew says: 'If you look after your staff, they will look after your customers who will in turn look after your profits.'

An ongoing, holistic process

Experience of helping both private and public sector organisations to achieve a customer focus shows that there is no 'quick fix' to creating a

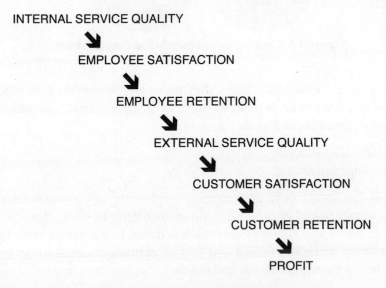

INTERNAL SERVICE QUALITY

EMPLOYEE SATISFACTION

EMPLOYEE RETENTION

EXTERNAL SERVICE QUALITY

CUSTOMER SATISFACTION

CUSTOMER RETENTION

PROFIT

Figure 1.7 The service/profit chain

Figure 1.8 Creating a customer-focused organisation

customer focus. Research shows that there are, however, a number of elements that need to be in place in order to create a climate and culture of customer orientation, as Figure 1.8 shows.

Business imperative and top team clarity

It is clear that unless there is a business imperative for customer retention and top management is fully committed to customer care, there is little chance of success. Customer orientation needs to permeate the organisation's mission, vision, values and key objectives. It needs to be visible both in senior managers' words and deeds.

Listening posts

Organisations with the best practices actively measure both internal and external customer satisfaction. They use the data to make improvements and drive change.

Service strategy and goals

To be successful, service-orientated organisations need to have a clear strategy and a set of specific and measurable goals for service improvements.

Customer-driven processes

The way an organisation does business with its customer should match the customer's needs, not its own. Technology can help here as new customer channels such as the Internet and contact centres have brought about new ways of doing business with the customer.

People development

Everyone throughout an organisation can benefit from training and development to enhance their attitude towards the customer – their behaviour, knowledge and skills. The quality of leadership in an organisation is often an indicator of its customer orientation.

Empowerment

Giving people responsibility for decisions affecting their work encourages a customer focus and ongoing improvement.

Communication

The lifeblood of an organisation, communication about customers, competitors and the best practice in customer service can help create an impetus for change.

Reward and recognition

Organisations with the best practices create a motivating climate for their employees by recognising and rewarding customer-orientated behaviour.

Sustaining a customer focus

World-class service organisations recognise the need to sustain a focus on the customer at all times.

Service quality initiatives should not be measured on a short-term basis – changing the culture of an organisation is a long-term process which needs to be approached on a continuous basis. Experiences of companies such as Virgin show that the process must be continuous. Achieving improvements in service quality is a never-ending journey.

SUMMARY

This book is designed to help you engender and sustain a customer focus.

In this introductory chapter an overview of service quality has been provided. The importance of customer service in an increasingly competitive environment has been discussed and the implications of increasing customer expectations and changes in trading patterns exposed.

A definition of *good* service is meeting customers' expectations. *Excellent* service is exceeding customer expectations. To provide *world-class* service, the need to improve the total relationship with the customer has been emphasised, improving the processes through which service is delivered to the customer.

The need for organisations to embrace change has been shown in the rise of contact centres, e-business and the Internet. Customer relationship management allows organisations to offer a personalised one-to-one service by using information to have improved knowledge, thereby targeting more effectively and providing the customer with a better service. However, businesses would be wrong to place all their faith in technology as a means to achieving customer orientation.

Total customer care will only be achieved when the needs of the 'internal' as well as the 'external' customer are considered. This involves capturing the 'hearts and minds' of all employees.

Managers play a key role in providing support and encouragement to their staff to achieve customer focus. Unless customer initiatives originate from the top of an organisation they have no long-term effect.

To help you begin the process of sustaining a customer focus the key points of this chapter are summarised in the form of an Action Checklist. (A checklist appears at the end of all but the last chapter.) Many of the ideas may seem self-evident; nevertheless, practical experience demonstrates the benefits of stressing the obvious. Use this list as a starting point to consider the service you currently provide and areas in which you can improve.

ACTION CHECKLIST

Practical exercises you can undertake after reading this chapter are to:

1. Put yourself in the customer's shoes and review the service you provide from his or her perspective.

2. Establish what changes are likely to take place in your marketplace in the future and their implications for your customer relationships.

3. Investigate the importance of service in customers' choice of your product(s).

4. Undertake a survey of your customers to establish their expectations, reasons for choice of products and services and satisfaction levels.

5. Establish what percentage of your business is repeat business and investigate ways of developing better relationships with your existing customers.

6. Analyse what percentage of your customers are advocates or frequent users.

7. Think of extra ways in which you can create goodwill for your company, such as better handling of complaints, showing concern for others, and providing better customer information.

8. Review your use of technology to enable customer orientation.

9. Assess how well your customers are dealt with over the Web or at your contact centre.

10. Use CRM and e-CRM techniques to identify customer segmentation.

11. Know your most profitable customers and tailor your service accordingly.

12. Encourage the sharing of customer information across departments.

13. Emphasise the fact that everyone has a customer throughout an organisation – establish 'internal' customer needs.

14. Ensure management involvement in all customer service initiatives.

15. Monitor internal and external customer satisfaction on an ongoing basis. Feed results back to everyone concerned and recognise success.

2

How Managers Need to Drive and Support a Service Strategy

The preceding chapter has illustrated the growing importance of customer service as a means of differentiation. This importance must be recognised by senior managers, as it is they who fashion the response of their organisations to this trend.

This chapter outlines how to create a customer-focused organisational culture where a customer service strategy underpins how the organisation conducts its business. It provides practical examples and advice on how organisational leaders can demonstrate their commitment to customer care and initiate and drive a programme of service improvements within their organisation.

START FROM THE TOP

An Institute of Management report reveals that emphasis on short-term goals, lack of commitment from top management and lack of training are seen as the main barriers to businesses achieving higher levels of customer care. Evidence shows that service excellence will only be considered a critical success factor in a business's long-term survival if senior management demonstrate their involvement in terms of time, money, effort, commitment, persistence and visibility.

Research conducted by Unisys into how more than 80 organisations world-wide have successfully embedded good customer service in their corporate culture reveals a clear message. Far from paying lip-service to the concept, leaders in the field put hard cash and considerable effort into building customer-driven organisations and, according to the research, best-practice organisations are those whose service improvement efforts are driven, directed and guided from the top.

Unisys UK chief executive, George Cox, stressed that words from on high are meaningless unless backed by actions: 'No CEO is going to say his company ignores the customer. But the top guy has to believe it in order to get the entire organisation soaked in the attitude that the customer really matters.'

Bob Hass, Chairman of jeans manufacturer Levi Strauss, explains that the challenge is to mix 'the hard stuff of getting jeans through the door with the soft stuff of worker empowerment'.

Service quality improvements are never-ending. Companies such as Scandinavian Airlines have been undertaking a programme designed to improve the quality of service it offers its customers over the past decade, and the programme is still ongoing. This programme, and many of those of other best-practice organisations, is sustained by the commitment and vision of the leaders of the organisation to a service philosophy and the development of a service strategy designed to sustain this philosophy. They each recognise that bringing about improvements in service quality often involves culture change and this can take up to five years to bring about.

Leadership is key

According to Professors Kotter and Heskett of Harvard Business School, the leadership style of the successful company is key to its ability to change. To facilitate a focus on the customer there first has to be a widespread acceptance among the workforce that the company faces losing customers unless it changes. Second, business leaders must communicate the need for change and act as positive role models.

Jack Welch, the ex-CEO of GEC, concentrated efforts on changing the culture of his organisation so that key values drove the business. These values include speed (in execution), simplicity (in concept and communication), self-confidence (through delegation and empowerment), ownership, impatience (for the results), candour (including constructive conflict), realism and agility (from a flexible and lean organisation).

In today's more responsive environment, leadership has shifted from the old command and control style to a new enabling approach which aims to release the potential of the workforce. A great deal has been written about leadership, style of leadership and the qualities that make up good leaders. Traditionally, leadership theories have fallen broadly into two camps – the situational and the visionary.

The *situational leadership* theory states that leaders assess a situation and manage it accordingly. The way they behave is contingent on their external conditions. Good leaders would particularly focus on two core issues: how much skill or knowledge their teams possess and the extent to which they require emotional support.

The *visionary leadership* theory is a much more recent development. On this view a good leader is seen in terms of a person with a strength of vision, who can motivate others to share that vision and to ensure that it is implemented. A more recent leadership theory, featured in Daniel Goleman's *Working with Emotional Intelligence*, claims that IQ is no longer the sole determinant of leadership success. Instead, it sees emotional intelligence as the determining factor. This consists of:

- self-awareness;
- self-regulation;
- empathy;
- motivation;
- social skills.

A survey conducted by KPMG showed that the most important leadership skills were thought to be the ability to motivate and to communicate. Despite this, 93 per cent of those questioned thought that communication skills were most lacking in British CEOs. Two of the characteristics strongly rated were the ability to attract the best people to the scheme and the skill to turn visions into reality. A recent poll by researchers MORI

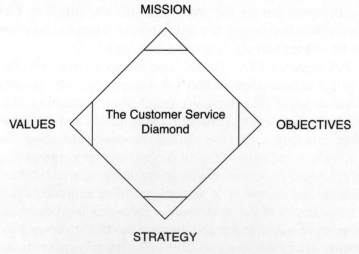

Figure 2.1 The customer service diamond

found that Richard Branson, Nelson Mandela and Winston Churchill are the three leaders that British people would like most to have a conversation with. The strong support for Richard Branson was on the basis of his clarity of vision and his ability to motivate others.

MISSION AND VISION

The first step on a journey to excellence is to establish a philosophy which has customer service at its core. This philosophy can be expressed in terms of a mission – a statement of the purpose or task of the organisation, or vision – a statement of where the business is going, its values and beliefs.

There is often confusion surrounding the terms 'mission' and 'vision'. Whatever the terminology used, a mission or vision should encapsulate what the employees accept and believe to be the main principles which guide their behaviour as employees.

On assuming the chairmanship of ICI, John Harvey-Jones set about creating a new sense of mission by a set of actions which had both a direct and symbolic effect on the company. He moved the meetings of the ICI board of directors from the imposing and highly traditional board room at Millbank and held them in his own office. The directors sat in their shirt-sleeves in comfortable chairs with side tables attached for their notes. This change facilitated teamwork and involvement of all concerned in the decision-making process. It was also a powerful message to convey to the rest of the organisation, which demonstrated far more effectively than any number of words that a new set of values was being fashioned.[1]

Surveys indicate that 90 per cent of large firms have written a mission statement in the last five years, making it more popular than any other single management tool. The average return on shareholder equity for firms with mission statements is 16.1 per cent; without mission statements it is 9.7 per cent, so there are powerful reasons for creating one. A mission statement is often helpful, but is only one of many steps to building a visionary company.

What are visions?

Peter Drucker, the management guru, states: 'One of the more important things an organisation can do is to determine what business it is in.'

A vision is a torch-bearer of the purpose of an organisation. It answers the question, 'What are we here for?' It provides a view of a future that is different and better than the present. Creating a vision should engender a common understanding of the principal tasks of the organisation. It should allow employees to identify with the objectives of the organisation and establish a common sense of purpose.

There are many approaches which differing organisations adopt to develop a vision. In general, the vision is no longer than a paragraph and is written in language which everyone can understand. Best-practice organisations consult with stakeholders including employees, before developing a shared vision. In this way everyone knows what goal they are aiming for and what is expected from them to help achieve organisational success. For example, financial services organisation Morgan Stanley Dean Witter's vision is to be 'a one firm firm'.

Harry Ramsden's is in *The Guinness Book of Records* as the world's largest fish and chip restaurant. When John Barnes, the Chairman of Harry Ramsden's plc, bought the business he recognised it had a tremendous reputation but that it had lost its way. His vision for the business involved re-establishing the values which had made it great in the past and then building on these to ensure an even brighter future. John Barnes spent the first few months in the business getting to know employee groups to learn about the best things that were done when 'Old Harry' was around. He formed customer groups to learn about their views of the organisation. Based on this research he and the management team established an ultimate vision for the business.

President Kennedy's vision of 'a man on the moon in the 1960s' turned NASA from a rather obscure agency into a national resource. Not only NASA's employees but also the thousands of assistants working for NASA, and the nation at large, were galvanised by this great vision. The commitment was to the vision, not to Kennedy. The vision was realised after his death – proof of the unifying nature of the vision.

Creating a vision

When writing a mission statement, an organisation, department or business unit must step back and reflect on what it is trying to achieve. It needs to focus on the fundamental elements that both define it and also make the difference between success and failure. Below are some examples:

- McDonald's is 'to be the UK's favourite quick service restaurant by providing great tasting food through excellent operations and by giving friendly service at a value price to our customers'.

- Wal-Mart's is to, 'give ordinary folk the chance to buy the same things as rich people'.
- 3M's is to, 'solve unsolved problems innovatively'.
- Disney's is to be 'the first in entertainment for people of all ages, everywhere'.

A vision needs the ownership and commitment of senior management within the organisation. The process of agreeing a mission or vision often takes place at a specially convened meeting. It can sometimes be helpful if this is led by an impartial facilitator who is not part of the management team.

The purpose of the meeting is to arrive at a team consensus on a vision statement. It is especially important that the vision does not include anything that senior management are not committed to, otherwise it will become meaningless. Likewise, it should be written in a language that everyone can understand.

A useful starting point in the development of a vision is to ask colleagues, customers, employees, shareholders and competitors:

- What do we want this organisation to be and to stand for?
- Where and how we are going to delight our customers?
- What do we want people in this organisation to be good at?
- How do we want them to behave?
- What do we have to be good at to succeed in this market or industry?

Involving employees

EC-funded research on HR development has found that the majority of chief executives fail to get across the message about the company's mission or vision to other groups of employees. Nearly half of those employees surveyed did not know what their organisational mission statement or vision was.

Often there is a danger that these are seen as empty words that convey little meaning to employees of an organisation. This danger can be avoided, however, if employees themselves are involved in the creation of the vision or mission. This can be achieved in a number of ways:

- Asking managers and staff to contribute their opinions on the vision using the same process of discussion and debate as senior management, and feeding results back to senior management forum.
- Establishing a representative body, drawn from across the organisation, to develop a mission or vision with senior management.

- Developing departmental visions that complement the organisation's overall vision.
- Reinforcing the vision via printed statements, posters, leaflets, booklets, etc.

One computer company, for example, developed a vision statement with its management team and then cascaded this throughout the company. Senior managers discussed the vision on a one-to-one basis with each of their managers who in turn discussed this with their staff. A small booklet was produced to aid the discussion, which was signed by both the manager and the staff member and left with them as a reminder. At the end of the meeting the manager summarised the discussions with each employee and fed this information to senior management, together with suggestions for improvement to the vision.

Other companies involve customers in the creation of a mission. NatWest Life was launched in January 1993. Starting on a green-field site meant that the organisation was able to benefit from detailed research into customer attitudes. The research told them that if they were to be successful in establishing long-term relationships with their customers, customer satisfaction had to be their principle role. This was therefore encapsulated in their vision statement: 'Our customers are the focus of everything we do . . . we value our customers and will deliver outstanding service and heed their feedback.'

When a statement is drafted the organisation should question if it is:

- memorable;
- meaningful;
- believable;
- motivational.

FedEx in the United States has developed the motto, 'People, Service, Profit', which summarises its business philosophy.

Continuously revisit the vision

Missions and visions should be regularly revisited (normally once a year) to ensure that they are still compatible with the organisation's internal and external environment. Tyre and exhaust replacement company, Kwik-Fit's commitment to its customers has been a priority since the company was founded by Tom Farmer in 1971. Its mission was to give '100% satisfaction 100% of the time'. Since then facilities have been provided for customers to register their concerns or suggestions – and for Kwik-Fit to keep in tune with its customers. Customer questionnaires are given out with receipts and a special free phone helpline is open round the clock. Every response is acknowledged and acted upon.

In the 1990s, the company reviewed and altered its mission statement. The word 'satisfaction' was replaced with 'delight'. Farmer explains:

> Satisfied customers have only been given what they expected. That's no longer enough. You have to go the extra mile and give something that isn't expected. Today, everyone is selling quality goods at the same price so you have to find other ways of being different – of adding value for the customer. It comes down to interpersonal relationships – how the person serving you relates to you.

As part of a review process, questions should be asked about the vision, such as:

- Is this statement still aspirational and motivational?
- How far are we attaining our vision?
- Which aspects of our vision are no longer relevant?

VALUES

To convert vision into reality, senior management have to be clear about what the organisation values. 'Values' in this context means those shared assumptions and beliefs which really influence people's behaviour. In other words, what is important to the way the business operates.

The vision itself may reflect a strongly held value. For example, the Body Shop's vision is clearly influenced by the value of using only natural products not tested on animals. The way the vision is developed also reflects organisational values. For example, is it the work of a few senior managers or a subject in which many have shared because the idea of participation and listening to colleagues is already a corporate value?

Values are sometimes called 'the cultural glue' of an organisation. Every organisation has its own culture. Culture includes what you see: the dress, tidiness the cleanliness of people and premises, and the way people behave; the words and jargon used; how welcoming people are, or how well they listen. Underlying these are the values that are common within the organisation. For example, what are the real priorities: is it customer service, or cost saving, or compliance with what the organisation wants? Culture is important because it can attract or lose customers, and it affects the amount of creativity and enthusiasm that people bring to work.

One company that recognises the contribution that corporate values can make to its commercial performance is NFC (The National Freight Corporation). Throughout the 1990s the company sustained high levels of performance. A key contribution to the success is what the group describes as its 'hidden plus factor' – the culture of employee share ownership and the enthusiasm which this has created in the company. This is enhanced by senior management's belief and commitment to its core values. NFC describe these values as: employee ownership, quality, internationalism, people development, social responsibility and premium performance.

Surveys reveal that up to 90 per cent of managers expect values to become even more important for organisational success over the next three years, with 85 per cent of those interviewed agreeing that 'in periods of rapid change, the staff need the stability and guidance of clear corporate values'. There is also evidence that superior financial performance depends on having values that help the organisation anticipate and adapt to changes in the business environment.

Online financial service organisation Egg has developed a set of values which underflows its corporate behaviour. Its six values are:

- Respect the individual.
- Get it done together and have fun.
- Make a difference in everything we do.
- Listen and learn.
- Do what we promise.
- Dance with customers.

When First Quench was formed from Thresher and Victoria Wine, senior managers recognised the urgent need for culture change. The board spent two days defining a mission, vision and values. A pilot group of 60 head office staff then took part in a team event designed to establish an understanding of the company's mission and values to ensure that people would buy into change. The change programme, called Alchemy, was subsequently rolled out to all employees. Reminders, workbooks, tapes and materials were distributed round the company so that the values were embedded in every part of the business.

The values were introduced to complement the organisation's enduring purpose (mission), 'Processing the power of information to offer individuals all the help they need', and its strategic intent (vision) for the next three years, 'creating a stunning and individual experience for customers and employees and driving extended value for shareholders'.

At retailer Wal-mart, the core values of the organisation are summed up by:

- respect for the individual;
- service for customers;
- striving for excellence.

At Hewlett-Packard 'the HP way' is the guiding principle of the two visionary engineer founders of the company, Hewlett and Packard, which has spawned hundreds of imitators. Although the founders are no longer involved in running the company their principles are so well known and accepted that employees are often said to make decisions according to what they think 'Bill and Dave would have done' in the same situation. These values centre on trust and respect for individuals, a high level of achievement and contribution, uncompromising integrity in the conduct of business, achievement of common objectives through teamwork, encouragement, flexibility and innovation. The company's objectives centre on profit, since that provides the finance for growth and the resources to meet the other objectives – customers; fields of interest that will offer opportunities for future expansion; growth that is limited only by profits and the ability to develop and produce innovative products that satisfy real customer needs; people, because they make the company success possible; management and citizenship.

Insurance company CGU, born out of the merger of two companies, recognised early on in the merger their different company values. They set up a series of workshops aimed at creating a new set of core values which focused on the needs of people in the business, business intermediaries and customers.

Ex-chief executive of telephone banking service First Direct, Kevin Newman, ventures a word of caution, however: 'Values will do no good whatsoever if people don't believe them. If there's a conflict between principles and practice, people will lose direction, but when it works it can produce powerful benefits.'[2]

OBJECTIVES

Office equipment company Xerox has four goals which it believes should influence all staff. They cover customer and employee satisfaction, market share and return on assets.

Each year, the board meet to decide how the company can work towards achieving these goals. They discuss their conclusions at a meeting with the company's top 100 managers who pass the message down to the next level within the hierarchy and so on. As well as being told what the objectives are face-to-face, each employee receives a written summary of them.

Sadly, all too often, although many senior managers pay lip-service to the value of customer service it does not form part of the stated corporate objectives – a key focal point for all organisational activities. Alternatively, it may appear as a key objective for year one, but in year two it has been relegated to the second division.

Best-practice organisations ensure that customer satisfaction always appears as a key corporate objective. When Motorola first went down the quality route in 1981 the company's senior management asked every unit in the organisation to improve quality tenfold in the next five years. Though each unit was given the freedom to decide on the measures most appropriate to its activities, the goal seemed impossible to those involved. By 1986, the company pronounced that the initiative had succeeded – albeit with more than a few hitches along the way. However, at about the same time, parts of the company became involved in benchmarking their service against competing and best-practice organisations. This led to the announcement in January 1987 of a three-pronged attack: another tenfold improvement by the beginning of 1989, a hundred-fold improvement by the start of 1991 and six 'sigma' qualities – 3.4 defects per million tasks – by the beginning of 1992. This 'crusade for quality' with clear and measurable milestones has led Motorola to win the coveted Malcolm Baldrige Award – set up to encourage US companies to match their Japanese rivals on the quality front – and the company has become synonymous with total quality and total customer satisfaction.

STRATEGY

Strategy makes up the final facet of the customer service diamond – mission, values, objectives, strategy. To convert vision and values into reality once customer service objectives have been established, senior management need to create a customer service strategy – long-range plans on such critical issues as customer-focused processes, human resources, innovation and so on to meet customer demands. The strategy should in turn lead to implementable actions.

The approach which many organisations adopt in formulating a customer service strategy can be outlined as follows:

1. Review and link to mission, values and corporate objectives.
2. Evaluate current position.
3. Formulate strategy.
4. Develop a specific action plan.
5. Establish criteria for success.
6. Identify obstacles to progress.
7. Implement.

1. Link to mission, vision, values and corporate objectives

We have discussed earlier the importance of an organisational mission and values and how vital it is to have customer service as a key objective for the organisation.

At Southwest Airlines, the low-cost US carrier, customer service is at the core of the business. From the start it set out to create a fun culture to distinguish itself from the competition. It specifically recruits fun people and gives its employees freedom to create fun.

2. Evaluate current position

Given this, in order to improve service quality senior management need to take stock of the organisation's 'fit' with the environment. This can take place via an external and internal appraisal. This process allows the managers to identify the gap between the desired and current state.

It is well to thoroughly evaluate an organisation's past performance and present position in order to have a measure of future potential. Indicators of past performance include historical financial results, competitor analysis, customer satisfaction measures, level of repeat and new business, as well as internal measures such as staff loyalty and attrition rates, motivation, structure and systems.

External appraisal

In evaluating current service performance senior managers need to be conscious of both the far and near environment in which the organisation operates.

The *far environment* can be defined as those elements which affect an organisation's business and over which a company often has very little direct control. These elements are often classified as the STEP factors – the sociological, technological, economic and political factors which affect a business. If one were to undertake an audit of the STEP factors which confront the current position of a coach company which wished to develop a service strategy, results may show:

Sociological factors:

- more people in full- and part-time work;
- greater car ownership;
- general desire for efficiency and speed in transport;
- growing awareness of environmental issues such as pollution and inner city congestion;
- higher degree of comfort and facilities expected;
- ageing population.

Technological factors:

- improvements in transport manufacture;
- automation;
- improvements in road networks,
- greater use of the Internet and e-business.

Economic factors:

- customers more cost conscious;
- staff retention low as a wide choice of employment opportunities;
- high cost of fuel.

Political factors:

- government backing for less car usage;
- EC regulations.

The implications of this analysis would then need to be evaluated in the light of customer expectations.

Taking as an example the sociological factors for the coach company, a service strategy would need to address customers' requirements for speed, frequency of service and comfort as well as their requirements for competitive prices and efficiency.

Next there needs to be an appraisal of the *near environment* which affects the performance of the organisation that is required. The near environment includes aspects such as the impact on the business of the size and structure of the industry in which the organisation operates, the competitive environment and bargaining power of suppliers and customers.

To conduct an audit of the near environment in terms of customer service one needs to look at the immediate industry and competitors within it as well as the power of existing customers.

Professor Michael Porter's concept of five forces which determine an organisation's competitive position is useful in this context and is shown in Figure 2.2.

Using this model in the hypothetical example of the coach company, when conducting an appraisal of the near environment it can be seen that the power of the customer is high – as there is a large number of alternative methods of transport and the threat of substitutes such as video-conferencing, car, rail, bus and tube transport is also high. Barriers to entering the market in our hypothetical example however are also high because of the cost of investment. The bargaining power of suppliers is poor and the rivalry amongst existing competitors is high.

On this basis a service strategy would probably need to address, among other issues, the need to benchmark competitors and comparable industries to meet growing customer expectations and to add value to the customer's experience.

Internal appraisal

To achieve true customer focus senior managers have to persuade the whole organisation to 'live the brand' rather than just produce, package and sell it. At Cadet Uniform Services in Toronto, research revealed that customers perceived the delivery drivers, who collected and delivered the laundry, as the company. The company gave up its salespeople and made its drivers the sole point of contact with the customer. The drivers' customer-handling skills now grow and develop the business: 98 per cent of success in business is down to repeat business.

American Express research shows that the manner in which a cardholder is handled when he or she is called to the phone, because his or her card limit is exceeded, affects the customer's satisfaction rating far more than if the card had been refused or denied.

When healthcare company PPP decided it wanted to deliver brand values such as openness, honesty, flexibility and personal service, it found

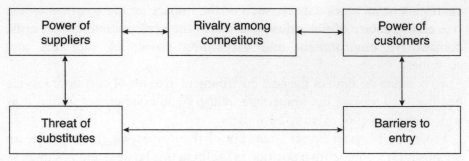

Figure 2.2 Porter's five forces

that it had to change not only its old insurance-based name, logo and advertising, but its insurance company mentality.

Organisations such as Barclays have invested heavily in bringing their brand to life by defining the desired customer experience and how leaders and team leaders can develop brand values through their behaviour.

Customers experience service in the way employees talk, behave and deal with them so that the company's own culture and values shine through everything it does. In preparing a customer service strategy, therefore, it is essential to appraise the internal organisational environment. This audit should include such aspects as:

Structure: analysis of the size and structure of the organisation and whether its configuration meets customers' needs. Many layers of hierarchy can block customers' access.

Shared values: what is valued in the organisation? For example, is there evidence of teamwork, communication and cooperation? Is there fundamental passion towards the customer, making money?

Strategy: what has been the organisation's strategy in the past? What successes or failures has this brought, and why? Is the strategy translated into action?

Systems: an assessment of the internal processes and the effectiveness of each of them in meeting customer requirements. Are the systems designed with the customer in mind?

Style of management: identification of characteristics of current management style and its appropriateness in a customer-focused organisation. What leadership style prevails?

Staff: an assessment of the organisation's performance in terms of human resource management – recruitment, training and development, career development, reward and recognition. How customer-focused are employees?

Skills: an audit of the skills profile of the organisation's staff and their competences in relation to customers. Are skills, knowledge, attitude and behaviour customer orientated?

Particular attention should be paid in the audit to how employees currently perceive the role of service within the organisation. To be successful, service quality must be integrated into the corporate culture of the organisation and become a natural part of working life.

Banks and building societies, for example, have undergone a revolution in the past decade to move from a bureaucratic to a service culture:

Past	*Future*
Organisational focus	Customer focus
Meeting audit requirements	Meeting customer requirements
Quality control	Error prevention
Hierarchical structure	Fewer layers
Limits on responsibility	Employee empowerment and responsibility
Individual responsible	Team based
Close communication	Open communication

This has involved moving away from a paternalistic and audit-controlled environment where the needs of the organisation came far above those of the customer, and creating a culture where enterprise and service-mindedness are promoted and the focus is on the customer.

3. Formulate strategy

Having undertaken an audit of the near and far environment and the internal organisation, senior management are then able to set a strategy for customer service to enhance service quality on a continuous basis. There are a number of examples of organisations which have created successful service strategies.

When Peter Bonfield was appointed as chairman and chief executive of ICL plc he was confronted with an organisation which faced going out of business. Bonfield and a top management team identified the company as being inward-looking without a clear vision of the future, lacking a consistent and appropriate culture, having a focus on technology rather than customers, and limited general management skills.

Having completed the analysis, the next step was to agree a critical strategy document called 'The ICL Way' which provided a culture blueprint and defined seven commitments to be made by all employees, especially in the areas of excellence and customer service. The document also featured 10 key roles for managers which focused on responsibilities for people and their development. A series of company-wide business performance initiatives was introduced:

Quality the ICL way – a top-down TQM programme aimed at building a quality culture focused on both internal and external customers.
The development of benchmarking to give objective external comparisons.
The creation of an in-company development programme.
Introduction of multi-skilling in the workforce.
The achievement where appropriate of standards such as ISO 9001.
A campaign to motivate the workforce through recognition, performance-related pay, employee surveys and annual and quarterly reviews, and criterion-based selection.

This strategy, aimed at focusing on customer satisfaction and excellence, has resulted in a strategic recovery which has been dramatic.[3]

The top team and leader of Braintree District Council outlined a simple statement of purpose as a focus for the organisation. Setting out its basic ambition, the mission led to operational principles for culture, quality, customer care and people development and contained four key statements:

1. Securing the best possible conditions for all who live in the district to lead a high-quality lifestyle.
2. Focusing on customers through providing quality services.
3. Ensuring staff development opportunities through training, appraisal, respect and support.
4. Operating in a business-like manner with clear accountabilities and insisting that targets are met.

These principles provided a strategic framework which had 12 priority themes: democracy, customer interest, quality, care of the disadvantaged, economic development, skills development, the environment, health, housing, leisure, transport, and management.

These policies were based on simple principles, such as customer focus, service delivery and continuous improvement and have become a bedrock of a successful quality programme which has earned Braintree consistently high scores in terms of customer satisfaction.[4]

An holistic approach

Quality and service cannot be seen in isolation. Senior executives should take an holistic approach to service strategy and not confine their plans to any one aspect of the business. Rather, a service strategy should encompass all areas of an organisation's activities which impact on the customer, including such elements as image, sales promotion, location and availability, timeliness, value, delivery, customer support, customer and supplier relationships. From internal perspectives, it should cover such aspects as: human resource management, recruitment, management information systems, marketing, processes, teamwork, communication, organisational structure, group interaction, competences and knowledge management.

Royal Mail has developed a 'Customer First' strategy which encompassed four aspects:

- employee involvement;
- customer satisfaction;
- continuous improvement;
- partnership building.

Seeboard is an example of an organisation whose customer service strategy has touched many aspects of business life. Since the 12 regional electricity boards were privatised in the early 1990s and forced to compete for business, they have had to sharpen their focus on customer service. Seeboard supplies electricity to 2 million customers in the south east. Each year, 10 million bills and reminders are sent out. Staff handle 3 million customer calls and 1 million letters and arrange 750,000 home visits. Seeboard set itself an aggressive service delivery strategy whose aim is to be 'simply the best'.

Improved staff communications, extensive training and the implementation of new technology form part of the strategy. Job-specific training is backed by courses on telephone excellence and how to achieve exceptional customer service. Other improvements to customer service have included extending office opening hours for customer enquiries, installing pay-as-you-go budget key meters in 180,000 homes, and arranging for people to pay their bills in cash, free of charge, at post offices. The strategy has brought improvements in customer response times and a decline in the number of complaints to the regulator.

Typical areas which a customer service strategy needs to address include the following:

Job design and competencies

Fortune magazine points out that, 'for all the improvements made possible by technology, the quality of service often depends on the individual who delivers it. All too often he is underpaid, untrained, unmotivated and half-educated.'

There is now greater recognition of the need to identify the skills, qualities and attributes needed to be effective in a customer-driven environment. Driven by a vision to 'create the best performing financial services business in the UK', Royal Bank of Scotland conducted a fundamental review of how it thought about its business. This involved a process re-engineering project and focusing the business more on the customer. It was recognised early on that if there was to be greater specialisation, the need for people to understand job content and behaviour was paramount. The HR team developed role definitions that laid the foundations for completely new career streams and job 'families'.

The key to this was a competency framework that described roles in far greater detail. For example, the role of customer services manager would have been described in the past in terms of *what* had to be done. Using the competency framework, the description included the definition of *how* the job was to be done by introducing factors such as planning and organisation. It was recognised that understanding staff skill could aid selection, performance management, training, the creation of a 'human asset' register and individual rewards.

Structure of the organisation

The structure an organisation adopts influences its strategy and in turn its strategy influences the structure it adopts (see Figure 2.3).

As businesses strive to move closer to their customers, many senior managers have begun to view bureaucratic organisations as inflexible, costly and a barrier between the company and its customers.

There is a growing awareness of the vulnerability of size where it is not accompanied by responsiveness and flexibility. In order to understand more fully the requirements and aspirations of customers and to respond to them proactively, organisations are becoming flatter, leaner and tighter. As one HR director of a high-tech company summarised:

> There is increased delegation of decision-making to the customer interface and fewer management layers between customers and decision points. There is more lateral communication and speedier decision-making in our de-layered organisation.

FedEx, the first US company to win the prestigious Malcolm Baldrige National Quality Award, has only five layers of management between its

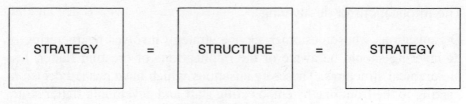

Figure 2.3 Structure

non-management people and chief executive officer and chief operating officer. According to the chief operating officer FedEx has, 'Truly made an effort to invert the traditional hierarchical pyramid and to put the emphasis where it belongs – with our customer contact people.'

Similarly, in the UK, BT has undergone a massive restructuring to become more responsive to the needs of the customer. Its intention was to create a more flexible, imaginative and entrepreneurial management culture to reduce organisational complexity and management costs. Ian Valance, BT's ex-chairman, has said:

> Our objective is to become a leaner and more subtle organisation, structured to meet the differing needs of our customers. We were organised by product and geography... that might have been convenient for us but it did not suit our customers.

Other organisations have found that de-layering helps break the organisation's paradigm – the way things are 'done round here'. When chief executive Archie Norman joined ASDA in 1991 the business was on the verge of collapse, having been one of the most successful retailers of the 1980s. The business centre had grown enormously and had become increasingly bureaucratic. It had also been extravagant in its spending as it tried to ape its major competitors.

> We had to break the head off this culture and cut layers of management so the stores were not so remote. We were trying to break the ingrained habits of having to function as an organisation which was highly centralised and controlling.

ASDA now has only two layers of management between the chief executive and the store managers. None of the managers wears a jacket on the shop floor; this is significant, as it says 'I'm not here to work, you are.'

The implications of de-layering

Organisations whose customer service strategy involves restructuring or de-layering should be aware of the implications of creating flatter, less hierarchical structures. Those organisations which have pushed decision-making to the front line by empowering staff and developing flatter structures have noticed knock-on effects in terms of employee and organisational development.

In flatter organisations there is often a need to:

- multi-skill the workforce;
- place greater emphasis on training and development;
- develop opportunities for career progression outside of the traditional hierarchical structure;
- enable individuals to become empowered;
- redefine the role of the manager within the new structure;
- place greater emphasis on teams;
- develop a sense of shared goals and values;
- motivate individuals towards organisational excellence.

Unless support and coaching are provided within new organisational structures, individuals can be left with a feeling that they are being asked to produce more for less. There is documented evidence that employees are suffering greater pressure and stress at work as a result of such changes. To counterbalance this, senior managers need to consider and to weigh up the benefits of bringing the organisation closer to the customer. They also need to consider the cultural impact of change.

Restructuring alone may not bring a greater customer focus. As Gary Hammel and C K Prahalad point out in their best-seller, *Computing for the Future*:

> Down sizing, the latest in attempts to correct mistakes of the past; it is not about creating markets of the future. Getting smaller is not enough. Down sizing, the equivalent of corporate anorexia, can make a company thinner; it doesn't necessarily make it healthier.

Companies such as Ford and Unipart are recognising that the new, flexible labour market requires a positive response from employers in terms of investing in greater training and development for their employees. They believe that because top-quality staff respond by giving commitment to employers that invest in them, this approach can be good for business.

Improved technology

As discussed in Chapter 1, information technology is now being used within a wide framework to deliver significant service improvements.

As customers become more demanding they often require access to services outside traditional working hours. Increased use of the telephone, together with the Internet, has made this possible, and those organisations which wish to gain or retain their competitive edge are recognising that technology is an essential part of business life.

The major benefits of technology in contact centres is the increased ease of making contact and reduced waiting time for the customer. However, most value is added to the caller during interaction with the service provider. The differentiator is the quality of call-answering staff. Staff selection, training and development therefore must be a priority.

First Direct is notable for its commitment to training. The company has an advanced approach to preparing banking representatives for managing customer relationships rather than simply answering calls. Banking representatives, the first point of contact for customers, undergo a three-hour selection process. Successful candidates are then put through a rigorous seven-week training programme.

This focuses on three main issues: systems, products and services, and effective communication. In the first week of training three days are spent evaluating trainees' communication techniques and helping them to recognise what communication is and what makes it effective. Communication models are used to provide a common language for discussing techniques.

During the last two weeks of training, banking representatives are allowed to take customer calls, but only with experienced staff alongside to provide additional coaching. Finally, before they can take calls unaided, they undergo a formal accreditation, taking simulated calls which span the range of enquiries they would encounter. Only after accreditation are they allowed to become part of the public face of First Direct.

One manager aptly summed up the use of technology to enhance customer service:

> IT is only as good as the people who use it. The best systems will only be as good as the quality of interaction between the customer service adviser and the customer.

Getting the processes right

One popular strategy to ensure that organisations focus on the customer is the adoption of such techniques as business process re-engineering.

A business can be seen as a series of activities with inputs and outputs, a result of which should service the customer. Business process re-engineering requires companies to focus on how they create and deliver value to customers. Each decision and action is identified to reveal the processes through which customers' needs are satisfied. The steps in the process are mapped out. This then helps to identify duplication of effort, unnecessary tasks, delays, opportunities for automation and so on. Wasted effort and delays can then be eliminated and stages at which value is added can be pinpointed for extra effort. The end result should be huge cost savings and productivity benefits, together with improved quality and faster time to market.

At Lloyds TSB, for example, the process mapping in their home-buying market resulted in a reduction of three separate processes managed across four functions to one process. This was then managed in a consistent and logical fashion by one function who reduced the time it took from an average of 30 days to formal offer to an average of 7 days to formal offer, reducing five forms with 167 questions and four or five interviews to one application form with one interview.

Business process re-engineering is commonly associated with clean sheet analysis – re-inventing a process from scratch – but such a radical approach is rarely necessary. Axa Sun Life, for example, achieved enormous benefit by focusing on those processes which it identified could deliver a sustainable competitive advantage. The company began to re-engineer its distribution and customer service processes in the 1990s. Customer focus groups and service staff closest to customers revealed that customers were looking primarily for improvements in speed rather than technical quality. Analysis of one process suggested that the turnaround time could be reduced by almost 80 per cent. Eliminating the backlog of work and taking a more proactive approach to managing capacity afforded a 21 per cent improvement. A further 25 per cent improvement came from managing third parties more effectively.

By improving the design of forms, for example, and with more direct contact with external customers, significant gains were made possible. Further improvements were brought about from streamlining the processes and reducing the number of people involved, and from increased quality through making fewer mistakes.

Analysis of processes for re-engineering, therefore, brings into sharp focus how efficient a company is in satisfying customer needs. It is a powerful part of a customer service strategy. However, like delayering it often involves dismantling functional boundaries and hierarchies, resulting in fundamental change which affects everyone within an organisation. Business process re-engineering has also been criticised for ignoring the people factor – a reduction in staffing levels is not inevitable. A re-engineered business asks a great deal more of its individuals.

People management

A customer service strategy must encompass, therefore, a philosophy on managing people within a service environment.

Richard Branson says, 'Look at your employees first, then your customers, then your shareholders.'

Southwest Airlines is a low-fare airline with 284 aircraft, based in Dallas. It is the United States fourth-largest airline, and the only one to continuously make a profit. Synonymous with fun, Southwest's mission statement concludes with these words: 'above all, employees will be provided the same concern, respect and caring attitude within the organisation that they are expected to share externally with every Southwest customer'.

This philosophy translates to the people-management strategy within the airline where individuals are hired for their customer orientation rather than their skills. They are then developed and encouraged to have fun at work, playing games and running competitions for passengers.

The role of the leader

It is over 10 years ago that Professor Benjamin Schneider of the University of Maryland established the direct relationship between customer and employee satisfaction. In one business a 5 per cent increase in employee satisfaction resulted in a 2 per cent gain in customer satisfaction and retention and a 2 per cent increase in profitability. To get the best out of their people, the role of the manager in a service environment is to coach, not to police. The characteristics of service style leaders are that they:

- are good listeners;
- encourage teamwork and good communication;
- delegate responsibility;

- require and recognise excellence;
- encourage problem-solving;
- request and welcome feedback;
- constantly seek out ideas and improvements;
- engender trust;
- are open and honest in their relationships.

This means greater consultation, involvement and regular communication with team members.

Boots the Chemist has established a string of new centres to offer the customer private health care and fitness services alongside its traditional pharmaceutical offerings. It expects its future managers to be able to manage a more emotional relationship with the customer and in turn with employees.

Managers at First Direct model the behaviours many organisations are aspiring to. Launched in February 1988, First Direct has made a significant impact on the financial services market. Market research suggested that it would have to offer four things to make the new bank succeed: speed, convenience, value for money and quality of service. Realising that the first three provided less opportunity for differentiation than quality of service, First Direct looked closely at this. Part of the definition of good service it came up with was composed of 'hygiene factors', what, when and so on, which again could easily be copied. But 'motivational factors' were also involved – how well the service is provided, how helpful, knowledgeable and efficient employees are and how much trouble they take to get it right. Says First Direct's ex-chief executive Kevin Newman:

> The moment of truth is when a banking representative takes a hundred phone calls towards the end of a busy seven-hour shift. Will they still be sufficiently committed to want to make this very last customer feel special – to feel that he or she has had a personal service?
>
> We convinced ourselves that the only element we could compete on was the motivational aspects of customer service. Broadly speaking, this company's only long-term assets are its people and the culture in which they operate.

First Direct's 2,000 staff are based at two sites in Leeds. They provide around-the-clock service, 365 days a year. It subsidises the cost of its 20,000 calls a day from customers, who pay only the local rate from anywhere in the UK.

First Direct's culture is designed to release the potential of the people who work in direct contact with customers. Newman explains:

Our managers are trying to move away from a hierarchical form of management to one in which people at all levels understand their roles, and managers perform more of a coaching role than a supervisory one.

Nobody has a reserved parking space, and the same applies to offices. First Direct is totally open plan and when senior managers want to have a private meeting, they must book a meeting room just like everyone else.[5]

People quality

A further consideration in the development of a customer service strategy is the need to develop quality people within the organisation. This can often lead to a re-evaluation of the recruitment, training and development processes, as well as career progression.

Car retailer Audi, for example, has developed the Audi Academy, a virtual university that delivers recruitment, training and personal development for every one of its 3,200 members.

At Eurodisney, the reward structure was revised so that front-line staff such as bartenders were paid more than their supervisors.

Other organisations, as we will see in Chapter 7, produce specific training and development in customer service and customer service competences to develop a customer-focused workforce.

4. Develop a specific action plan

Whatever the strategy an organisation develops to enhance its customer care, it is essential that a plan is drawn up of how the strategy is to be implemented so that management can systematically measure its progress. A plan of action provides employees with a clear set of goals to aim for.

It is advisable to establish long-, medium- and short-term objectives and implementation actions and to review these at regular intervals. For example, the long-term objective of a service quality programme may be for an organisation to 'distinguish itself from its competitors by providing a superior standard of customer service'. Senior management may agree that this objective will take three years to attain. In the first year the milestone may be, for example, attaining a score of 85 per cent in terms of customer satisfaction compared to competitors. A medium-term objective for year two may be to increase that score to 90 per cent and a three-year objective may be to move to 95 per cent on very satisfied customers.

To help achieve each objective there may be specific actions needed. For example, year one's actions may be:

- to develop leadership training for all managers;
- to ensure that all team members attend a service workshop;
- to establish improvement teams in each internal department to undertake process reviews across all aspects of the business.

5. Establish criteria for success

At the same time as developing a plan of action to sustain the strategy, criteria for measuring the attainment of these customer service objectives must be determined. These criteria could include such indices as:

- increased market share;
- high levels of customer retention;
- increased profitability;
- greater staff motivation.

They could also include measures as behavioural pointers to change: the number of customer visits made by members of management; the number of problems solved by members of staff in their workplace, etc.

Lex Services is an example of an organisation that is using the 'balanced scorecard' approach to measuring business performance. Developed by Professor Kaplan, the balanced scorecard provides organisations with a system for measuring performance in terms of:

- customer satisfaction;
- development of staff;
- financial performance;
- organisational learning.

This provides a more holistic approach to performance than looking back only at financial results.

European Quality Award

Many organisations are turning to the European Foundation for Quality Management (EFQM) model of organisational excellence to help them develop a service strategy and assess their progress. There are three main models which are generally used for assessment: Deming, which has six elements of assessment; Baldridge, which has seven; and EFQM, which has nine. Many companies such as Hewlett-Packard and Milliken have developed their own.

Normally the models provide a framework for critically examining the organisation's method and performance. The EFQM model is now widely accepted as a benchmark for Europe and is linked to the European Quality Award. The model is a tool which can be applied at various levels within the organisation to measure the impact of service delivery. The model encompasses the following as customer service enablers:

- leadership;
- people management;
- policy and strategy;
- resources; and
- processes.

It measures results in terms of people satisfaction, customer satisfaction, impact on society and business results. For the customer satisfaction and employee/people satisfaction categories as well as, to a lesser extent, the impact on society, most weighting is given to perception rather than other measures. For business results, financial and non-financial measures are used. Figure 2.4 shows the EFQM model:

Organisations such as the Royal Mail have used the European business excellence self-assessment method to evaluate the contribution its customer service department is making to overall business excellence.

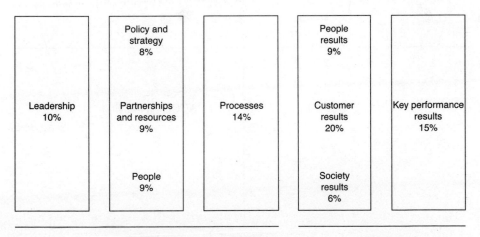

Figure 2.4 The EFQM self-assessment module

6.   Identify obstacles to progress

Creating a customer service culture within an organisation involves change. Models such as the European Quality Award provide a useful tool to monitor the degree of change that is taking place.

In every process of change – a new job, a move from home, a new baby, divorce, bereavement – many people experience a sense of loss of security and familiarity. The same is true in a major organisational change such as instilling a service quality philosophy.

People's reaction to change is often dependent upon their status within the organisation, their attitudes towards their employer, past experiences and organisational norms. A typical pattern of response to change is vacillation between initial *resistance*, followed by a period of *denial* where

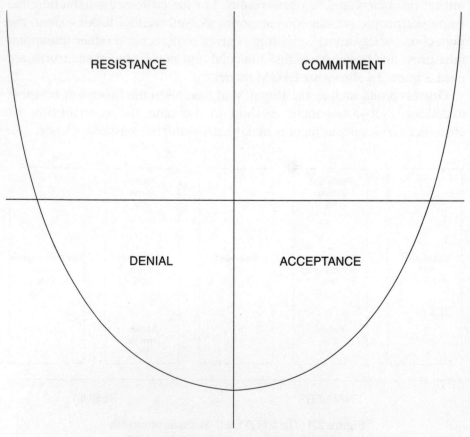

Figure 2.5 People's reaction to change

people refuse to face up to the implications of change. The transition period should lead to exploration of the effect of the changes and final *acceptance* and *commitment* to the new way of working (see Figure 2.5).

People's reactions to change can often be classified into those of an innovator, a conservative or an inhibitor.

Innovators welcome change and see it as a challenge. They are stimulated by new ideas and concepts and are willing trialists. *Conservatives* wait to see the results and effects of change before accepting alterations to power bases and positions. *Inhibitors* are those people who, through reasons of insecurity, fear or inertia, resist change and are slow to adapt. They will only accept change when it is part of standard practice and the changes have been fully adopted by the rest of the organisation, and it becomes increasingly difficult for them to 'hold out'.

At the beginning of the development of a service quality programme, senior managers need to identify the innovators, conservatives and inhibitors within their organisation. Innovators are those people who are most likely to accept quickly a service quality philosophy. Conservatives will adopt the philosophy once they see its tangible results. Inhibitors will be slow to change. Inhibitors often express their hostility towards a programme in terms such as:

'We're already doing it.'

'We've tried it all before.'

'It's flavour of the month.'

'It's all American hype.'

'Why don't they spend the money on increasing our salaries?'

'It's someone else's problem.'

Middle management

Middle management are often identified as the main obstacle to service improvement.

Surveys show that whereas team members overwhelmingly favour service improvement programmes because they gain more say in improving the way they work, organisations often experience a problem in the task of changing management behaviour.

In a process of change it is the middle ranks of the organisation who often feel squeezed as they become sandwiched between senior managers who have issued a directive to change and know clearly where the organisation should be going, and those members of staff who may be cynical and sceptical about the change. In this situation middle managers may vacillate between their commitment to the goals of the organisation and their identification with the sentiments of staff.

Developing a customer care strategy disrupts the lines of command and control, threatening functional power bases. Empowerment, a key feature of a service strategy as well as business process re-engineering and re-structuring, means delegating power. There is a new focus for management on facilitating ongoing improvement, demanding a new range of skills, and closer scrutiny of performance. Resistance to change, particularly in a business which has operated successfully for many years, is generally the biggest obstacle to creating a customer focus.

It is critical, therefore, to develop a service strategy which ensures the involvement of middle management from the start of a programme. Likewise, demonstrating tangible benefits early on in the programme is important in order to prevent disillusionment creeping in.

Failure to engender management commitment is often attributed to the lack of explanations provided to lower and middle management, from the outset of a programme, about how the service strategy is intended to work and the role they will be required to play. Typical comments made by middle managers who are involved in service quality improvement programmes are:

'A great concept but difficult to put into practice.'

'I believe in it but I can't always give it any time.'

'Difficult to monitor.'

'It's not easy to see any tangible evidence of success.'

It must be stressed to middle management, therefore, that they are the key to bringing about the necessary radical changes required as part of a successful programme.

It can be helpful to use analytical models to assess the power of the driving forces for change and to identify potential allies and competitors. Two such models are the actor/issue matrix and force-field analysis.

Actor/issue matrix

This concept allows managers to evaluate the issues affecting individuals as they face a period of change and therefore their likely reaction to change.

A matrix is drawn to identify on one axis the key participants, or actors, in the organisational arena, and on the other axis the issues that are likely to be of direct concern to participants when a service programme is introduced. Using this matrix, senior managers can consider the attitudes of each participant to each of the issues related to the introduction of a service strategy and highlight any possible obstacles.

For example, where service improvements are likely to include greater involvement of team members, the actor/issue matrix in Figure 2.6 could apply.

For each of the issues identified it is possible to postulate who is likely to be for or against, neutral or indifferent to each goal and why this might be so.

Senior managers can then identify how each actor is likely to react in the event of such changes and establish a strategy for dealing with these reactions. In this way, the chances of getting a programme implemented are improved.

Force-field analysis

Force-field analysis provides another useful model for analysing the likely reactions of people throughout the organisation to the desired change. It is based on the idea that any situation can be regarded as a result of two sets of opposing but balanced forces. Force-field analysis allows senior managers

Actor/Issue	Person A	Person B	Person C
Loss of status derived from position	*		
Opportunity to develop skills		*	*
Easier control of service quality			*

Figure 2.6 Example of actor/isse matrix

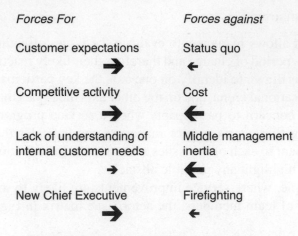

Figure 2.7 Example of force-field analysis

to identify and assess the strength of the forces that are likely to be opposed or to support the change. In putting the change into effect, the forces in favour of the change need to be increased and the forces opposing it minimised. Figure 2.7 shows an example of a hypothetical force-field analysis for the introduction of a quality programme in an insurance company.

The role of senior management in service quality

A service philosophy will not become part of the culture of an organisation unless service is seen to be valued by the leaders of the organisation. Essentially leaders need to champion culture change.

'You do what you value and you value what you do' is a maxim which can be applied to service quality programmes. Senior managers, therefore, need to be seen to visibly support the service programme if employees are to recognise its importance. If senior managers say 'do this' and employees see them applying other rules to suit their own needs and circumstances, it is hardly surprising that employees do not take service seriously.

A manager in a bank, for example, serves no purpose in putting a service statement on the wall and exhorting his or her staff to give good service to customers if he or she then shuts themself away in the office and is reluctant to help out on a till when the counter is busy at lunchtimes and the branch is short on staff. The manager is not reinforcing a service ethic because he or she probably in turn does not perceive that his or her area manager is encouraging them to do so. Typically, the area manager may only mention service (and then in a critical fashion) if the branch's 'mystery shopper' results are poor. He or she may not provide encouragement and support, or recognition of good efforts, or demonstrate through his or her behaviour that he or she wishes everyone to focus on the customer. The CEO of First Union Corporation explains, 'Service sinks in when managers talk and act service, service, service day in and day out in obvious and subtle ways.'

Many senior managers fail to appreciate that customer service requires a different approach to business. The traditional controlling style of management, in which staff's role was to help the manager do his or her job, needs to be abandoned in favour of a facilitating role, where the manager enables members of staff to perform their key task of serving the customer. Managers therefore need to 'lead by example'.

When Xerox Corporation was fighting back against the Japanese copier onslaught in the early 1980s, CEO David Kearns led a culture change in which customer satisfaction became the number one corporate goal. He reinforced it powerfully by insisting that he and his senior executive colleagues took it in turn once a month to answer customer complaints and queries on the phone.

The role of leaders should be to help workers to know what their firms stand for, and to facilitate the identification of employees' aims with those of the organisation. A good leader is able to engender the belief in his or her staff that they are running their own business, while still working towards the overall objectives of the company.

The Chinese sage, Lao-Tse wrote 25 centuries ago:

> A leader is best when people hardly know he exists. Not so good when people obey and acclaim him, worse when they despise him. Fail to honour people and they fail to honour you, but of a good leader, when his work is done, his aim fulfilled, they will say, 'We did this ourselves'.

In a service-oriented organisation, leaders need to appear throughout the business, not just in a senior management role.

Service champions

Just as every crusade requires its champion, service heroes and sponsors are required to bring about successful change. These are people of sufficient status and influence within the business who can challenge the organisational paradigm and create and communicate a new vision for the organisation.

Ideally a service champion should be at the head of the organisation itself and have sufficient faith in his or her beliefs to be able to persuade other followers to join him or her and to 'spread the word'.

Charles Dunstone, founder of Carphone Warehouse, has built a business which makes more than £600 million a year by putting himself in the customers' shoes and trying to understand their needs.

The chairmen of both IBM and Ericcson report spending more than 50 per cent of their time talking with customers.

In every organisation there is likely to be resistance to change brought about by inertia and fear. It is important that this resistance is not smothered – people should be allowed to voice their concerns. A service champion and his or her followers, therefore, needs to set a positive example for fellow employees and to encourage dialogue and feedback.

Behaviour patterns and skills are not inherited, they are learnt and copied, so senior managers in particular must set a shining example. They especially need good communication skills. Experience shows that often those people at a senior level who do champion a service quality cause can also be those who identify intellectually with the concept – but they may not always be particularly articulate when communicating the philosophy to their more practically minded subordinates.

Having established a mission or vision for the organisation, therefore, the management team need to create and communicate an expectation among fellow employees that a customer care strategy is ongoing and not just a one-off campaign. Frequently organisations begin initiatives which last for a short period of time only. This causes a heightened degree of cynicism.

7. Implement

Successful management teams build customer care into all the actions they take as managers of the company. Here is a selection of practical actions which senior managers can undertake to bring a service philosophy to life.

a. *Integrate service quality into all management activities*

The most powerful way a management team can show visible and verbal commitment to service quality is to integrate customer care into all management activities. This means:

- putting customer service on top of all management agendas;
- including customer satisfaction scores on all profit and loss statements;
- including customer service on all job descriptions;

- including customer service in all appraisals;
- talking customer service at all company updates, briefings, departmental meetings, presentations and training sessions.

Introduce some ways in which customer care can become integrated into a business's activities so that it becomes the number one factor in organisational life.

b. Give time to spearhead the service programme

The value management put on an activity is often perceived by employees as directly related to how management spend their time.

During British Airway's 'Putting People First' campaign, Sir Colin Marshall delivered the closing speech at two-thirds of the first 430 sessions. Another airline chief, Jan Carlson of SAS, has also been deeply involved in his company's quality programme, to the extent of having written a book on the subject.

It is essential for senior management to make time to spearhead a customer service strategy by attending launch events, communication forums, training sessions and reviews, and to be open to questions and involvement in debate.

c. Initiate regular customer contact

How many senior managers in this country have regular contact with their customers? When was the last time the marketing director of one of the rail companies had to check the tickets of hot and angry commuters forced to stand in a late and overcrowded train where the air conditioning had broken down, or a supermarket boss soothed the nerves of a frustrated shopper?

The remoteness of many senior managers leads them to be shut off from honest feedback and dragged into internal politics. An important method of demonstrating visible commitment is for management to have direct contact with customers. All ASDA senior managers are committed to a programme of 'listening groups' where they meet customers on a regular basis, for example.

Tom Farmer, Chairman and Chief Executive of Kwik-Fit, and every one of his management team, spend one week a year working in one of the Kwik-Fit depots. They fit exhausts, change tyres and, even more importantly, are seen by the staff dealing with customers. They are observed working to Tom Farmer's customer policy:

I am your customer, satisfy my wants – add personal attention and a friendly touch – and I will become a walking advertisement for your products and services. Ignore my wants, show carelessness, inattention and poor manners and I will simply cease to exist – as far as you are concerned.

In addition, Tom Farmer regularly visits each one of his depots and commits one evening a fortnight to telephoning customers to enquire how they had found the service the previous day.

Tom Pritzker, President of the family-owned Hyatt Corporation in America, insists on putting his management in the field as doormen, front desk attendants and food servers. For two years running Hyatt Hotels have held an 'In Touch Day'. Originally conceived as a morale booster for lower-level employees, the company's managers have discovered how vital and often difficult is the role of the service provider.

With most hotels providing a similar service, Hyatt's executives believe it is the employees in the front line who determine the fate of the company. Tom Pritzker believes that this type of corporate 'upstairs-downstairs' role-reversal has changed managers' decision-making. Tom Pritzker himself works as a porter, doorman and a waiter at his family's Washington DC Park Hyatt Hotel as part of the 'In-Touch Day.' The day following the 'In Touch' programme, lower-level employees go to the corporate suites to see how the other half live.

This type of involvement, of getting on the shop floor, experiencing the service itself and keeping close to the customer, has three major effects:

- It helps avoid the imposition of procedures and policies which in fact hinder staff in delivering good service.
- Obvious involvement helps strengthen the commitment of management to staff.
- It avoids the double standard of managers talking about the quality of service and not acting by example.

Organisations ranging from Avis to Mrs Field's Cookies recognise the benefits of 'visible management', when head office managers spend time each year on the front line. MBNA America Bank requires each manager to spend four hours a month listening to customers' phone calls.

Richard Branson's active participation in his airline, Virgin Atlantic, is a benefit for customers. After a Virgin flight, Branson faxes his Crawley head office with comments, suggestions and criticisms gleaned from talking to passengers and observing the in-flight service. All are investigated and reported back to the Chairman.

d. *Monitoring customer satisfaction*

Coming into direct contact with the customer is only one means of listening to customers. It is also important that senior management spend time and effort in monitoring customer satisfaction on an ongoing basis.

Pret A Manger is an example of an organisation which does both. Pret A Manger serves thousands of customers a week in sandwich bars throughout the London area. Director Julian Metcalfe sums up the company's philosophy:

> Quite rightly with hindsight we realise that what brings customers back is a good product at the price and with the right service. That is 95 per cent of the battle, what makes us a success is repeat trade. You can fool a customer once or twice but after that they won't come back. . . . We tend to look at what we are trying to achieve from the customer's perspective, not from the shop's perspective. We are also reminding our staff that it's not we who pay them their wages, it's the customer, and that every single sandwich that they make is someone's lunch.[6]

It keeps in touch with the front line by shutting down the entire Fleet Street head office for one day every quarter, giving all head office staff the chance to spend a day preparing sandwiches, serving behind the counter or cleaning tabletops. In addition, a message from Julian Metcalfe is printed on all sandwich wrappers and carrier bags, extolling customers to phone him directly with any comments or suggestions they may have on any aspect of the product, price or service. In this way, Julian Metcalfe and his co-directors hope to keep closely in touch with their customers.

Senior managers in other best-practice organisations regularly monitor the levels of customer satisfaction and spearhead initiatives to bring about service improvement.

A personal promise and commitment to customer satisfaction from senior management emphasises the organisation's dedication. The then-CEO of Birmingham Midshires Building Society advertised his home phone number for customers to call with their concerns.

e. *Take a personal interest in complaints*

Although, as we will see in Chapter 3, complaints are not a reliable measure of customer satisfaction, senior management should have a process in place to deal effectively with complaints and take a personal responsibility and interest in their resolution.

J Willard Marriot, founder of the US hotel chain, personally read every customer complaint card and his son, Bill, the present chairman is reputed to read about 10 per cent of the thousands of letters that pour in each month.

Marriot not only benchmarks competitors' innovations but questions its customers on them: 'If Holiday Inn offers a free continental breakfast, Marriot will know within weeks whether its customers would like one too.'

All managers at mobile telephone company Orange were given the experience of what it is like to be on the receiving end of customer complaints. About 200 spent a day listening in to customer calls. It was hoped that this experience would make them more customer focused and improve the status of the firm's customer service staff.

f. Regularly buy your goods and use your services

A further means of getting close to the customer is for senior management to experience the treatment received by customers when they buy the goods and use the services that their organisation provides.

If it is not possible to directly purchase goods, managers can telephone their company to make an enquiry to see how it is handled. For example:

- How quickly was the telephone answered?
- What was the attitude of the service provider?
- Did you receive all the information you expected on the products or services you wished to purchase?

Alternatively, they can visit the company's Web site. This simple method allows senior executives to put themselves in the customer's shoes to gain an independent perspective of the organisation.

g. And those of your competitors

As we will see in Chapter 3, it is useful to benchmark the quality of the service that is provided by an organisation against that of competitors.

A simple means of monitoring how well a company is performing is for senior management to buy the goods or use the services of competitors. Where this is not possible, managers can make similar enquiries about products and services.

Not only does this bring about greater awareness of the choice available to customers, but it also provides direct comparison of how different companies deal with enquiries.

h. Publish a service statement for customers

Once a service philosophy has been established within the organisation and employees are trained in customer care, a means of demonstrating both senior management's and the organisation's commitment to service is to publish a statement or charter.

Private Patients Plan (PPP), for example, has published a Customer Service Charter setting out the rights and entitlements of their customers. This includes courtesy, helpful advice and guidance, fair and equitable service, confidential handling of personal details and affairs, and advance notification of change in cover.

The Co-operative Bank issued a set of customer service guarantees. They say:

Should any of our services not live up to any of the following promises we will put the problem right, say sorry and give you £10:

1. *Account opening*. We promise we will deal with your current account application within 48 hours of receiving it.
2. *Statements*. We promise not to make any financial errors on your statements – no ifs or buts.
3. *Cheque book and cards*. We promise we will automatically issue you a cheque book and cards to make sure you always have them available.
4. *Standing orders and direct debits*. We promise to set up and pay your standing orders and direct debits as instructed and without any mistakes.
5. *Personal loans*. Any requests from our current account customers for an overdraft or personal loan will be dealt with and, if approved, made available within one hour.

Service promises can be made in every business; for example, here is a customer guarantee printed by a local baker on the shop's paper bags:

Mr Coughlan's guarantee

At Coughlans we strive at perfection.

Our master craftsmen produce top quality products by using only the finest ingredients put together with traditional skills acquired in over 50 years of baking.

We believe that you, our customers, have the right to demand the very best. At Coughlans, we have pledged ourselves to provide it.

P J Coughlan, Master Baker and Confectioner.

In Burger King outlets a large poster advertises 'A customer care hotline' where customers are invited to phone in with their comments on the quality of products and services at Burger King restaurants.

Statements and advertisements such as these serve two useful purposes. First, they reinforce the company's commitment to service in the eyes of their customers; second, they reinforce to employees the importance of customer service to the organisation.

However, on a cautionary note, it is advisable not to publish such statements, pledges or charters unless the organisation is certain of delivering what it promises, as such communications often inflate customers' expectations.

i.   *Publish a service philosophy statement for staff*

Senior managers send a powerful message by publishing their own commitment to service quality.

In keeping with the company culture of informality, Virgin Atlantic Airways have very little paperwork relating to customer care. However, a key document is the 'guiding principles from Richard' which spells out the customer care philosophy in the Chairman's own words. This is:

> You must meet the passenger on his or her terms. They are individuals and require different things.

> As a rule we should be friendly and informal but always taking account of what the individual wants.

> Other airline staff are hidebound by rules. We should give ours guidelines and encouragement to solve a passenger's problem.

> First to know is best to deal with.

> The only way to make our staff trustworthy is to trust them. We must begin to trust people to use their judgement to resolve problems whilst being mindful of any cost to the company.

> Mistakes are inevitable; dissatisfied customers are not.

> Our staff should be happy, cheerful, smiling, friendly and enjoying their job. It is a manager's job to motivate the staff and create this atmosphere. Their role is to support their people in doing their best for the passenger. Money is not the answer but good leadership is.

We must give our staff responsibility and authority. Responsibility is the obligation to act, not just accept the blame. Authority is resources to deal with the situation.

We want our staff to bring their personalities to work and put it into their job, bring individuality, freshness and care to their work.

We need our staff to be comfortable with the exceptions, to think outside the framework and to do what is right for the passenger, not just 'the job'.

We want our staff to anticipate a passenger's problem. Think beyond the immediate, recognise the implications of their actions.

The only purpose in having frontline positions is if the passenger experiences service excellence. Otherwise, why not use machines?

We have two competitive advantages – product and service. We invest much time and money in keeping our product different, fun, interesting and high quality. We must now invest in the same way for our service.

We must communicate with our staff. If we change things we must tell them and tell them why.

We must listen to what our staff has to say and act on it. If we can't do it we must say why not.

We must improve in line with our culture, not at the expense of it.

We must never design what we do by assuming the worst in people.

Car hire company Avis has published a set of four 'People Guarantees' for all employees. These set out the organisation's promises to give everyone opportunities for personal development, regular communication, performance reviews and opportunities to contribute to improvements in service quality.

j.   *Publish your own standards of code of behaviour*
An effective means of setting an example throughout the organisation is for senior managers to publish their own standards of service/codes of behaviour. Here is an extract of standards of service published by a team of senior managers from an engineering company:

Our standards
Meetings
- Show up for meetings on time.
- Issue agendas for meetings well in advance.
- Come prepared for the meeting based on the agenda (time and subject).
- Be prepared to offer alternatives to any recommendations you make.
- Do not allow interruptions of meetings.
- Do not interrupt when someone else is talking – let him/her finish.

Likewise an individual's personal standards can be published. Here is an example of personal service standards set and published by a senior manager at a building society:

Bob's personal standards
Phone
Answer in three rings.
Greet callers with name and 'How may I help you?'
Accept all calls, if in.
Take and act on messages.
Always ring back when I say I will.

Correspondence
Respond accurately and politely.
Answer correspondence within two working days or quicker if in.

k.   *Feedback to staff the results of the programme*
Management can show their commitment to service quality if they regularly feed back to staff the results of any action taken to improve and enhance the quality of service provided to customers.

Team briefing, where information is cascaded throughout the organisation and fed back to senior management, is helpful in this process.

Organisations such as House of Fraser have produced videos for employees where their chief executive has personally endorsed service programmes and reported on their progress.

In other organisations such as freight carrier, The Lane Group, a newspaper has been regularly produced with comments from the senior management team and members of staff on the progress of its service initiative.

l. *Welcome feedback from staff*
Successful service leaders make time for their customers, suppliers and staff and seek out and welcome feedback. For example, Pete Harman, the

chief executive of Harman Stores, the largest Kentucky Fried Chicken concessionaire in America, spends 50 per cent of his working time talking to staff and listening to customers.

Other executives make time in their diaries each week for personal visits to customers and staff.

The CEO of a computer company, for example, holds working lunches on a weekly basis with six different members of staff. This allows employees an opportunity to question and give feedback to him on their opinions and concerns. The CEO in turn encourages his team of managers to hold regular get-togethers on an informal basis with their staff.

At Nationwide Building Society members of staff were invited to a series of events called 'Talkback', which allowed employees the opportunity to question senior managers of the society about philosophies and policies. A free exchange of ideas and views was encouraged by holding these regular forums.

m. Encourage teamwork

Encouraging teamwork from the top of the organisation downwards helps build an atmosphere of openness and trust. Senior management of an organisation must be seen to work as a team to set a positive example for their subordinates. It is often a useful exercise at the beginning of service quality initiatives for the management team to review their team effectiveness by honestly replying to questions such as:

- How does the team make decisions?
- Are all the potential resources and creativity of team members used to the full?
- How well organised are the team in approaching a task?
- How effective is the interaction among team members?
- Are disagreements and conflicts used constructively in the team?

In this way team members can understand and complement each other's roles.

At National & Provincial Building Society, for example, a major change programme to focus the organisation more on customers was initiated by developing a network of teams throughout the organisation to encourage greater ownership and openness.

n. Recognise success

Senior managers need to be aware of the power of recognition.

At Richer Sounds, the hi-fi business founded in 1978 by Julian Richer and featured in *The Guinness Book of Records* as Britain's busiest retailer,

Julian Richer recommends 'building recognition into your system as the quickest fix to start motivating people'. In many companies junior staff do not even know what their chairman looks like. At Richer Sounds, staff start their careers with a three-day training course at Julian Richer's house.

Every month employees in the three winning branches in the customer service competition, the Richer Way, win a car for a month. Two get Bentleys and one a Jaguar XJS convertible. The car is theirs to use as they wish; the company pays the petrol, and if the winners cannot drive, the company provides a chauffeur for two days. Richer's philosophy is that as many people as possible should be recognised – recognition should not only go to the high-fliers. 'If you want your staff to give great service, reward them for great service'.[7]

SUMMARY

In this chapter the steps needed to create a customer-focused culture have been discussed, including the development of an organisational vision and values.

The need to include customer service in the organisation's key objectives has been stressed. The chapter outlines a methodology for developing a customer service strategy.

Managers are the key to the successful implementation of the strategy and a variety of ideas on which managers can model their behaviour are suggested.

The next stage in the evolution of a service philosophy is the implementation of the strategy itself, and different approaches are outlined in the next chapters.

ACTION CHECKLIST

The action which can be taken as a result of this chapter is to:

1.   Develop a mission and vision for the organisation.

2.   Involve staff in the evolution of the mission and vision – regularly review this.

3.   Encourage the development of organisational values to implement the corporate mission and vision.

4.   Review the past performance of the organisation and evaluate its current position in terms of customer service.

---

5. Undertake a review of the factors in the near and far environments which impact upon service quality.

6. Identify organisational paradigms – discuss with your colleagues what words you would use to describe the culture of your organisation.

7. Establish objectives for your customer service programme – be clear about the criteria for success.

8. Identify obstacles to progress – develop a plan of action to overcome these.

9. Utilise innovators – they can become service champions for the organisation.

10. Ensure speedy and visible successes for the first stage of a quality programme.

11. Identify service leaders – encourage them to develop a following.

12. Spend time communicating and encouraging the implementation of the service strategy.

13. Stay close to your customers, monitor customer feedback and develop innovative ways of obtaining this.

14. Take responsibility and ownership for complaints – make sure an efficient complaints procedure is in place.

15. Purchase your products and services and those of your competitors – be a 'mystery shopper'.

16. Develop a service charter for customers and make sure you can adhere to this.

17. Publish your own personal standards.

18. Encourage teamwork throughout the organisation. Review the effectiveness of your own team.

19. Develop a service strategy that encompasses all parts of the business. Ensure that middle managers are involved in its design.

20. Review the size and structure of your organisation to bring it closer to the customer.

21. Review the job design of each role within the organisation. Develop customer service competencies.

22. Investigate how improved information technology can aid the service you deliver your customers.

23. Develop an implementation plan for the service strategy.

24. Review your organisational processes – how customer-friendly are they?

25. Review your people-management policies – how people and customer orientated are they?

26. Consider using the balanced scorecard or the European Quality Award as a measure of your business performance.

3

Listening to Customers

An essential first step in the development of all service initiatives is gaining feedback from customers. Listening to customers is vital if organisations wish not to only attract new customers but also to retain existing ones.

The use of market research is an important ingredient in developing a customer care programme and also a powerful means of monitoring the progress of customer service initiatives.

Many organisations fail to build hard measures of the effectiveness of service quality improvements into their customer care programmes. This chapter outlines the range of techniques for listening to customers and the advantages and disadvantages of each approach. It also demonstrates how to measure external as well as internal customer satisfaction.

BARRIERS TO LISTENING

The editor of *Business Week* summed up many companies' attitudes to the customer when he wrote:

> Probably the most important management fundamental that is being ignored today is staying close to the customer to satisfy his needs and anticipate his wants. In too many companies, the customer has become a bloody nuisance whose unpredictable behaviour damages carefully made strategic plans, whose activities mess up computer operations, and who stubbornly insists that purchased products should work.

A recent survey found that 86 per cent of company executives see themselves as being customer-centric. Yet often employees stop being consumers as soon as they walk into their place of work.

Often organisations believe that they have an understanding of their customers' requirements; this may however be based on a subjective rather than an objective viewpoint.

The barriers which prevent organisations getting close to their customers include:

- the evidence of anecdotal events which occur on a one-off basis and can cloud a manager's opinion;
- the views of complainants which are often not counterbalanced by non-complainants; a high percentage of customers do not complain – only one in 26 people is the figure often quoted, based on research undertaken in America;
- the opinions of a strongly articulate group of customers which may cloud an organisation's view of customer requirements;
- preconceptions within the organisation – the 'we have always done it this way and this is what the customer wants' syndrome.

These are all factors which prevent companies from gaining a true understanding of how well their products and services match customers' expectations.

It has been proved that by actively listening to customers companies can save, rather than expend money. The 1-10-100 rule illustrates this point. This says:

> For every pound your company might spend on preventing a quality problem, it will spend ten to inspect and correct the mistake after it occurs. In the worst case, the quality failure goes unanswered or unnoticed until after your customer has taken delivery. To fix the problem at this stage, you probably pay about 100 times what you could have paid to prevent it from happening at all.

A useful means of evaluating the cost of errors which go unheeded is to compile a cost diary and to estimate both the professional and personal costs of each error that occurs and the savings which could have been made based on prevention.

Organisations with the best practices actively encourage complaints. As business guru Theodore Levitt explains, 'One of the surest signs of a bad or declining relationship with a customer is the absence of complaints. Nobody is ever THAT satisfied, especially not over an extended period of time. The customer is either NOT being candid or NOT being contacted.'

THE MONITORING OF COMPLAINTS AND COMPLIMENTS

As on average only a small percentage of an organisation's customer base actually bothers to complain and fewer people take the trouble to compliment an organisation, the measurement of complaints and compliments is often misleading.

Furthermore, customers' perceptions of an organisation are often based on their dealings with front-line staff. These members of staff represent the organisation in the eyes of the customer, and any complaints that customers make are normally directed at this level. It takes a serious incident for the complaint to escalate beyond front-line staff. Consequently, it is often difficult for senior management to gain a true understanding of customers' concerns as they may have little direct contact. Complaints that organisations do receive are effectively the tip of the iceberg. For every *bad* experience of service, however, research shows that customers tell 10 other people. These figures are sure to explode with the advent of an increased use of the Internet.

It is important, nevertheless, that organisations give due consideration to the minority of customers who do contact them directly by instigating an effective system for dealing with both compliments and complaints. In fact, research by MORI indicates that customers are more likely to complain *if* they want a continuing relationship with the service provider. It is well worth therefore promoting a willingness to hear complaints. Camden Council regularly send out publicity material about its complaint process and has used the local press to promote its complaints procedure.

A customer who complains is giving the organisation another opportunity to put things right, and will be fair if treated fairly. A customer who makes a compliment allows an organisation an opportunity to recognise the efforts of the service provider and to publish the compliment as an example of good practice. Roadside caterers Little Chef took a novel approach to complaint management. It trained its employees to actively seek feedback from its customers. The results demonstrated a greater commitment by employees subsequently to action service improvements.

It is useful to analyse both complaints and compliments in terms of their source, type of complaint or compliment and the frequency with which they occur. It is also useful to track the time it takes to acknowledge a complaint – a speedy response or preferably a telephone call to acknowledge receipt of the complaint is important – and the amount of time it takes to resolve the complaint. Car hire company Avis has investigated company repurchase intention. It discovered that 92 per cent of customers who experienced no problems would repurchase from it again. Customers who experienced a problem and who complained and were satisfied had a repurchase intention of 91 per cent. Among customers who experienced a problem but didn't complain, repurchase intention fell to 78 per cent. However, only 46 per cent of customers who experienced a problem, complained and were not satisfied, would repurchase again from the company.

Customer care balance sheet

To gain a better understanding of the impact of complaints, a customer care balance sheet is a useful tool. It tells the organisation how much business it is losing both from customers who do not complain and from customers who do complain and are not satisfied with the way their complaint is handled.

Postal surveys can be used periodically to ask customers who have not complained and those who have, how satisfied they are with their experience, how many people they will tell if they are not satisfied and whether they intend to use the services of the company again, as a result of their experience.

The answers from these surveys are converted into annual lost sales revenues using the formula shown in Figure 3.1.

The first element is sales lost from customers who experienced a problem and who did complain but were not entirely satisfied with the way their complaint or enquiry was handled. (Sales lost include sales lost from negative word-of-mouth advertising and sales lost from customers who will not purchase the service again.)

The second element is sales lost from customers who experienced a problem but did not complain. Again, the sales lost include sales lost from

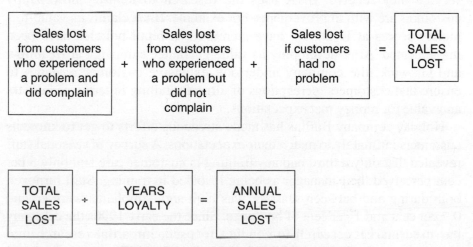

Figure 3.1 Customer care balance sheet

negative word-of-mouth advertising and sales lost from customers who will not purchase the service again.

From these two elements sales which would in fact have been lost anyway through normal attrition are detracted.

In the formulation, sales gained from positive word-of-mouth advertising are not taken into consideration because the formula deals with market damage rather than market opportunity (yet another area worthy of consideration).

To make the calculation accurate for each type of business, the formula is applied over the reasonable period of loyalty of the customers. The final calculation then takes the total sales lost over this period of loyalty, divided by the period of loyalty to arrive at annual sales lost.

This type of customer care balance sheet can help win the financial support of senior management to developing a means of ongoing customer measurement which allows employees throughout the organisation to determine how well they are performing.

THE VALUE OF LISTENING TO CUSTOMERS

Service quality improvements come about as a direct result of listening to customers, and proactively going out to generate feedback, rather than just relying upon complaints analysis.

British Airports Authority, for example, interviews around 120,000 customers a year. They are asked to give scores to different aspects of service they receive. BAA uses the research to identify how happy customers are with improvements. For example, BAA claims its value-for-money scores at Heathrow have increased as retail policies have been implemented. After developing its value guarantee campaign at Heathrow and Gatwick, the company undertook extensive customer research to ensure that customers' perceptions of airport retailing in terms of fairness and value for money met expectations.

Holiday company Butlins has made strenuous efforts to get to know its customers intimately to match their expectations. A survey of seasonal staff revealed that only a third had any training in customer care and only 5 per cent perceived their manager as being involved in training. Staff turnover, both during and between seasons, was high and complaints were around 0.9 per cent and 1 per cent of bookings. Since the early 1990s the company has used market research to conduct focused, impartial research into customer satisfaction and the kind of product people want from it. From that research comes the nucleus of a product which changes annually based on what customers tell the organisation. NOP research now shows that Butlins is achieving the highest level of customer satisfaction since its foundation nearly 60 years ago. Record numbers of customers are visiting its centres and the number of complaints has dropped to well below 0.3 per cent of bookings. Information technology is harnessed to analyse research, identify trends, measure repeat business and record and track the resolution of customer complaints.[8]

Electricity company Seeboard regularly canvasses the views of its customers about the service it provides. The research is carried out in the high street, on the doorstep and by telephone using detailed questionnaires. A customer service newspaper is produced for all customers to feed back results of the research and to explain what the company is doing to meet and exceed customer expectations.

Begin by listening

Successful service quality programmes, therefore, begin by listening to customers.

To gauge the quality of service an organisation provides, it is important to gain the views of customers *before* a service initiative begins. Likewise it is critical that customer satisfaction measures are based upon a customer's perceptions of what is important, rather than those of the organisation. Conducting surveys of customers before a service improvement programme begins provides a benchmark against which to monitor the progress of a service campaign.

Organisations such as Jaguar Cars have successfully applied this approach. At the beginning of the quality initiative instigated at Jaguar, Sir John Egan commissioned telephone research to gain customer's opinions on the quality of the product and service provided. Recordings of these conversations were played to senior management to demonstrate the areas of customer concern.

Often there is a difference between the 'perceived' and the 'received' levels of service. That is the quality of the service received by the customer and the perceptions of the quality of service given by the service provider. Research conducted among customers of Jaguar Cars illustrated that the company needed to take urgent steps to bridge this gap.

Canvass internal as well as external customers' views

Listening to customers does not have to be restricted to those outside the organisation. As well as conducting regular surveys of customer satisfaction among policy holders, NatWest Life tracks satisfaction levels among a second set of customers – the parent bank's dedicated sales force of personal financial advisers.

The first survey provided a startling benchmark of the level of service provided by the 12 major life offices. This survey indicated that 64 per cent of the sales force were satisfied with the service provided by these offices. The company set an initial target to achieve at least 70 per cent satisfaction among personal financial advisers in its first year of trading. By the end of the first year, 76 per cent of sellers stated that NatWest Life service was 'excellent' or that they were 'extremely satisfied'. The feedback from the sales force has been so positive that NatWest Life has stopped grouping the categories of 'excellent' and 'extremely satisfied' together and is now focusing on 'excellent' as a target.

MONITORING CUSTOMER SATISFACTION

Starting point

Monitoring customer satisfaction is a pointless exercise unless management are committed to the process and likely to act on the results. The objectives of monitoring, therefore, need to be clearly defined before a programme begins, together with a budget and timetable.

First, managers must decide which areas of customer satisfaction to measure. Different customers have different expectations and therefore different satisfaction levels with the service provided by an organisation. It is important to identify market segments – the groups of customers who should be included in any research – whose needs, expectations and satisfaction levels may alter greatly. Look, for example, at the different needs of a business and tourist passenger of an airline.

Next, the sample method for the research must be decided, before research is conducted and analysis takes place. Results can then be interpreted and disseminated to all those involved (Figure 3.2).

The presentation of results is often an area which is neglected in developing a measurement plan. Results will be ignored unless they are presented in a manner which is manageable and readily understandable to the recipients of the report. The objectives of the report should be to allow

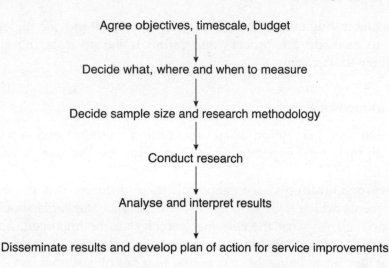

Agree objectives, timescale, budget

Decide what, where and when to measure

Decide sample size and research methodology

Conduct research

Analyse and interpret results

Disseminate results and develop plan of action for service improvements

Figure 3.2 Sequence of activity

managers and staff to take action as a result of the surveys. Research results become meaningless unless they are fed back quickly to the organisation. At Dominos Pizzas in America, for example, customer satisfaction results are posted publicly within 24 hours of the analysis being completed.

Review existing research

Before beginning a new programme of monitoring, it is useful to review any existing information or research data which the company may have collated in the past concerning customers and customer satisfaction. Typical questions to ask are:

- What do we know about our existing customers?
- What do we know about their expectations?
- How well are we meeting these expectations?
- What will happen in future to customer requirements?
- How do we compare to our competitors?
- How is the market likely to change in the next three years?

Other information may be obtained from the media, through published reports, forecast centres and competitive material.

Pilot scheme

We strongly advise that prior to commencing full-scale customer research a pilot is conducted to test the waters. Talking to customers, holding focus groups and testing questionnaires on a small scale all provide the opportunity to evaluate the process and refine it before it is introduced throughout the company.

What to measure

The customers' perception of an organisation's product and service is based on their total experience over time, not just the sale or one-off encounter.

Every organisation's customers will have different sets of service requirements which need to be measured. Service standards should be monitored against what the *customer* perceives to be important, not the organisation's perception. Many companies concentrate their measurement on what they see as being the 'risk points' in terms of customer service – it is important that these areas are also seen to be critical in customers' eyes.

A useful starting point is to identify:

- What are our customers' expectations?
- What standard of service do we currently provide our customers?
- Does this service meet our customers' expectations?
- If not, what are the problems?

Importantly, both customer satisfaction and loyalty should be measured. Customer satisfaction is only one piece in the jigsaw; customer loyalty must be the ultimate goal. Research by Xerox has shown that customers must be *very* satisfied (not just 'satisfied') to not seriously consider moving their business. An article in *The Harvard Business Review* stated unequivocally that 'completely satisfied' customers are – to a surprising degree – much more loyal than 'satisfied' customers. These findings are substantiated by AT&T, which had traditionally measured customer satisfaction using monthly surveys. The company added together the scores of customers who rated it as 'excellent' to those who rated it as 'good' to arrive at an overall customer satisfaction score – usually totalling around 90 per cent. However, in spite of these scores, many parts of the business were losing market share. It was only when the 'excellent' ratings were separated from the 'good' ratings that the true picture of customer loyalty emerged – 95 per cent of customers rating the service as 'excellent' subsequently remain loyal compared with only 15 per cent who rate it 'average'.

It may also be useful to see who or what influences your customers' expectations, for example advertising material, comparative service levels of competitors, reputation, etc. It would also be useful to ask: why do customers defect?

There are a number of variables which can be measured as part of a customer satisfaction survey. These include not only customer satisfaction in terms of performance against service standards but also repeat business and increase in orders. Other variables which can be measured include:

- reliability – ability to keep promises on a consistent basis;
- flexibility – speed in changing and adapting to new requirements;
- accuracy – lack of mistakes and defects, precise corrections;
- responsiveness – willingness to help and provide what's needed;
- empathy – giving individual attention to customers;
- tangibles – equipment, communication media, physical environment;
- time – minutes, hours, on time, overtime, time saved;
- quantity – over-budget, under-budget, profit, loss, break-even;
- quality – type of material, finish and durability.

Overview of methods

Telephone banking company First Direct monitors 5 to10 per cent of all calls and provides continuous feedback on measures such as:

- voice quality;
- rapport-building;
- ability to spot opportunities;
- average call duration;
- achieving income targets.

It is possible to monitor both hard and soft measures of customer satisfaction. At the AA, customer satisfaction has traditionally been monitored through retention rate, complaints and customer research. Hard data on performance within the service delivery operation such as fix rate – the proportion of members' vehicles fixed out of total workload; service levels – percentage of jobs attended within one hour; and jobs per shift – the number of jobs a patrol completes within a standard shift pattern, are also used as measures. The AA also wanted to be able to add softer data on members' expectations of performance and their opinion of what was actually delivered to get a more rounded view of the service delivery operation.

Importantly, it needed to be certain that it was focusing on what its customers wanted, not what the organisation thought they wanted, which often can be a trap businesses fall into when they gauge performance solely on the basis of internal measures. The softer data approach was constructed using a customer satisfaction index which was designed by the people who would have to use it. The index is based on customer perceptions of performance and opinions and each factor is weighted, reflecting the relevant importance that customers place on a range of elements within the service chain, such as waiting time, ability to fix a vehicle, and perceptions of the control and telephone operator.

Research has also shown that customers believe that there are a number of attributes that patrol members should demonstrate, such as efficiency, professionalism, helpfulness, courteousness, whether they provide reassurance, whether they are concerned about the customers' problems, are friendly and respectful. These attributes are weighted according to the relative importance placed on them and an aggregate figure is produced. This score comprises 50 per cent of the customer satisfaction index. The other 50 per cent is made up of customers' opinions on the service they have received, benchmarked against their expectations.

The index is generated by taking a sample of breakdown jobs and mailing members (customers) with a questionnaire four to six days after they have received the service. On average 6–8,000 members are mailed a month, which represents 1 in 32 incidents. The response rate to the questionnaire is around 50 per cent.

The customer satisfaction index programme enables the AA to highlight where they are under- and over-achieving. It also serves to motivate and develop the front-line staff's performance, with each team taking ownership of the results and producing an action plan.[9]

FedEx has built a unique service quality index (SQI). The SQI identifies the 12 major categories of customer dissatisfaction. Points are weighted to each category. The greater the total number of points, the higher the aggravation for the customer.

Cross-divisional root-cause teams were formed to identify problems and come up with solutions for each of the 12 SQI categories. The focus on customer service measurements has helped FedEx reduce the SQI points by 50 per cent over a four-year period, with volume growth of 80 per cent. At the same time as SQI points have been declining FedEx's customer and employee satisfaction levels have increased.

Market research companies

On some occasions companies find it is useful to employ the services of an outside market research agency to help in the preparation of the research, collation of the data and its interpretation. The Market Research Society, based in London, is a useful source of information on such agencies.

Specialist research companies can be particularly useful when large-scale research is to take place and when the client organisation does not have the resources to deal with this. Likewise, independent agencies can sometimes lend a degree of authority to a research project or ensure confidentiality, particularly where employee research is being undertaken.

Prompted by the Citizens' Charter, the Inland Revenue launched a major survey programme based on a four-year cycle. Concentrating on service delivery and not policy, each year a separate group of major customers has been surveyed to discover their experiences of dealing with the Inland Revenue and what they want from the service. The four groups comprise individuals (employed and self-employed), employers, pensioners and professional advisers.

The surveys are conducted on an annual basis and the Inland Revenue has used a professional market research firm for each one. Although it acknowledges that it needed the outside expertise for the first couple of surveys, it felt it could probably manage the techniques itself once these had been established. However, it made a deliberate point of continuing to use outside firms for three reasons:

1. It thinks respondents speak more freely to independent researchers.
2. The independent researchers brought an additional perspective to bear.
3. The results had more creditability.

The methodology used for each survey was to hold focus groups to identify the issues which were relevant to the survey population and to then hold internal discussions to identify the issues relevant to the Inland Revenue. At this point a questionnaire was prepared and piloted before the main survey was conducted, results disseminated and action taken on the findings.[10]

Sample sizes

To gain a representative sample of customer opinions it is not necessary to speak to all customers.

Sampling allows companies to gain information from a small number of customers who will represent the total universe of their customer base, thus ensuring shorter timescales for research and reduced costs.

Sample sizes are worked out on a mathematical basis using square roots. Therefore, the sample size needed to produce results within 5 per cent accuracy (when the universe size is known) for a range of universe sizes is, for example:

Universe number	Sample size
500	222
1,000	206
5,000	370
10,000	305
50,000	397

A word of caution is required, however, as the smaller the sample size the higher the probability of a range of error being present in research results. For example, a sample size of 100 customers gives an error range of 10 per cent. Therefore, when 50 per cent of customers respond that they are satisfied with the service, the true range of customer satisfaction figures could be anywhere between 40 and 60 per cent. This figure decreases the higher the sample size. Hence:

Sample size	Range of error (%)	Range of true figures (%)*
300	6	44–56
500	5	45–55
1000	3	47–53

*When the figure obtained is 50%.

This is why, for example, opinion polls are always read with a degree of caution by political parties.

Qualitative and quantitative methods

There are two main methods of gathering information from customers, qualitative and quantitative:

Quantitative Research (Hard issues and facts)	Qualitative Research (Soft issues and opinions)
Telephone surveys	Focus groups/user
Self-completion questionnaires	groups/customer panels
(comment cards)	Face-to-face interviews
Postal surveys	Videos
Mystery shopping	Freephone
Third party surveys	Suggestion schemes
Online surveys	Online discussion forums

Qualitative methods provide feedback from customers on 'soft issues and opinions' and give the organisation an opportunity to probe customers' feelings and attitudes on an in-depth basis. Typical qualitative techniques include user panels, customer groups, and personal interviews.

Quantitative methods allow the organisation to quantify customer opinions in a numerical fashion. Typical quantitative techniques include telephone surveys, self-completion questionnaires, the monitoring of compliments and complaints, and mystery shopping.

Care is required in the choice of the best methodology. The best plan is to adopt a variety of these techniques – an organisation is wise not to restrict itself to just one method. Forte Hotels, for example, uses mystery guest reports, quarterly telephone surveys and biannual guest-satisfaction postal audits to measure customer retention. It is normally possible to gain a greater degree and depth of information from qualitative methods, although quantitative routes reach a wider audience and often prove more cost-effective. Best practice shows that organisations need to use qualitative research to first gain insight into customers' attitudes and behaviour before using quantitative methods. In 1993, Eurodisney was not in an enviable position; its customer visits had dropped by 1 million and the newly opened theme park was in danger of making a loss. The first step to recovery was the setting up of focus groups in its target markets. The resultant data helped to reshape the 50,000 customer satisfaction questionnaires issued onsite each year to show a true picture of customer satisfaction.

Choosing an appropriate research method

The accuracy and appropriateness of the methods an organisation chooses to conduct research among its customers determine the reliability of the results.

There are advantages and disadvantages of both qualitative and quantitative research. To aid the process of deciding on the most appropriate research method, typical opportunities and pitfalls are outlined below.

Telephone surveys

Many companies in the service sector use telephone interviews as a means of gaining first-hand feedback on customers' experiences. Kwik-Fit customer services department telephones at random 100 customers per month to check on customer satisfaction, for example.

BT interviews 13,000 business customers each month to check that they are satisfied with the service.

At car dealership Daewoo all customers are telephoned after they have brought their car in for a service to gauge their satisfaction levels.

At FedEx random telephone interviews with lost accounts produce valuable and honest feedback to help the company develop specific targeted programmes to reactivate lost customers.

The advantage of this method is that it allows an immediate response from customers in a short space of time. It is also a useful PR exercise for the company undertaking the survey, which can be effected at a relatively low cost.

The major disadvantage of telephone interviewing is the invasion of privacy. How the call is introduced often determines whether the customer will give the caller his or her time. It is also difficult to conduct a lengthy interview with customers. Some customers may also find it difficult to answer scalar questions or to give considered responses if caught 'on the hop'. Likewise, the telephone clearly cannot be used in a visual manner.

Self-completion questionnaires

The most popular method of gaining feedback from customers at the beginning of a customer service programme is the use of self-completion questionnaires. These can be sent to the customer by post or e-mail or distributed at the branch or at point of contact with the customer.

Many such questionnaires are found in hotels and restaurants. However, unless the design is particularly eye-catching, completion rates can be low. Another disadvantage of questionnaires at point of contact is that they do not allow a complete representation of customers' viewpoints to be canvassed. They can therefore sometimes be biased towards particular customer types. They are also open to abuse by staff who may fill them in themselves!

However, a major benefit in providing self-completion questionnaires at the point of contact with customers is that they demonstrate to both customers and employees that the organisation is serious about the service it provides. Asking employees to personally hand out questionnaires to customers also increases completion rates, as do incentives.

McDonald's has successfully used customer questionnaires to canvass opinion and since the early 1990s staff and customer opinion surveys have been conducted like never before. One research programme tested the views of both staff and customers concurrently. Customer opinions were gathered using focus groups and cards available in all restaurants, which asked people to rank food and services used on a scale of 1 to 5. This method, called 'Food for your Thoughts', encouraged a high response by offering food vouchers to those who completed a card. The results of the research pointed to one major area for improvement: although people appreciated quick and efficient service, a defining characteristic of McDonald's, it was in danger of becoming robotic and impersonal. The research results provided McDonald's with the impetus to move forward in offering a more personal service.[11]

Guidelines for self-completion questionnaires

The guidelines for developing a self-completion questionnaire include:

- Explaining the benefits of completion to the customer by making sure that the objectives of the questionnaire are clear.
- Making the questionnaire easy to complete – ensuring the design is airy and simple in its layout.
- Keeping questions short to allow speedy completion.
- Leaving room for additional comments if required – however, experience shows that this space should not be too long as those customers who have a particular point to make normally also accompany the questionnaire with a letter.
- Making return easy – ensuring there is a freepost address or a posting box available to customers.
- Signing the request – the request should be as personal as possible. It is particularly helpful for a member of senior management to ask for customer feedback as this lends authority to the request.
- Thanking customers for their participation.

Questionnaires should be laid out in a logical sequence, grouped by subject and have general questions set out before specific ones. Likewise it is helpful to include easy questions before difficult ones and to put particularly sensitive issues at the end of a questionnaire where customers are more likely to answer them than at the beginning. Personal customer details are generally included at the end of the questionnaire.

Here are some examples of self-completion questionnaires found at the customer point of contact in a variety of retail outlets, banks and catering establishments.

Tesco

We value your comments!

Please let us know any comment you may have about your shopping trip.

This leaflet invites customers to tell the store manager how satisfied they are with different aspects of the store, what they like about the store and any other products/services or facilities the customer would like to see at the store. In addition, customers are asked for any comments or ideas on how Tesco can improve its customer service.

Virgin Hotels

Virgin Hotels uses a novel way of incentivising customers to complete a survey about their stay: all those who complete the survey are entered into a prize draw for a trip by Virgin Airlines to the United States. Clearly the greater the incentive the customer has to complete a questionnaire the higher the response rate is likely to be.

Thomas Cook Customer Questionnaire

A customer questionnaire is handed out by members of staff at Thomas Cook travel agents when a customer makes a booking.

The questionnaire asks for customers' impressions of the way their booking was handled and in addition asks for an overall satisfaction rating with the shop.

The leaflet includes a useful question regarding repurchase intention:

> Would you book with Thomas Cook again?
> Yes __   No __   Undecided __

A further question asks:

> If you have ever had reason to make a complaint through Thomas Cook, were you satisfied with our handling of the complaint?

This is a helpful means of allowing the organisation to gauge reaction to its complaint-handling procedures.

NatWest Bank

A NatWest Bank questionnaire gives customers further opportunity of expressing their dissatisfaction by asking, 'Have you complained, *or felt like complaining* about the service you have received from NatWest within the last six months? If so, what was it about?'

Likewise, NatWest can track the quality of service it provides over time by including a question which makes a comparison with the service now to that of a year ago.

The bank also includes a question on whether customers, if asked to recommend a bank to someone who is considering opening a bank current account, would be likely to recommend its branch.

When preparing a self-completion questionnaire it is often useful to compare the different approaches that organisations take to this exercise and the different types of questions asked. On every customer receipt it issues, Virgin includes a questionnaire asking customers to rate its service.

Kwik-Fit, for example, includes a customer satisfaction questionnaire as part of its Kwik-Fit guarantee. The questionnaire is signed by Tom Farmer, Managing Director, and the response goes directly to him.

Viking Direct, a stationery supply company, enclose a postcard-size questionnaire which customers can return to the Chairman, Ian Helford, with all its deliveries. The postcard is headed, 'If we've goofed lately, please let me know. You'll get it out of your system. And we'll get it out of ours', and had four categories for comments – quality of merchandise, promptness of service, courtesy of service, and other comments or suggestions.

Odeon Cinemas includes specific questions on the range of facilities offered to customers, as part of its customer surveys. Other questions are more general such as:

Is there anything you particularly *like* about this Odeon cinema?

Is there anything you *dislike* about this Odeon cinema or which you think needs improvement?

Information such as this on the best aspect of the service an organisation provides and the one area most in need of improvement can be particularly helpful to aid understanding of customer perceptions. It is advisable to hold a customer focus group prior to designing a questionnaire so the organisation has the opportunity to hear from customers what is important to them.

We value your opinion

As a valued customer we welcome your comments on the standard of service our agency provides. Your opinions are very important to us and will allow us to continually improve our total service to you.

Please complete this simple questionnaire and return it to us in the reply-paid envelope. Your comments will be used confidentially and we appreciate your time and help.

Yours sincerely,

Elizabeth Davies

Marketing Director

Please indicate your opinion by ringing the mark which corresponds to your views.

4 = Very good 3 = Good 2 = Fair 1 = Poor

a) On the last occasion you contacted our office, how would you rate the:

1. Speed of response in reacting to your needs   4 3 2 1
2. Accuracy of our understanding of your work requirements 4 3 2 1
3. Standard of work carried out for you   4 3 2 1
4. Contact we maintained with you during the period of
    the contract   4 3 2 1
5. Attitude of our staff   4 3 2 1
6. Ability of staff to problem-solve, when appropriate   4 3 2 1
7. Accuracy of our invoices   4 3 2 1
8. Satisfaction overall with the service we provided   4 3 2 1
9. Did you have reason to complain, or feel like complaining during the period of the contract?

    Yes, Complained __, No __, Don't Know __,
    Felt like complaining __

10. If yes to question 9, was your complaint dealt with to your satisfaction?

    Yes __, No __, Don't know __

11. What, in your opinion is the best aspect of the service we provide?

12. What is the one aspect of our service, above all others, that we should improve?

13. How does the service we provide compare to other agencies you have used or have heard about?

    Better __, About equal __, Worse __

14. Why do you say this?

15. How likely are you to use the services of our agency again in the future?

    Very likely __, Not likely __, Unsure __

16. Please use this space for any other comments you may wish to make on the quality of our services.

On the facing page is an example of a self-completion questionnaire handed out by an employment agency, covering the different aspects of the service it provides.

The design and layout of a questionnaire affect response rates. Often, the opening sentence of a questionnaire can either attract or detract customers from completing the rest of the questionnaire.

Postal surveys

A more systematic understanding of customers' opinions can be obtained via postal surveys.

Postal surveys have been used for some years by the financial sector to provide feedback from customers who may not regularly come into a branch or whose account may be held at a different branch to the one which they visit. NatWest, for example, regularly surveys its customers. Its literature advertised:

Frankly speaking

We always set the highest possible standards on the service we provide, but there may be times when you feel we haven't got it right. If you ever have a problem, we would want to hear about it. More importantly, we can work together to do something about it. With your help we will get it right.

Advantages and disadvantages of postal surveys

The principal advantages of postal surveys are that they are easy to administer and allow organisations to reach a large number of customers quickly. Postal surveys can be inexpensive if response rates are high.

The disadvantages can be the quality, accuracy and timeliness of the list of customers that the organisation is working from. Furthermore, response rates can be unpredictable. Typical response rates range from 15 to 20 per cent for a postal questionnaire where there is no incentive, compared to an 85 per cent achievement rate on a face-to-face interview.

There is also a danger that postal surveys may seem impersonal. Customer response rates increase if there is a high level of interest and it is helpful to motivate respondents via an accompanying letter or to consider offering a reward or incentive for completion. Ensuring the accuracy of the customer list is of vital importance, as is the use of the customer's name – a personalised questionnaire has much more customer appeal.

It is also important to guarantee confidentiality to customers and to ensure that they can return the questionnaire anonymously if required (although pre-coding does allow the organisation to identify those questionnaires which are returned).

It is useful to keep the questionnaire relatively short and to include closed questions – that is those giving customers a range of predetermined responses eg, Yes, No, Don't Know, with tick boxes, and open questions – Who, What, Why, Where, When and How – when additional comment or explanation is required.

Scalar questions allow comparisons to be made of customers' replies. These are questions asking customers to rate service factors on a scale of 1 to 4 or 1 to 6, where 4 or 6 equals very good and 1 equals very poor, or alternatively where a predetermined scale of responses is given, eg very satisfied, fairly satisfied, not very satisfied, not at all satisfied. It is best practice to give customers an even rather than uneven number of choices so that they don't opt for the neutral, middle choice.

Organisations should take care not to use questions open to misinterpretation in questionnaires, such as 'frequent', 'useful', 'often' or 'recently', as these need to be further qualified – one person's view of 'recently' may differ from another's for example.

Online surveys

The increased use of the Internet as a method of communication provides organisations with the opportunity to post customer satisfaction surveys online.

At Network Equipment Technologies in the United States, the server automatically e-mails a personalised invitation to take part in a Web-based survey to all customers who have purchased from the company. If the customer wishes to take part in the survey, he or she clicks on a hyperlink which takes him or her to the online questionnaire.

The results of the completed questionnaires are automatically posted on the company's Web site for all to see. The advantage of this system is that it is quick and easy to use, being done in 'real time'; it also alerts employees to customers' perceptions of problems or successes.

Importance rankings

A useful method to get closer to customers is to understand not only their level of satisfaction with the service provided but also the importance factors of particular aspects of the service. A sample customer opinion survey* in the car hire industry shows levels of satisfaction as follows:

Service area	Performance (%)*
Reservations in order	77
Good mechanical condition	75
Clean cars	65
Express car return	61
Short walk to cars	60
Makes and models	53
Express pick-up	47
Cares about the customer	47
Quality frequent hirer programme	34
Non-smoker cars	11

Opion Research Corp survey, reported in *Managing Service Quality*.
*Percentage giving a satisfaction rating of 8, 9 or 10 on a scale of 1 to 10.

The obvious assumption from this table is that the areas needing most attention are those that appear low on the list. However, an enhanced survey asked customers to rate the importance of a given service to them, as well as to rate the company's performance – both on the same scale. This comparison produces a further set of data where the third figure shows the gap between expectations and performance:

Service area	Importance (%)	Performance (%)	Gap (%)
Cares about the customer	68	47	–21
Good mechanical condition	96	75	–21
Express pick-up	66	47	–19
Non-smoker cars	30	11	–19
Reservations in order	88	77	–11
Clean cars	76	65	–11
Express car return	71	61	–10
Short walk to cars	60	60	0
Frequent hirer programme	24	34	+10
Makes and models	23	53	+30

Now a new set of priorities emerges, based either on the gap between expectations and performance, or just on the importance rating.

Questionnaires such as those used by Standard Life, for example, allow customers to rank the overall importance of the factors involved.

Customers are asked to rank whether the way Standard Life handled their recent communication was very important, fairly important, not very important, or not at all important, as well as their satisfaction with the service levels provided on a scale of very satisfied, fairly satisfied, not very satisfied, or not at all satisfied.

In this way, organisations can prioritise the actions needed to be taken to improve their customer service.

Mystery shoppers

This is a research method which is often used in the retail area, but which has now been successfully applied in such sectors as catering, financial services and the automotive industry.

Mystery shopping is a useful technique to supplement customer feedback because it provides independent monitoring of service levels. However, it does require careful handling, and the Market Research Society has recently developed a code of conduct for mystery shopping.

An anonymous assessment and evaluation of employees is made by a 'mystery shopper' posing as an ordinary customer in person or on the telephone. In this way a measurement can be made not only of a particular outlet's service quality but also a comparison can be made across site locations and companies.

Victoria Wine, part of the First Quench organisation, has been using mystery shopping on a regular basis. A rolling programme covers all outlets: 50 elements are used to assess the service including cleanliness, acknowledging customers within 30 seconds and how questions are handled. Feedback is given to each shop and includes its performance relative to previous mystery shopping assessments and to other branches. Overall trends and areas for improvement are incorporated into company training programmes.

It is not advisable to utilise mystery shopping as the sole measure of the effectiveness of customer satisfaction. An organisation may have different perceptions of the importance of various aspects of its relationship with customers to customers themselves. This can result in whoever conducts the mystery shopping being wrongly briefed.

Only when mystery shopping is used together with other forms of direct customer feedback can the method be validated. It is best practice, for example, to conduct research among customers to identify key measures which will form the basis of a mystery shopper checklist, eg:

- greetings used;
- warmth of welcome;
- product knowledge;
- caring attitude;
- telephone manner, etc.

There can also be resistance among employees to the concept of mystery shoppers. Employees may see them as snoopers, spies or detectives, who are out to catch people getting it wrong, rather than catch them getting it right. The ethos of mystery shoppers should be to reward staff for good service, not to castigate them for poor. Staff members therefore should not be identified in mystery shopper reports unless it is in a positive light.

Post Office Counters undertook mystery shopping surveys four times a year, using an external research company under contract to them. The prime function of the survey was to test clerks' knowledge and product availability with a view to identifying whether a problem existed in the network and to look for regional variances. This information was used to see whether discrepancies were due to a lack of insufficient staff training, late distribution of information to counter staff or other factors. In addition, the mystery shoppers evaluated a short range of service issues, such as:

- approachability of staff;
- attentiveness of staff;
- atmosphere of office;
- welcome from staff.

Other organisations find it beneficial to use their own staff to 'mystery shop', as in this way members of staff experience the quality of service from a customer's point of view.

The Ritz Hotel held a 'get to know your customer' event by inviting members of staff to be customers for the day. Staff learnt to appreciate the different roles undertaken by their colleagues, and what it felt like to receive the services that they provided.

Other organisations canvass their customers to complete a mystery shop survey the next time they do business with them, regardless of who they do their business with or why it is undertaken. US medical company Respironics has canvassed 15 per cent of its customer base as mystery shoppers.

Focus groups/user groups/customer panels

A powerful technique in allowing members of staff and management to gain first-hand feedback from customers is the development of customer service groups, focus groups and user panels. Focus groups are useful for gaining insights into customers' attitudes and behaviour. They can be run prior to the development of a customer questionnaire, for example, to help an organisation to understand customers' perceptions better. This is done by inviting customers to attend an informal gathering at the service provider's premises to express their opinions on the quality of service provided. The employees of the organisation often attend the meetings to hear customers' views.

Such groups have been successfully applied by organisations as diverse as British Telecom, Boots, Nationwide Building Society and Safeway. Many computer companies have also successfully developed the concept of user panels.

It is best to use a facilitator to run a focus group and to have a structured agenda – without being too prescriptive so that customers have a real opportunity to express their views. Groups should be held at a time of day to best suit customers.

Typical topics which can be discussed in customer focus groups and user panels include:

- usage of the organisation's product and services;
- use of competitive products and services and reasons why;
- customers' likes and dislikes;
- areas for improvement;
- ideas and treatments to new products and services.

Customer service groups can also be a very useful PR tool. Safeway held a series of groups for customers in its stores on a local basis and followed up the event with national press coverage, stressing that it was listening to customers' needs. Customers had been invited by the management to check out the store facilities and question Safeway's top executives, as part of the country-wide 'Customer Seminar Programme' headed by Alistair Grant, the Chairman and Chief Executive of Safeway.

An example of focus groups run on a large scale is the two-day meetings of 300 people at Walsall Town Hall which took place to focus on customer issues. The attendees were seated at tables of eight people. Each table consisted of a mix of customers and employees from all levels and departments. Discussions took place around the table about what participants were 'glad, sad and mad' about and looked at the service the Council provides. Ideas were shared by putting stickers on points of agreement. This was fed back to the whole group using flip charts.

In the afternoon the group was divided into six workshops sharing information about change initiatives. The following morning all participants reassembled to recap on areas of concern and to consider the way forward. The result was sharing of ideas, action plans and commitments between customers and employees of the Council.

A possible disadvantage of customer service groups and user panels is that it can sometimes be difficult to recruit customers to attend these groups. Customers who participate may either already be advocates of the company or alternatively, particularly strident in their criticisms. The customers who are recruited, therefore, may not truly represent a cross-section of the organisation's customer base.

In addition, if these groups are run on a regular basis, it is important that action is taken both at a local level and nationally to address any areas of service weakness that customers in the groups identify. Otherwise, both customers and staff become quickly disillusioned with the concept and see no benefit from the listening process.

At Lloyds TSB, 'customer panels' are held throughout the country, where groups of customers join staff from their branch to discuss what improvements can be made to the branch's service. Improvements made by branches as a direct result of suggestions from customers include:

- changes to queuing systems;
- improved signage;
- better lighting in cashpoint lobbies;
- lunchtime staggered over a longer period to reduce queues;
- new banking hall furniture;
- bell systems at enquiry desks.

Most panels are held in the evening, and involve 8 to 10 customers and key members of staff of the branch. As well as discussing service issues, there is usually a 'behind the scenes' tour of the branch and a demonstration of the latest banking technology.

After Hewlett-Packard held its first customer focus group, participants were invited in to see what had been done as a result of their suggestions. The goal was to demonstrate that HP is serious about taking action on the issues that participants had raised. Time was spent talking them through the corrective action plans and how the business is run.

The benefits of focus groups are that they provide a more in-depth and qualitative feel about what customers say about the service. The organisation gains a wealth of data rich in anecdotes and verbatim quotes by asking key questions such as:

● What do you think of when we talk about (the company)?
● If you were the head of xxx what would you do to improve service?
● What else would you like to do with xxx?

Electronic focus groups

Experiments by Carnegie Mellon University in the United States show that open discussions on the Web about service conducted among an organisation's customer base can often be more fruitful than those which are carried out face-to-face. People in the electronic focus groups which were monitored as part of this research, tended to:

● talk more frankly and more often;
● have an equal share of remarks to contribute (in face-to-face focus groups, one or two can sometimes dominate the discussion);
● make more suggestions and proposals for improvements.

Mystery Web Shopping

Many organisations are now using mystery shop techniques on the Web to assess their service. Employees from Boots and Granada acted as mystery shoppers when the companies' joint Web site www.wellbeing.com was in development.

Suggestion schemes

Organisations such as the Body Shop successfully monitor customer opinions by the use of suggestion schemes, which can be used effectively to monitor how well products and services meet customer requirements and to identify areas for improvement. Web-based service providers such as lastminute.com are promoting suggestions from customers online by inviting comments as part of their Web sites.

Videos

Video points allow customers to video their views. One was established for a short period by British Airways in Terminal 4 at Heathrow. Customers who had reason to complain went into a small booth to video their comments. This allowed managers who did not come into face-to-face contact with customers to see the type of complaints dealt with by front-line staff.

Some shopping centre developments are considering a variation on this scheme by placing computer points in large shopping malls so that customers can again feed back their opinions on the service levels provided by typing in their views on the computer.

Face-to-face interviews

Other organisations, particularly in the high street, supplement postal and telephone surveys with face-to-face interviews to monitor service levels. A major advantage of this method is the speed of response; the disadvantage can be the cost involved. Face-to-face interviews, however, can be longer and less structured than telephone or postal surveys and allow more subtle questioning.

Many organisations conduct 'in-depth' interviews with key customers to ascertain their attitudes and opinions.

Face-to-face interviews are often a useful technique prior to compiling a postal or telephone survey; they allow a better feel for and explanation of issues and enable a subsequent questionnaire to be developed.

London Underground finds that the best and most cost-effective way to achieve a sample of customers that is consistent and representative of all underground users is to conduct an interview at underground stations. The maximum length of the interview must be less than 10 minutes or the sample will consist of more infrequent users of the service. The constraints on the length of the interviews limits the customer service index to 22 measures. These include frequency of service, cleanliness, staff, public address and ease of ticket buying. The customer service index is an exit study relating to the perception of the journey just made, the train from which the customer has alighted and the entry station.

Freephone

A technique which is growing in popularity is free customer phone lines.

This is an idea which was first started by companies such as P&G in the United States and is said to be the most popular means there of gaining feedback from customers. Eighty-five per cent of consumer brands in the United States have care line numbers on their products/parts, compared to

8 per cent in the UK. The General Electric Answer Center, for example, offers a 24-hour-a-day hotline and handles over 2 million calls a year, only a small proportion of which are complaints.

In the UK this technique is now being used by organisations such as Coca-Cola, American Express and Burger King. At Burger King restaurants customers wishing to comment on any aspect of the service in their outlets phone a designated number free of charge.

Petrol retailer Shell has established a Shell customer service centre free enquiry service. A leaflet at all Shell stations advertises for 'enquiries, complaints, compliments and anything you want to know about Shell'.

Set to grow in popularity in this country, freephone care lines should be an enhancement of, not a replacement for, customer enquiries or complaint processes. Proper training needs to be provided to staff answering the calls as a poor telephone response can in fact do more harm than good in terms of adverse PR for the organisation.

Third party surveys

Another means businesses adopt to monitor customer satisfaction is to make comparisons between the quality of service provided by their own organisation and that of competitors.

This is normally achieved via syndicated research where a number of companies in the same industry commission independent surveys of customer satisfaction and share the results, thus allowing direct comparison of service levels to be made.

Alternatively, managers can purchase independent industry reports. The Consumers' Association, for example, publishes independent surveys of many industry sectors.

WHERE AND WHEN TO MEASURE

Where and when to measure customer satisfaction depends upon the type of business and the prevailing market conditions.

Measurement can take place in any location that the customer is based – in the organisation's own outlets, at home, at their office or place of work, in the street, in a shopping mall, at competitors'.

Every organisation must decide when it will receive the most accurate picture of customer opinions. Some companies prefer to take a snapshot or to evaluate customer satisfaction before and after a pilot service quality scheme. Others undertake ongoing monitoring on a monthly, quarterly or yearly basis.

One disadvantage of undertaking too frequent monitoring, eg weekly or monthly, is that trends do not have time to emerge. Our experience is that managers tend to react to individual survey results rather than looking at the bigger and longer-term picture. It is helpful, for example, to set specific improvement targets on a quarterly or six-monthly basis and to monitor the effectiveness of these improvements. Importantly, customer research results need to be communicated to employees so that improvements can be made. One research study showed that this only happened in 40 per cent of cases.

When the Grid System Management Division of power supplier National Grid undertook a survey to establish customer perception, what emerged was a high regard for Grid System Management by their customers and satisfaction that their system worked. However, GSM was seen by some as rather arrogant and not offering good value for money. Managers within the business did not like the criticism but recognised its value. The survey became the impetus of a customer care programme, whose key aim was to reinforce the organisation's professionalism and raise the awareness of customer issues by involving as many staff as possible in focusing on customer requirements and perceptions. The measurement became an ongoing and critical feature of the programme which has enabled the organisation to successfully monitor and manage the change process.

CONTINUOUS IMPROVEMENT

Once a measurement system has been developed it needs to be continuously reviewed to ensure that the information it provides is valid. It is also advisable to adopt a range of 'listening' mechanisms to obtain a wide variety of views. Air Miles, for example, uses a mix of customer panels, staff panels, mystery calls and field or desk research as feedback tools.

According to a paper given by John Markham, Rover, at the MRS customer care seminar, customer care research at Rover Cars[12] has been used to measure the effectiveness of its customer satisfaction initiative. The objective of the initiative is to help and encourage Rover dealers to provide extraordinary customer satisfaction. The customer care research project began with research which was conducted among customers of Rover Cars. This indicated poor service standards at some UK dealers. An extensive mystery shopping survey conducted by Rover Cars also confirmed that there were opportunities to improve the customer service provided by dealerships.

Subsequently, qualitative group discussions identified key areas of dealer service of importance to customers. At the same time, Rover undertook a benchmark survey which quantified the relative positions of Rover and its competitors against key measures. Next, an individual dealer customer care survey was undertaken among a sample of the largest Rover dealers (25 per cent of the network). In addition, an independent survey among a sample of after-sales customers for each dealership was undertaken. Further qualitative surveys were conducted to identify good, average and poor dealers and to gain a further understanding of the detailed causes of customer satisfaction and dissatisfaction. Also, interviews with individual customers tested alternative questionnaire formats in terms of colour, layout and design.

As a result of this background work, a pilot survey was conducted among selected dealers to test alternative sampling methods. The pilot survey was then evaluated to identify the best method of rolling out the research on a nationwide basis. The findings from this pilot identified that although the level of response varied between dealer types, the overall response rate was high – on average over 60 per cent.

In the pilot some questionnaires had been distributed by dealer staff and these were discovered to cause bias in the sample. In addition, opportunities to refine the questionnaire were identified. It was discovered that the response rate improved if an introductory letter to customers was signed by the Marketing Director of Rover Cars.

An additional survey to compare responses was conducted between responders and non-responders to the pilot survey and only minimal differences were found in the profile of customer satisfaction. In addition, feedback from participants in the pilot survey demonstrated that the exercise was seen to generate a caring, positive image for Rover Cars among customers. One learning point identified from the pilot, however, was that better procedures were required to handle associated customer queries or complaints, which were sent in together with the completed questionnaires.

As a result of undertaking the pilot, Rover Cars was able to improve the method and content of its customer care research. The customer satisfaction initiative research now runs on a quarterly basis and acts as a monitor of customer satisfaction with dealer performance. Separate surveys are completed for both sales and after-sales.

Although Rover Cars undertook both telephone and postal surveys of customers in the initial pilot, in the subsequent roll-out of the research it was decided to restrict customer satisfaction surveys to postal questionnaires of Rover dealers only. Individual service reports are completed for every Rover Cars' UK dealer. Rover Cars are able to monitor performance trends by gaining a direct measure of customer satisfaction with its dealer performance, encompassing individual dealer measures, as well as customer satisfaction with sales and after-sales.

Detailed reports on individual dealers and consolidated reports for dealer groups were produced on a regular basis. Summary management reports based on the total UK network sales regions, dealer size and classifications were also produced, together with extra analysis as required.

Customer research has been continuously refined by Rover Cars. Quality action teams set up as part of the customer satisfaction initiative have continuously reviewed the research process. In particular the quality action team identified that internal customers who received copies of the research reports – Rover Cars' dealers and management – required a quicker turnaround time and the research process was subsequently streamlined and fieldwork time reduced to meet this demand.

INVOLVING EMPLOYEES WHEN YOU MEASURE

The Rover experience illustrates the importance of gaining support and ownership for a measurement system. Customer satisfaction surveys are most effective when people are informed about the monitoring system which is to take place and the reasons for measuring. It is also vital that people understand what will happen with research results and that measurement is undertaken unobtrusively, without affecting performance. Involving recipients of the research in an audit of the usefulness of the results is also an effective technique.

At pharmaceutical company Glaxo SmithKline, customer service representatives undertake follow-up calls to customers each week to monitor their satisfaction. Rather than employing a research company to undertake the discussion, the company believes that it is important to use employees to conduct the process as this helps to engender understanding of customer issues.

RECOGNISING ACHIEVEMENT

As more companies measure customer satisfaction, measurement results can be used as the basis of awards for good customer service to emphasise its importance throughout the company.

Avis, which surveys over 100,000 customers resident in 15 countries, from the once-a-year holiday car renter to the weekly business car renter, provides over 1,100 monthly reports of progress back to the individual Avis offices and departments which delivered the service. In countries where local management practice supports it, front-line managers participate in incentive programmes which reward them with bonuses based on specific revenue improvements, sales efforts, cost reduction measures and customer care performance as measured by the customer care research.

Such programmes position customer care as a critical and essential element of business activities.

INVOLVING HEAD OFFICE DEPARTMENTS IN THE MEASUREMENT PROCESS

As the quality of service provided within the organisation has a direct effect on external service quality, it is also possible to measure internal customer service.

Nationwide Building Society measures its success based on how it is rated by its customers, its staff and financial analysts. Employee ratings are judged through staff surveys. Two measures – financial indicators and customer and employee perceptions – are used to establish the size of the annual staff bonus.

Organisations such as Eurodollar regularly surveyed head office departments. They used the results of their customer service index to attack the fundamental issues of service quality within the organisation.

There were four key components to the internal measurement:

1. Senior management visit.
2. Internal comment card.
3. Inter-departmental service questionnaire.
4. Directors' assessment.

Senior management visited each department and assessed a wide range of issues. The process demonstrated tangible commitment from senior executives and ensured that staff understood and appreciated the importance of the programme. Internal comment cards systematically measured internal telephone responses. Here each department was asked to monitor five telephone calls per week from other departments on a planned basis and to feed back the results.

The third element of measurement was inter-departmental service questionnaires. These were completed on a monthly basis and covered such elements as:

- telephone service;
- written communication;
- ownership of problems;
- general treatment of others.

Then the directors made assessments of each department to ensure that exceptional contributions to customer service over and above expectations were recognised. Each element of the measurement system contributed towards a total score. A regular roll of honour was created, based on departmental teams who received gold, silver and bronze awards, with badges, scrolls and some tangible recognition items.[13]

CANVASS THE VIEW OF OTHER STAKEHOLDERS

In many organisations the range of stakeholders is wide. This could include not only members of the public but suppliers, shareholders, government bodies and consumer groups. A firm principle of measuring satisfaction can be applied to all stakeholder groups in order to gain a fuller understanding of the expectations and satisfaction level of each segment.

Employee attitude surveys

To bring about successful change, the views of employees at all levels throughout a company need to be canvassed before a service quality programme can begin to bridge the gaps in employee and customer perception.

Employee attitude surveys are one means of canvassing the opinions of the workforce. One company discovered through research, for example, that a major customer criticism was the poor level of communication between staff and the customer. In turn, through employee research, it was discovered that employees of the company criticised the lack of communication internally, the absence of team spirit and overall lack of direction for the company. Before improvements in external customer service could be brought about, improvements in internal customer relations needed to be addressed.

Seeking out employees' opinions is a means of showing that organisations care for their internal customers. Employee attitude surveys are also a useful means of gauging internal service levels and of assessing the general climate of the organisation. They can act as a barometer of change in culture, particularly where organisations are moving from a traditionally paternalistic to a more commercial environment. Companies in the utilities sector, for example, regularly undertake staff attitude surveys to monitor the progress of their service initiatives. The results are normally published to employees. Staff at Boots the Chemist are given an opportunity to register their feelings about their employer in a regular staff opinion survey.

The principal benefits of attitude surveys are that they provide evidence to the organisation of employees' current opinions and any changes in opinion that take place over time as a result of alterations in policies and practice. They allow suggestions for improvement to be made by employees and can also uncover particular grievances, allowing employees to release pent-up feelings. Importantly, staff attitude surveys also demonstrate management's commitment and concern for their workforce.

As in external customer research, it is useful to explore issues initially via loosely structured interviews or focus group discussions prior to developing a structured survey format. At Disney, regular employee attitude surveys are conducted each year, preceded by 200 focus groups with 'cast members'. All employees also have access to 'what's on your mind?' suggestion forms.

Also, like external measurement, a variety of sampling methods can be used. It is important to decide early on who should be included in the survey. Normally, a survey takes place via a self-completion questionnaire requiring 20–45 minutes to fill in. Response rates vary but 66 per cent is an average. The response rate increases if employees are given time to complete the questionnaire at work. Alternatively, questionnaires may be sent to employees' homes. Some surveys can be quickly completed at conferences or presentation events. In other instances, telephone surveys can be conducted among employees.

Traditional written questionnaires are only one of the approaches that Barclays Bank is using to survey its employees. A feedback process has also been developed using team briefings, and smaller focus groups and surveys. Focus groups in the bank's regions, chosen because they represent the bank as a whole, set the agenda for larger team briefings in which the bank's change programme is cascaded through the organisation at each level. Focus groups are run by external consultants to ensure confidentiality and accurate feedback. In larger team briefings line managers present a video where members of staff express the views raised in focus groups as part of their presentation. In the second half of these meetings staff are split into small discussion groups to give their response.

SmithKline Beecham intersperses its attitude surveys with much quicker measures. The organisation aims to change the prevailing culture towards greater empowerment. In order to monitor the change, a 'culture capping' system was designed. This involves taking regular soundings into the culture. One method used was a card-sorting approach, rather than questionnaires or interviews. Forty statements drawn from research about the conditions needed to create a 'learning organisation' were drawn up. The individuals taking part in the survey were handed a set of cards which they had to post into four labelled boxes to show to what extent they agreed with the statement on each card.

Whatever the method, the confidentiality and anonymity of surveys must be assured to allow employees to express their views frankly.

When Anglian Water carried out its first employee opinion survey it commissioned an external research organisation to help design a questionnaire after first interviewing small groups of staff drawn from a cross-section of the workforce. The 112 questions finally included in the survey form were formulated around the concerns raised by these groups. The questionnaire was then tested for clarity on a sample of the workforce before going out to all 5,000 employees. Although forms were distributed through the internal mail system, returns were made directly and anonymously to the research company which also analysed the results and compared them with surveys carried out in similar companies. No one in Anglian Water saw the completed questionnaire or the comment sheets that the company had done.[14]

First Direct believes in continually understanding the needs of its employees. It has introduced a 'culture critique', using staff focus groups and one-to-one interviews, not just with current employees, but with past ones too.

Typical questions included in staff attitude surveys include:

- those relating to employees' attitudes towards the customer and service quality – both externally and internally – within the organisation;
- questions regarding the understanding and communication of the mission and vision of the organisation to employees;
- the leadership style of managers within the organisation;
- the structure of the organisation and its appropriateness;
- the degree of teamwork and cooperation;
- career opportunities and personal development.

Royal Mail also included a question in its survey on which areas of improvement should be tackled first.

Importantly, a summary of the findings of the surveys should be fed back to all employees, together with action which will be taken as a result of the survey, to prove that the exercise has been worthwhile. Feedback is normally cascaded throughout the organisation or can be given to individual groups. Typically, 97–98 per cent of all FedEx staff takes part in the organisation's annual employee attitude survey. Results are published within 14 hours of the cut-off time. Everyone has access to the feedback, and if poorly performing managers fail to improve their performance in the eyes of the internal customers after a second year, they are asked to stand down.

Anglian Water created a road show of its survey results and invited every employee from around 80 sites into five main centres. Presentations were backed up by written details of the results and by focus groups. Two hundred volunteers covering a cross-section of employees were brought together in groups of 10 to discuss the results and what should be done about them. About 300 suggestions resulted, which the company then took and began either to address or explain why they could not be achieved. Directors were put in charge of particular issues of concern, such as employee involvement and career development.

When Hewlett-Packard began its first employee survey, it put together four taskforces in response to the main findings. The groups met and agreed a one-year implementation plan to bring about significant change. Like other organisations, HP is aware of the need to avoid 'over surveying' its staff and plans to hold surveys on a yearly or 18-month cycle.

Where questions on customer service in a staff attitude survey mirror those asked of customers, the organisation is able to assess gaps in perceptions which may need to be addressed.

Attitude surveys do not need to rely solely on lengthy paperwork. At Brighton Healthcare NHS Trust, the chairman put a short slip with a handwritten top and tail into wage packets, asking staff to list two or three things that they would fix if they could. Several hundred ideas came back and to date the Trust has spent £1.8 million on their implementation. A monthly report on the progress of this fix-it scheme is circulated so staff know their ideas are being listened to and to encourage staff to come forward with further ideas for improvement.

BEST PRACTICE BENCHMARKING

Many organisations are now taking listening to customers one step further via the use of benchmarking.

The principles

Best practice benchmarking is the systematic appraisal of the 'best practices' in order to identify areas for improvement. It allows organisations to set standards according to the best practices that they can find.

Benchmarking enables companies to compare themselves to 'best in class' organisations and to identify differences in performance, to document why these exist and to identify steps to meet and surpass the 'best in class' by developing a set of standards and an action plan to bring about improvements. The process is shown in Figure 3.3.

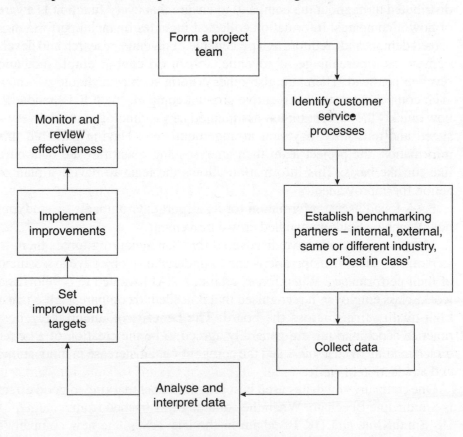

Figure 3.3 The benchmarking process

The first step is to establish who to benchmark against. Asking customers and suppliers who they consider as offering best practice should identify approved organisations. Next, a project team needs to be set up to manage the process. It is best if the team is drawn from different parts of the business. Before benchmarking can begin the team need to map out the organisation's customer service processes so that direct comparisons can be made with other businesses.

Many organisations face the problem of how to collect information. A raft of methods is normally adopted by companies, such as asking customers, consulting industry observers or trade associations, through to reviewing international journals and using business libraries. The direct exchange of information among the benchmarking partners is probably most effective.

ICL benchmarks more than 20 of its competitors both on company performance and product technology. The information it gleans is distributed throughout the company to ensure that every function is aware of how it compares. Information collected includes financial performance – aged debtors and creditors as a percentage of revenue, research and development as a percentage of revenue; return on capital employed; and revenue per head. There are also other criteria such as technology – how each component in the competitive product compares with ICL standards, how quickly the competitor has assimilated new technology; and delivery – speed and reliability, payment arrangements, etc. Having gathered this information, the project team then analyses and quantifies the data on a like-for-like basis. This information allows the team to devise a plan of action for improvement.

BAA found useful information for its airport environments by studying how Wembley Stadium handled crowd movement.

Many organisations have discovered that benchmarking forces them to step outside their own operations and to undertake an objective assessment of their performance. When forces retailer NAAFI wanted to develop as a world-class employer, it recognised that it needed to compare itself against high-quality firms across the board. The benefits of undertaking best practice benchmarking are generally agreed to be the creation of a better understanding of customers and the competition, an increase in innovations and a reduction in waste.

One company which has used best practice benchmarking to good effect is SmithKline Beecham. When the company was formed from a merger of US SmithKline and UK Beecham in the late 1980s, the new company's chairman was determined to get the merger right from the beginning by fitting the two cultures together. He decided against imposing changes or bringing in outside consultants. Instead, more than 160 committees or 'project teams' were set up consisting of staff from each company. Rather than one company imposing its working practices, the teams were told to find the 'best practice in the industry' (and in some cases outside it) and to copy it, thus ensuring that the best culture would emerge.

As in other service initiatives, senior management's commitment to best practice benchmarking is important, along with training and guidance for project teams in how to identify and analyse results. Also time is often needed for project teams to successfully gather and analyse data and develop a plan of improvement.

Before a benchmarking activity takes place, agreement needs to be reached on areas of the business which need to be benchmarked. It is useful to prioritise these areas to ensure that processes and operations which are most critical to the operation are benchmarked. These areas can often be identified from discussions with external and internal customers and industry sources. Key areas are normally those in need of significant improvement in external customers' eyes or those which may affect a company's profitability. However, internal measures such as the effect on a company's performance of staff turnover and absenteeism can also be benchmarked. Often priorities will change over time and it is important that these are reviewed and that likewise performance standards which are set against best practices are constantly monitored as service quality may be improving on an ongoing basis in other parts of the industry.

Most companies benchmark quantifiable 'hard' measures such as speed of service, on-time delivery, sales per employee, and work in progress. Each measure can then be broken down into variables which can be compared on a like-for-like basis. Speed of service in an insurance company, for example, can be broken down into response time on the telephone, length of time to send an acknowledgement of a customer's request, etc.

It is more difficult to benchmark softer measures which are difficult to qualify. Often best practice benchmarking helps organisations improve their own management information systems, as before comparisons can be made, key measures need to be obtained within the company.

There are four basic methods of benchmarking:

- against direct competition;
- against parallel industries;
- against other parts of your own organisation;
- against different industries or 'best in class' organisations.

Xerox began benchmarking over 10 years ago at the beginning of its 'Leadership Through Quality' programme. It is currently reviewing its empowerment process against benchmarking partners such as Digital and Hewlett-Packard. Shell and Chevron have benchmarked their quality programme against Xerox's achievements.

SUMMARY

Listening to customers is a vital element of customer care. The more direct feedback an organisation receives from its customers, the better it can develop its relationship with them.

Research should be used to establish customer needs, both externally and internally, and to act as a benchmark against which to measure the effectiveness of progress in creating a customer focus. In addition, monitoring satisfaction levels on an ongoing basis is an important method of sustaining a customer focus.

A mixture of both quantitative and qualitative research methods helps provide a balanced approach to customer feedback.

Research should be used to recognise and reward good service at regular intervals. Internal customers should also be encouraged to measure their own service performance and their opinions should be regularly sought.

Best-practice organisations are now turning to benchmarking as a means of gaining external comparison.

Market research can play an important part in the journey to excellence only if actionable changes are proposed as a result of customer care surveys. To create a service culture, customer research results need to be communicated throughout the organisation and integrated into business plans. Management and staff training and development can then concentrate on those aspects of service quality identified via research as most in need of improvement.

ACTION CHECKLIST

The action which can be taken as a result of this chapter is to:

1. Assess the barriers which exist in your organisation to listening to customers – develop a plan of action for overcoming these.

2. Ensure senior managers are fully committed to measuring service quality before monitoring begins.

3. Develop a customer care balance sheet to measure the annual cost of lost sales revenue.

4. Pilot a measurement system.

5. Review the organisation's complaints procedure – ensure customers receive a speedy and complete response.

6. Decide which customers, what aspects of service and when, to measure.

7. Decide the most appropriate research methods to meet your objectives – regularly review their effectiveness.

8. Develop a self-completion questionnaire for your customers.

9. Undertake a postal survey.

10. Include importance as well as satisfaction rankings in all customer surveys.

11. Conduct a telephone survey among customers.

12. Undertake face-to-face interviews with customers.

13. Develop a suggestion scheme for customers.

14. Offer a freephone facility to customers.

15. Introduce a mystery shopper scheme.

16. Investigate novel means of listening to customers – such as videoed and taped comments and computer points.

17. Investigate third party surveys.

18. Hold customer focus groups and user panels.

19. Link the results of customer satisfaction surveys to rewards for good service.

20. Undertake an attitude survey among employees.

21. Encourage internal service providers to measure their customer satisfaction.

22. Listen to customers on a regular basis – and regularly feed back the results of this process to employees.

23. Establish a help desk for customer queries in your organisation.

24. Undertake a benchmarking study.

25. Offer a facility online for customers to feed back their comments on to your Web site or by e-mail.

26. E-mail your customers with an online survey or invite them to join an online discussion forum on service improvements.

27. Post customer and employee survey results on your Internet or intranet site.

4

Implementing a Customer Care Strategy

When an organisation develops a customer service strategy, the means by which it is introduced to employees will determine its effectiveness and success.

In this chapter we investigate methods of implementing a service strategy and the need to design and market a programme throughout the organisation, starting with management and cascading throughout the company.

CONTINUOUS IMPROVEMENT

Research into organisations which have successfully applied a customer-focus programme reveals that the approach adopted in first introducing the strategy often determines its success.

In order for a service quality philosophy to be readily assimilated into the company, service excellence must not be presented as a novelty – rather as a logical extension of what the company is already doing. Those companies which are most successful in installing a service philosophy ensure that this is marketed throughout the organisation as a continuous process rather than a one-off campaign.

Restaurant chain TGI Fridays, for example, has no customer service programme which they run specifically for employees and managers. They believe that service quality has no start or end dates; it needs to be something that is totally integrated and ongoing within the business. At US department store Nordstrom, the company's preference is to 'hire nice people' whose attitudes are customer focused – customer care is so much a part of their culture that they do not need a customer care programme!

Engender ownership

The more employees feel involved in the development of a service strategy, the more successful will be the ownership of its principles. Ideas owned by staff are more likely to be accepted and implemented. It is vital to involve employees in the design of the programme and to communicate clearly to them its objectives and key success criteria and the timescale for implementation.

When the RAC recognised radical change was needed to exceed its customers' increasing expectations, it decided that customer-driven quality (CDQ) had to permeate every aspect of the business if expectations were to be met. Vision, mission and values were established and it was recognised that systems, people and processes needed to be brought in line to meet customer requirements and implement the vision successfully.

First, the RAC set about upgrading its systems, in particular its computerised rescue service which handles the 3 million calls at the organisation's five control centres. Having established new systems, senior management were involved in developing a framework for the CDQ strategy. A quality management system was put in place and quality councils were set up at group level, meeting every month. At the same time process councils were established to facilitate improvements. RAC board members committed themselves to regular site visits to talk about the CDQ strategy and obtain feedback from staff. This ensured that consistent messages were communicated at all levels. In addition, 'bottom-up' communication was encouraged, including a 'best ideas' programme for staff to bring about measurable improvements, and customer service and quality improvement schemes to encourage system developments.

Test the waters

One useful means of introducing a service philosophy is to demonstrate its effectiveness by running a pilot scheme. A pilot scheme is particularly helpful where resistance to change is likely to be high. To ensure the success of the programme it is useful for employees to see the benefits of a new approach. Through identifying part of the organisation which is typical of the business in size and structure in which to pilot an approach, a useful example is often set which can then act as an illustration of the success of the programme. A comparable control situation should also be chosen which will not undertake the programme but which can also be monitored and the achievements of the pilot can be assessed.

Senior management of National Mutual Life developed a service quality strategy to ensure differentiation in the marketplace. This relied on empowering people within the organisation to use their experience and knowledge to solve specific business problems and in so doing improve their own performance and that of the organisation as a whole.

National Mutual decided to implement the strategy, called 'Customer Care', on a pilot basis to provide a taste of how the programme would work. Two project teams, one in the new business area, the other in pension claims, took part in a two-day workshop which introduced the concepts of customer care. The team then focused on ways of analysing and improving how they completed their activities. The pilot projects were hugely successful, demonstrating the potential improvements which can be generated from small-scale activities, such as making computer input screens more user-friendly. A wide range of benefits emerged, including higher staff motivation and greater levels of teamwork and cooperation. The pilot was the impetus therefore for change.

Employees who are involved in a pilot need to understand that as this is the first time that such an initiative has taken place, the strategy may not be perfect. A time-scale should be set for the pilot and the initiative evaluated. Importantly the comments and feedback of employees involved in the pilot scheme must be sought to ensure that, when the strategy is rolled out throughout the organisation, the learning points from the pilot can be incorporated.

A national chain of estate agents which was considering introducing a customer care programme selected one branch from each of its 10 regions throughout the country to act as a pilot and also chose one branch in each of the regions to act as a control.

Concern was expressed that because of regional variations and different working practices it would not be possible to introduce a customer care strategy on a uniform basis throughout the country. A pilot scheme was developed in one part of the business typical of the organisation. The pilot was subsequently evaluated, and it proved that 90 per cent of the pilot branches showed significant improvement over the control branches as a result of the customer care programme in terms of both customer satisfaction (based on pre- and post-customer research) and employee morale. The pilot branches then acted as champions for the strategy and were used as examples to overcome resistance by other branches as the programme developed.

Establish a steering group

A useful means of beginning a programme designed to make the service strategy come alive is to establish a steering group whose members can be drawn from all parts of the organisation and whose role is to spearhead the implementation of the strategy.

The steering group need not be large, but its members need to be sufficiently influential within the organisation and should be drawn from across job grades and functions.

Steering group members must possess good communication skills. It is also beneficial for team members to understand group processes so they can successfully work together. An open and honest discussion among team members to establish individuals' expectations and motivations prior to the team beginning to work together is often a useful exercise.

Hotel group Queen Moat Houses set about making its staff the driving force behind its move to improve customer service by appointing three members of staff as service champions from each hotel. Staff acted as mini steering groups for the service initiative and were used to train other employees and also act as coaches.

When Audi recognised that it needed to develop its distinct personality in the UK, it set up a vanguard of 20 Audi centres. These centres were recognised as strong advocates of change. Their task was to identify and refine the best aspects of customer care, acting as a steering group for the rest of the dealer network.

MARKETING A SERVICE STRATEGY

When developing a service quality programme, successful organisations remember not only to create the right environment to encourage service improvements but also to market and sell the strategy to employees.

Employees are the first market of the organisation. If staff are told about new products or services by customers before being informed by management, it is hardly surprising that they have little faith in what managers say. So, for employees to believe in and act by the principles of a service philosophy, they need to understand not only the reasons for the programme but what is expected of them. A service philosophy must be marketed and sold *internally* before it can be presented to the external customer.

Many organisations begin their customer care programmes by giving them a name so that these can be branded and recognised throughout the company. Although this approach has its advantages, care should be taken in the selection of a name as there is a danger that branding can create the impression that a programme is a separate entity rather than being integrated into the culture of an organisation. In addition, a name has to be long-lasting. It is often difficult to revive a strategy by giving it a different name if other programmes with other names have been unsuccessfully introduced in the past.

Names that are often given to service quality programmes include:

Focus on the Customer	Putting service first
Success through Service	First service
Customers First	Partnership Programme
You Make the Difference	Partners in customer service
Right First Time	Team service
Profit through Service	In touch
Putting the Customer First	Excel
Caring for Customers	Winning for Customers
To be the best	Service to Succeed
Leadership through quality	Making the Difference
Quality pays	First Class Service
Service Excellence	Customer-driven Service.
Who cares wins	

These names then lend themselves to communication material (see Chapter 8).

Introducing the programme to employees

The first task of senior management and members of the steering group is to decide how to introduce the programme to employees.

Experience shows that educating management first is more successful than introducing a programme to all employees at the same time. It can prove effective to hold workshops and seminars that introduce the service philosophy to all employees. However, separate events should also be held first with managers to explain their roles and to gain their commitment. Leadership training may also be needed to help bring about change.

British Airways started its quality service initiative with a programme called 'Putting People First'. This was a two-day event bringing together a carefully constructed cross-section of staff who deliver service. Members of staff gathered together, 150 at a time, at a large conference centre. The seating was prearranged in small groups and organised into gatherings of eight people. The subject matter for the event covered a wide range of issues from personal experience of dealing with service organisations to feedback on research and the importance of giving attention to customers. The events were rounded off by a talk from Sir Colin Marshall who gave visible support to the messages on the course.

Feedback from the event identified the need for greater management commitment to the principles of service quality. Subsequently British Airways instigated 'Managing People First', a one-week residential course for managers to give them experience of managing in a service industry. Here managers received detailed feedback on their strengths and weaknesses by means of a questionnaire which had been completed by both associates and subordinates. Also, managers had the opportunity to work in small groups which provided support and encouragement to investigate the need for change and to formulate a detailed plan for improvement.

When the NAAFI (the Navy, Army and Airforce Institute) underwent a change programme to bring it back into line with the needs of its customers, a 'listening survey' among NAAFI staff reported low levels of morale and self-esteem.

The first step in the change process was a development programme for front-line managers to discuss the need for change and the key behaviour that would support this. The management development programme supported the organisation's three key values of: aiming for the best; open and honest communication; and effective teamwork. The programme subsequently underpinned its customer focus.

Include everyone

Senior management often approach a customer service philosophy by directing their initial efforts at front-line staff. This can be a mistake, as a customer service philosophy needs to be integrated into all aspects of the business. Training front-line staff alone will not tackle the underlying issues of improvement in service, nor does it engender understanding of the internal customer.

Service improvement programmes should always begin with management. This has the dual effect of bringing about involvement, participation and ownership at management level as well as ensuring that before staff take part in the programme, managers have an understanding of the process in which everyone will be involved. Staff then will know that their managers have also undertaken similar activities. At Xerox, for example, managers went through an initial quality programme twice –

once to learn about the programme and once to be trained to be able to teach their subordinates about the strategy.

A company-wide initiative

If a customer service philosophy is seen to belong to one person, one department, or one part of the business, the success of the programme will often be dependent on the political standing and influence of that particular department or person within the organisation.

Particularly where customer care programmes are marketed to employees as a short-term campaign rather than an ongoing philosophy, there is great danger that employees see the introduction of service improvement programmes as 'flavour of the month'. In the same way, although it may be useful to employ the services of an outside consultant to aid the development of the company's programme, it is important to ensure that consultants are used only as facilitators for change and that the strategy itself is seen to emanate from senior members of the company and is tailored to the organisation's specific requirements.

'Off the shelf' customer care programmes often have a major failing in that their content and setting are irrelevant and not tailored to the organisation. Likewise, there has been a move away from a 'sheep-dip' style of training which all employees attend in an almost evangelical style, towards more tailored and practical programmes, often run in-house.

Lloyds Bank, for example, established a programme called 'Developing Service Excellence' which involved every employee in retail banking from front-line to the top team. Moving away from the traditional method by which they had introduced programmes in the past, 'Developing Service Excellence' was not delivered by a series of classroom-based workshops; instead Lloyds trainers trained managers and team leaders to lead a team-based process in the branches and business centres around the country.

A series of team sessions was held involving all employees undertaking some self-managed development and the facilitation of team action planning sessions during the course of team meetings.

When IBM Asia Pacific agreed to the target of delivering a world-class service to its external and internal customers, it meant reaching 8,000 people in 12 different countries. Their approach was for local teams to train themselves and then facilitate small group training sessions to improve peoples' relationships with the customer at a local level. In this way, all employees across the region took part in the programme.

MANAGERS LEAD THE WAY

Best-practice organisations, therefore, engage managers to lead a service strategy forward. Emphasis on customer care has led Lex Retail Group, one of the largest motor retailer groups in the UK, into a major programme of change. The key to this was the realisation that managers in the business needed to value their relationships with their people as much as they valued their relationships with their customers, as it was believed that only people who felt valued could give value. Research shows that the most talented managers receive high ratings in the employee survey question: 'At work I have the opportunity to do what I do best every day.' Where employees agreed with this statement, customer retention and loyalty scores were appreciably higher.

Lex's vision focused on three main areas: delighting customers, empowering people and optimising performance. It was realised that to achieve this vision front-line employees needed to be supported by managers and allowed to take responsibility in order to provide outstanding service. This meant a change in the top-down style of doing business that had evolved in the organisation. The main board sponsored a programme which involved residential workshops for all managers on facilitating change. This in turn has led to managers encouraging greater ownership and responsibility for problems.

One DIY retailer drove home the message about the need for good customer care by forcing managers to experience rotten service themselves. Managers were invited to attend what they thought was just another sales meeting, held at a distant hotel and starting at 8.30 am. When they arrived nothing was ready for them. An hour later, still minus any coffee, the executives were ushered into a filthy conference room. Cigarette ash and broken biscuits littered the floor where the remains of earlier meals had not been cleared away. Coffee, when it arrived eventually, was served by surly, unhelpful staff who argued among themselves.

At this point the doors to the conference room opened and the assembled managers were asked to move into another cleaner room. Here they were greeted by their directors and asked what they thought of the service provided by the hotel. The day then continued by emphasising the importance of customer care. Five similar one-day road shows were held, each catering for 65 people. Participants at four road shows were store managers and regional managers, the fifth was senior head office staff, including directors. A customer service programme was introduced at the road shows which involved syndicate work. The approach was cascaded to train junior staff using examples of bad service and team discussions as a way of highlighting areas of improvement.

Legal & General sent all its staff, from directors down to raw recruits, on a two-day training course. The importance of everyone providing a good service throughout the organisation was emphasised by senior management presence.

Electricity company, Norweb, has responded to privatisation and increased customer expectation by becoming slimmer, faster and more efficient. The company's top 40 managers attended sessions called 'Breaking the Chain'. They used the analogy of an elephant which never forgets. Tethered as a baby, it tries to break free; it cannot and it suffers great pain. Even as an adult, tethered by a chain it could easily break, the elephant does not forget the pain and does not try to break free. The session focused on breaking free from the past and trying to create a customer-driven future.[15]

It was followed by 'Get it off your chest' sessions with a wider selection of 300 staff from each of the branches and 20 customer services sections. Here people were encouraged to say how things could be improved at work. The result was over 800 suggestions which were all looked at and acted upon quickly to bring about improvements in service quality.

HIGH OR LOW KEY?

Various techniques have been used by different organisations at the beginning of service quality initiatives, including holding workshops and seminars with senior management and day or half-day events which both members of management and staff attend. Other organisations make customer service part of ongoing training and development.

There is merit in bringing together groups of people who would normally never meet, to discuss service quality. NatWest, for example, held a series of management workshops to introduce their quality service programme involving all executives downwards from every unit and department. Three hundred and thirty such workshops were held within two months; the objectives of the workshops were to provide input and introduce the service quality programme to managers and led to a huge increase in communications. In addition, a series of seven one-day events for all employees was held in seven purpose-built auditoria in locations throughout the country to introduce the programme.

At the Woolwich Building Society, a customer service programme was developed which was initiated via a research programme designed to establish not only what Woolwich staff but also customers thought about the kind of service the building society offered. Subsequent to this research a team of people were sent around the country to explain in person the aims of the campaign and to quantify initial reactions. This included detailed analysis of employees' attitude to service and service delivery. The basis of this work founded a major educational programme involving 3,500 people, including everyone from the chief executive to the newest recruit. The programme for more senior staff was extended to include those aspects of leadership necessary to ensure the perpetuation of the process.

Other organisations introduce a programme in a more low-key fashion using vehicles such as team meetings, staff announcements and videos. Nationwide Building Society chose to hold a series of evening party events for employees *after* its customer service strategy had been launched as a thank you to staff.

Whatever the method chosen to introduce a service strategy, organisations need to ask some key questions:

● How does the introduction instil the values of the organisation?
● How does it fit the needs of employees?
● How is management commitment being demonstrated?
● How suitable is the approach?
● How will we measure success?

One successful service excellence programme, for example, resulted in an increase in customer satisfaction from 69 to 87 per cent in nine months and an increase in staff morale in the same period of 22 per cent.

SUMMARY

This chapter has described the need to successfully market and introduce a service quality strategy to employees.

Whatever the methods adopted for introducing a customer service strategy, the learning points of the most successful companies are to:

● develop a detailed plan for the introductory phase of the programme;
● position this phase as the beginning of an ongoing process;
● introduce the programme to managers first;
● market the programme with the same vigour as a service or product which is to be introduced to an external customer.

In the chapters that follow, techniques for engendering ownership and empowerment are outlined, together with methods for improving internal customer relationships, providing education and training, ensuring consistency of communication and sustaining a customer focus.

ACTION CHECKLIST

The action which can be taken as a result of this chapter includes:

1.   Providing leadership training to managers who will spearhead change.

2.   Establishing a steering group to mastermind the introduction of a customer service strategy.

3.   Developing a name for the programme and a logo, if felt appropriate.

4.   Investigating the benefits of employing an external consultant to aid the process of introduction.

5.   Deciding on a pilot and control area to test the programme.

6.   Reviewing the effectiveness of a pilot scheme before it is developed elsewhere, so that weaknesses can be overcome.

7.   Involving managers in the introduction of a programme before other members of staff.

8.   Ensuring that everyone, not just one department or function, is involved in the development of the programme.

9.   Developing a means of introducing the programme which will best match the needs of employees and the values of your organisation.

5

Empowerment and Ownership

Organisations where employees are empowered and take ownership of service quality are more likely to deliver excellent service to their customers.

This chapter outlines methods of engendering ownership of service initiatives including the process of empowerment and teamwork. It considers the myths surrounding empowerment and the need for preparation and support to bring it about. Finally the chapter outlines the importance of service recovery and describes a process for achieving this.

VALUED PEOPLE VALUE CUSTOMERS

Surveys reveal that people are happiest at their work when they feel valued and important, when they are involved in the business and when they feel knowledgeable about what is happening.

A MORI survey of organisations with more than 1,000 employees, found that two-thirds felt undervalued. Fewer than 1 in 10 felt that their views were valued and only 1 in 4 were actively committed to help the organisation succeed.

A customer service philosophy offers employees an opportunity to participate in a programme which will determine the success of their organisation. However, many initiatives fail because the philosophy is owned by only a few and is not incorporated into the culture of the organisation so that it becomes a natural way of doing business.

There are many approaches that can be adopted to encourage ownership of a quality philosophy. One of the most used today is empowerment – the devolving of decision-making and responsibility to employees throughout the workplace.

Empowerment is in danger of becoming a management 'buzz word' and many myths surround it. One of its major benefits has to be that employee involvement does make a difference to the bottom line, according to research findings from the United States, but the incidence of empowerment is disproportionately low relative to the hype it receives. Nevertheless, those companies which are adopting this approach find it a powerful means of providing excellent service in a customer-friendly and un-bureaucratic way. The Involvement and Participation Association investigated the success of companies which established employee involvement and empowerment in a supportive environment. It claims that within a year of a shift to employee involvement, overall financial improvements of between 10 and 30 per cent could be achieved.

The customer benefits from empowerment because an empowered organisation tends to be:

- less bureaucratic;
- more flexible;
- more responsive;
- more considerate of customers' needs;
- easier to do business with.

MYTHS ABOUT EMPOWERMENT

As is common with much management rhetoric, there are many myths surrounding empowerment. These include:

- empowerment is appropriate for all organisations;
- everyone will welcome empowerment;
- telling people they are empowered will make them be empowered.

Jack Welch, ex-CEO of GE, puts much of the success of the transformation of the company down to empowerment – freeing up people to focus on the customer by sharing information and taking decisions with the support of their manager.

Empowerment is appropriate for all organisations

This is probably not the case. Those businesses which have a need for strict regulatory control will not benefit greatly from empowerment. Others, whose management style and culture tends towards 'command and control' will also find empowerment inappropriate if they wish to continue this way. Also, the degree of empowerment different organisations wish to achieve will vary according to the circumstance and the individual.

EMPOWERMENT

LEVEL 1:	LEVEL 2:	LEVEL 3:
Some involvement but manager makes overall decisions	Greater involvement Manager makes strategic decisions	Total involvement in all decisions

Figure 5.1 The range of empowerment

Jan Carlzon, former CEO of SAS Scandinavian Airlines, describes empowerment as, 'to free someone from rigorous control, and to give that person freedom to take responsibility for his ideas, decisions, actions'. It is useful to see empowerment as working along a spectrum as shown in Figure 5.1:

Level 1 – employees are encouraged to own decisions and get involved in improvement initiatives. However, the manager takes overall control.

Level 2 – teams and individuals have more say and take ownership of decisions affecting their work but strategic decisions are still made by management.

Level 3 – teams are completely self-managing and make all decisions about not only how they operate in terms of task but also structure and reward.

Level 1

There are many examples of organisations which involve employees in a service strategy. However, at this level, members of staff still have to put ideas for improvement forward to their manager for approval or they can make decisions within certain areas, eg issuing a refund. At FedEx, all call-centre agents have six weeks' training before taking live calls. As part of this training, it is explained that they can give up to $200 on the spot at their discretion when a customer complains. Another frequently used method of involving employees in service quality initiatives is via the adoption of 'improvement teams'.

Garden centre retailer, Jardinerie, is typical of organisations which encourage service improvement groups as a means of promoting good ideas for service quality. These work on the basis that staff identify areas for improvement, generate solutions to problems and are involved in the implementation of the solutions.

Typically, service improvement teams are made up of between four to eight people who are involved in delivering the service. The stages in the team process are:

1. Identify problems and issues affecting service quality.
2. Establish the root cause of the problems.
3. Generate ideas for solutions to the problems.
4. Evaluate and select best ideas.
5. Implement chosen solutions.

(There is more information on problem-solving techniques provided in Chapter 6.)

At Jardinerie Garden Centres, project improvement groups, known as 'piglets', have been working on projects ranging from information-sharing to tightening up on security. Each piglet team shares responsibility for planning, implementing and controlling their project. There is a team leader, who acts as internal facilitator rather than the boss and, as teams gain experience, they are free to elect their own leader or even to rotate the leadership role. Team members set their own agendas. This, Jardinerie believes, differs from the conventional approach where, after a few months, people lose interest and the concept loses credibility.

Level 2

This middle level of empowerment is where teams and individuals have more say and take ownership of decisions affecting their work, but strategic decisions are still made by management.

One example of this is the Oriental Hotel in Bangkok, which for the 10th year running has won the best hotel in the world award. The General Manager attributes this to giving all employees the authority to say 'yes' to any customer request. The only time members of staff need to refer to a manager is when they want to say 'no'.

In the air express industry, DHL wished to introduce a sophisticated hand-held bar code scanner with a small keyboard to improve the speed and quality of service. The scanner was used by the courier who was responsible for accurate capture of shipment data. In the UK a cross-functional team of representatives from various departments was established to discuss how improvements from using the scanner would help customer service and to investigate the best way of introducing the new scanner to the business.

By the time the scanner was finally rolled out the multi-functional team had involved others throughout the organisation in feedback on its use in the field. They had incorporated many of the suggestions of the launch initiative and the scanner was received favourably by many couriers. By comparison, when the scanner was implemented in other European countries, it took much longer to implement and at a greater cost as employees had not been consulted prior to its launch.

Empowerment at this level can also involve members of staff working on an individual basis to bring about improvements in quality. At Marriot Hotels a concerted effort was made to empower all staff so that they would go out of their way to help the customer. This became the message of a long-standing advertising campaign designed to show that Marriot service was excellent.

At supermarket chain Tesco, restructuring has taken place to restrict the level of management in each store to one senior manager and one front-line manager in order to make the management team more accountable. The company introduced a service quality whose aim was to apply a natural approach to customers and to take away the rules and regulations which restricted members of staff from making decisions – essentially empowerment. Senior managers decided not to wrap the initiative in fancy words: this is a simplified debureaucratised organisation, more customer-facing and driven by customer needs.

Level 3

Department store Nordstorm in the United States issues this statement to all new employees:

Rule 1 Use your good judgement in all situations.
There are no additional rules.

Organisations which encourage employees to adopt total control of their work and working patterns are usually those which have undergone a period of change, probably involving delayering to transform them into flatter, more flexible and customer-focused units.

At Allied Dunbar, for example, levels of management were cut to three. The customer service department was restructured into autonomous teams of five to six people. It was felt that this would not only create a greater sense of shared ownership but ensure that employees' jobs were more interesting because of the greater width of tasks they would be responsible for.

Dutch bus company Vancom has found that teamwork encourages loyalty and ownership of customer issues. It has developed its reputation for high-quality service at low cost through self-managed teams, with few managers. Interestingly, although the organisations in the examples have gone down the route of self-managing teams, these sometimes run alongside other parts of the organisation where individuals do not wish to take on the same degree of empowerment, or it is not appropriate for the organisational context (eg, the unit is staffed by temporary workers).

Everyone will welcome empowerment

This is a fallacy – not everyone will want to be empowered and many people are happy with the status quo. This can apply to members of staff as well as managers. It is important that this is recognised and that support and encouragement are provided to those people who wish to change.

As responsibility and decision-making are devolved further down the organisational structure, studies show that managers' reaction can be one of fear. They may lose their power, their standing may be reduced and they lose control of decision-making. It is vital therefore that support is provided to managers to help them through the transition so that they see a role for themselves as coaches and facilitators and so that they do not block the decisions of their teams.

At restaurant chain Harvesters, a 'COPS' planning model was used to help the organisation devolve into self-managing teams. A strategy was established to change the Culture, Organisation, People and Systems within the business. It was agreed that the culture needed to move from a closed and secretive, conservative and risk-adverse style of working with low team spirit and high task orientation, towards a high-quality concern which was open and trusting, more entrepreneurial and where team spirit was high and orientation was on results. This meant changing the organisation from a top-down formalised structure to one where there was looser role definition and where people worked in autonomous, collaborative work groups. Each Harvester restaurant is run by a self-managing team with the manager acting as coach to facilitate team decisions. The change in emphasis has meant the need to improve managers' and staffs' skills and engender a more cooperative and flexible organisation. In turn, systems have had to be reviewed to enable them to support rather than hinder the business.

At pharmaceutical company Glaxo SmithKline, the move towards becoming more customer focused is being assisted by team coaches. The role of team coach has been specially created so that support and encouragement can be given to team members and so that they can achieve their team and personal development goals. The coaches have been given training in coaching, facilitation and counselling skills.

Telling people they are empowered will make them be empowered

Those organisations which have successfully introduced an empowering environment within their organisations have done so as part of a structured approach. Empowerment will not just simply happen overnight – telling people that they are empowered and can take additional responsibility does not mean that they will necessarily do so.

Empowerment works best where it is part of a customer service strategy and where guidelines are set down for the degree of responsibility that employees can take. For example, how far can decision-making go? What areas does it cover and which does it not?

In all cases, in order to encourage empowerment there is a need for greater training and support of employees. Often, empowerment involves multi-skilling. At car manufacturers Ford, business centre hotline service staff are trained to pick up any call and take responsibility for that call, no matter what the query. This has involved a heightened need for training and development of staff including a greater breadth of knowledge of products, customers and the organisation, and increased technical support.

Training needs therefore revolve around information as well as attitude and skills (see Figure 5.2).

At car company Avis, 'intelligent' empowerment has been encouraged so that both front-line and support employees know what is the right thing

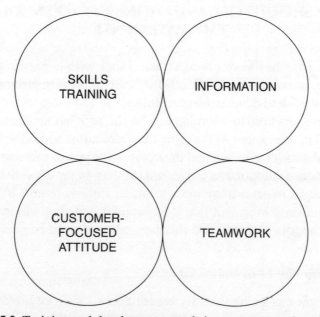

Figure 5.2 Training and development needs in an empowered environmet

to do and why. Using an acronym, ACTORS, the company has encouraged employees by giving them the *authority* to satisfy the customer by making them *competent* in their job so that they can exercise empowerment in confidence; by creating mutual trust between employees and the company and by giving them *opportunities* to exercise their empowerment as well as the *responsibility* to ensure this takes place with the support of senior management and the employee's manager. An extensive programme of training and development has been provided to help employees achieve this aim.

There is more emphasis placed on teamwork in an empowered environment and this also requires training.

When pharmaceutical company SmithKline Beecham overhauled its export ordering department, it went from a staff of 34 to 16 by merging three departments into one. In order to empower staff and motivate them to take additional responsibility, a self-driven team was established and training provided in multi-skilling. A team development training programme was established to help employees to work together in a supportive environment.

Chapter 7 outlines a variety of approaches to training and development that can help create an empowered, customer-focused organisation.

WHAT SHOULD ORGANISATIONS DO TO ENCOURAGE EMPOWERMENT?

The first step that businesses need to take if they wish to encourage empowerment is to assess the degree of empowerment in the organisation now and how far they wish to devolve responsibility.

Next, managers need to be brought on board, which often means extensive training and re-education. At the same time structures and information technology need to be considered and the symbols of power taken away.

Only when a supportive environment has been established should managers begin to set a framework in place with their staff by discussing the degree of empowerment that the manager and the individual wish to have. Then ongoing support and encouragement should be provided.

Creating the right environment

Empowerment can be assisted by creating a working environment which engenders cooperation and support. Organisations such as First Direct and

Alliance & Leicester have discovered that office layout has an impact on how employees behave. Taking away traditional symbols of power, such as directors' dining rooms, separate offices and car parking spaces, puts everyone on the same level.

Managers have an important role to play in listening to staff's views and acting on them where at all possible. Channel ferry operator P&O Stena involved its employees in creating an environment where empowerment and customer service would be more prevalent. Increasing pressure from competitors and newcomers such as the Channel Tunnel led Stena to create an entirely new restaurant concept on board its ships. Called 'Globe Trotters', the concept was developed by managers working in small groups after visits to best practice organisations. Employees were invited to a Mad Hatter's Tea Party to discuss the new concept. Here a workshop took place which included employees becoming entertainers for their customers, the audience. The atmosphere of participation encouraged members of staff to come up with ideas for improving the concept and the style of customer service which would really make a difference. Importantly, the ideas which came out of the party were listened to by managers and included in the implementation of the new restaurant. These comprised ideas for service delivery, environment and uniform.

Teamwork

Teamwork is often an integral element of empowered customer service and is a proven means of encouraging the acceptance of greater responsibility. Organisations such as Cussons, makers of Imperial Leather soap, have discovered that engendering a culture where people work in teams has helped them achieve greater results in the knowledge that groups are more likely to solve problems more effectively than individuals. Businesses use teamwork, therefore, as a way of flattening the corporate structure and developing the skills of all staff, as well as breaking down departmental barriers and getting close to the customer base.

Whether it be cross-functional teams, self-managing teams or project groups, higher productivity is reported through teamworking than through working in the traditional silo, vertical types of organisation. So convinced were organisations such as SmithKline Beecham of the benefits of teamwork, for example, that it turned its organisation 90 degrees on its side to work in cross-functional teams.

P&G reports 30 to 40 per cent higher productivity in those plants with team-based structures rather than vertical ones. When Levis encouraged

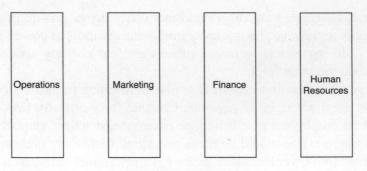

The silo organisation

The matrix organisation

Figure 5.3 Silos versus matrix organisations

one manufacturing plant to work as teams it found that shipments of jeans could be turned around in one day rather than six.

Characteristics of a successful team

The characteristics of a effective team are:

- There is a common sense of purpose and a clear understanding of the team's objectives.
- The team have or can obtain all the resources they need to achieve their objectives.
- There is a range of skills and know-how among the team members to deal effectively with the team's tasks.
- There is a range of team types within the team – each member of the team has different aptitudes for the various team roles required for effective team working.

- Team members have respect for each other both as individuals and for the contribution each makes to the team's performance.

However, the fact that a team's membership has all the necessary knowledge and expertise does not guarantee their success. Teams do not always work together effectively.

Pioneering research on team performance and team types, carried out by Dr Meredith Belbin, has produced one of the most widely used typologies for teams. The Belbin team types are:

Coordinator	mature, confident, balanced
Plant	creative, imaginative, unorthodox
Resource investigator	extrovert, enthusiastic, exploratory
Shaper	dynamic, challenging, outgoing
Monitor evaluator	serious, strategic, discerning
Teamworker	mild, perceptive, accommodating
Implementor	disciplined, reliable, efficient
Completor	painstaking, careful, conscientious
Specialist	single minded, self-starter, dedicated.

Forming teams of different types affects the output of the team. Putting plant, implementor and coordinator together, for example, gives a combination of bright ideas, practicality and direction.

Whatever method is used to assess potential team behaviour, it is important to recognise that individuals rarely fall neatly into team-type categories. The shaper, for example, may also have characteristics of the completor, and so on.

It also needs to be remembered that teams often go through a cycle of group behaviour which involves joining, exploring, challenging and operating together effectively, often known as forming, storming, norming and performing (Figure 5.4). Each team needs to go through this process before they become effective.

The make-up of any particular team should take account both of its optimum size and the specific characteristics of its task. Teams of more than eight people, for example, may find it difficult to ensure every team member's participation. Here it is often better to sub-divide the task and work in smaller groups and then meet to review and coordinate progress as a team.

Even when teams have a high degree of autonomy and the skill and maturity to supervise and direct themselves, teamwork can break down. It is helpful, therefore, to encourage regular reviews of team performance and

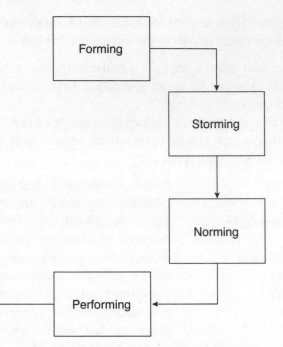

Figure 5.4 The cycle of team behaviour

not to fear conflict in a team – when this is open and constructive it can enhance team performance.

SERVICE RECOVERY AND EMPOWERMENT

Empowerment plays an important part in service recovery and many organisations are moving towards devolving responsibility and decision-making powers to front-line staff who are responsible for dealing with customer complaints.

At the AA, for example, staff are empowered to commit the organisation to pay the member up to £100 where service has been poor. If, for example, a stranded motorist has had to wait for an over-long period for a patrol to arrive, the patrol person can pay the customer money in compensation and reclaim this from the AA. Staff are also empowered to refund membership fees when service is poor.

At BT the customer's first point of contact – the operators – are now empowered to offer 'goodwill gestures' in the form of cash payments to recompense the customer if something goes wrong.

The move towards empowerment in complaint management situations coincides with the general trend towards viewing customer complaints in a more positive light. The reasons behind this are that complaints point to improvement areas which businesses should address; they give organisations a chance to put things right for the customer and they can also strengthen customer loyalty.

Royal Bank of Scotland discovered the effect of service recovery when it measured how much customer satisfaction dictated future buying intentions. It divided its customers into three categories: those with a problem that had not been resolved, those with a problem that had been efficiently dealt with, and those whose experience of the Bank was nothing but smooth.

Those who were dissatisfied were the ones least likely to buy any more of the Bank's services, but there was a marked difference in attitude between people who had complained and had quickly been given satisfactory answers and the happy, everyday customers. Those who had settled grievances were, by a good margin, more likely to buy Royal Bank of Scotland products in the future. Settling the problem openly, politely and speedily resulted in the customer being more positive about the bank, even when the final decision over something like a disputed bank charge may not have gone in the account holder's favour (see Figure 5.5).

Organisations such as British Airways found similar results through their customer research. They believe that a 'right first time' attitude and effective complaint management lead to maximum customer satisfaction and loyalty.

BA has encouraged employees to take responsibility for complaints, which together with process improvement, enhanced technology and greater listening to customers has created a more efficient service recovery. The first step was to develop a listening-post plan – increasing the number and means of gaining feedback from customers including an international freepost comment card, customer listening forums where BA executives and customers could discuss service issues, and a 'fly with me' programme where members of British Airways and customers fly together to experience problems first-hand.

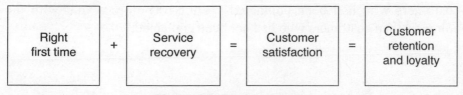

Figure 5.5 Service recovery

BA changed its style of dealing with complaints from a back office function to a proactive customer retention unit. It instigated interpersonal skills training and greater empowerment for all staff, coupled with a process improvement review where 13 steps in complaint management were cut down to 3, and the introduction of a £4.5 million image-based system to eliminate the need for copying letters and faxes.

Empowerment in the context of service recovery, therefore, means ensuring that employees not have only the skills but the knowledge to be able to resolve the complaint and to work to establish the underlying cause of the problem. Typical skills in empowered service recovery include:

- Apologising and owning the problem – the customer doesn't want to be passed from pillar to post or to be made to feel guilty for complaining. Empathising with the customer and appreciating the customer's situation often takes emotion out of the complaint.
- Doing it quickly – studies show that the ability to satisfy customers through service recovery dips after 5 days and the possibility drops to under 20 per cent after 28 days. Therefore the quicker the response to a complaint, the more likely it is to be resolved satisfactorily.
- Doing it by phone – customers' attitudes against use of the telephone are now largely gone, and a personal apology by phone allows the organisation to show that it really cares and provides a speedy response to the customer.
- Knowing how to fix it – empowered employees need to know about the organisation, its products and services, in order to resolve a complaint quickly.
- Fixing the root cause of the problem – collecting and analysing meaningful data on complaints so that the underlying causes for these can be identified and improvements made.

Organisations with the best practices are also empowering their employees to prevent complaints. At Gracie Golf, a US mail-order catalogue company, staff identified two categories of customers at risk. They were empowered to call these customers and fix any problems by offering a range of gift vouchers and free-delivery options. Research subsequently showed that the customers who had been contacted spent $100 more a year with the company than customers who had not been contacted.

SUMMARY

This chapter has outlined how empowerment and ownership can encourage employees to provide the customer with excellent customer service.

We have exploded some of the myths about empowerment and demonstrated that it will only work in a supportive environment where people are receptive to change.

Service recovery plays an important role in retaining customers and creating goodwill.

ACTION CHECKLIST

Ideas which can be implemented as a result of this chapter are to:

1. Establish the degree of empowerment and involvement in your organisation now.

2. Ask managers and staff for their opinions on what additional responsibilities they would like to accept.

3. Agree a framework for empowerment.

4. Provide training for managers in the role of coach and facilitator.

5. Review your structures to see if they are appropriate for empowerment.

6. Improve your IT systems.

7. Discuss the concept of empowerment with your staff and canvass their views.

8. Provide information on a regular basis to your team.

9. Ask your team what additional information they require.

10. Provide training to your staff to improve their knowledge and skills.

11. Act as a positive role model to your team.

12. Review how you currently handle complaints.

13. Set guidelines for how to deal with complaints.

14. Deal with as many complaints as possible by phone rather than in writing.

15. Raise the profile of those people who deal with complaints.

16. Set up a complaints-prevention team and empower staff to contact customers who are likely to defect and win them round.

6

The Internal Customer

Anita Roddick of the Body Shop has publicly recognised that 'my people are my first line of customers'.

The quality of service delivered to external customers is often determined by the quality of service that internal customers – employees – provide each other. This chapter demonstrates how companies can create an 'internal customer' philosophy by everyone recognising they have a customer and by encouraging participation of employees in service improvements.

It deals with how to develop understanding of internal customer needs, teamwork and employee care, as well as looking at methods for generating suggestions and ideas from employees and process improvement.

EVERYONE HAS A CUSTOMER

The concept of customer care becomes more accessible to many people when they recognise that everyone throughout the organisation has a customer. The quality of service supplied to people within the organisation often determines how well the external customer is served (Figure 6.1).

If organisations wish to improve the quality of their service they need to overcome the 'them and us' attitudes prevalent in many companies among both management and staff. To foster a service philosophy, therefore, organisations need to recognise the importance of the internal customer

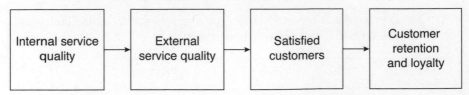

Figure 6.1 The link between internal and external customer care

and the need for greater information-sharing and problem ownership by employees.

In best practice organisations each department undertakes surveys on how well they are meeting internal customer needs. They then take action to improve the quality of the service they are providing.

DEVELOPING UNDERSTANDING OF INTERNAL CUSTOMER NEEDS

Recognising the supplier/customer chain is pivotal to service improvement and forms the basis of the concept of total quality management. Awareness and understanding, therefore, of who are the internal customers and what the internal customer needs is vital to cultivating employee commitment.

British Airways, for example, helped break down the barriers between departments and create a greater understanding of people's roles by holding 'A Day in the Life of' event for all its staff where each function gave presentations and displays for other members of staff on their role within the organisation.

Similarly, Dow Chemicals in the United States held 'Special Emphasis Days' to allow individuals to become better acquainted with each other's day-to-day responsibilities and problems. Participants were purposefully seated next to people they did not know and at the beginning of the day asked to interview their neighbours to gain a greater understanding of others' roles within the organisation and to get to know them as individuals. Throughout the day, group work took place to investigate typical customer problems and the day included feedback and demonstrations of service areas which caused frustration to customers.

One way to encourage greater understanding at the beginning of service programmes is to organise a series of workshops for all staff where the chain effect of service can be emphasised. Employees can be given a series of typical problems to work on which cut across departments and functions to illustrate that everybody is part of the service quality chain.

Another method is for each department to listen to its customers, then develop a customer charter and standards or service-level agreements and an action plan for improvement.

At Hyundai Car UK, a customer service training programme involved all members of staff and their managers. As part of the two-day workshop, each department received feedback from their internal customers on what they perceived to be their strengths and weaknesses, and where the service could be improved. This formed the basis of departmental action plans.

Service quality steering groups

In an effort to generate greater understanding of the internal customer, many organisations establish working parties or steering groups drawn from many parts of the organisation to spearhead service initiatives.

At One2One, the telecommunications company, a new kind of teamwork based around total quality management was introduced. Eleven managers sat as members of the total quality culture steering team. Below this, six process quality teams were responsible for reviewing the process of particular functions. The people process quality team, for example, set up 11 quality action teams to prioritise and develop new systems. This involved over 800 people. In this way a spirit of cooperation was developed across functions and departments.

Service champions

Another means of engendering ownership of a service culture across functions is via service champions (sometimes called service coordinators or representatives). Here, individuals, normally at staff level, represent their department or function and spearhead improvements in service. In this way a network of service champions is formed throughout the organisation.

These employees are normally 'influencers' within their teams and act as a useful channel to bring information upwards to management as well as acting as a conduit for information on customer service initiatives to their colleagues. Where service champions work successfully, these people also form informal links with other service representatives who can provide an interface with departments or supply information on aspects of service quality.

For example, in one insurance company with a large head office and branch network, service coordinators were formed from each branch and function. These met on a regular basis to discuss issues of concern to their function and to coordinate customer care activities across the organisation. The meetings were voluntary, organised by the service coordinators, and the agenda for the meetings was their own. Guest speakers were invited to the meetings from other parts of the organisation to bring in specialist help and advice. Useful suggestions were brought up as part of the meetings and ideas filtered back to the various functions via the system of coordinators.

As part of their quality initiative, Joshua Tetley, the brewers, successfully established service team leaders from all parts of the company who were able to influence their peers.

When Nationwide Building Society introduced a customer service programme called 'The Partnership Programme', a partnership team was established. Team members were drawn from both branches and support departments. The purpose of the team was to visit individual locations to explain on a personal basis what actions employees could take to help improve service, and to act as positive role models.

At South Ribble Borough Council, 20 customer care 'champions' drawn from all levels across the organisation helped to facilitate customer care training and improvement groups.

PROCESS IMPROVEMENT

There is a growing recognition that in order for organisations to be more responsive to customers, processes have to be streamlined and straightforward. Many businesses are using process improvement or business process reorganising to help them become more customer focused. A process is a sequence of activities which leads to an output for the customer (internal or external), as shown in Figure 6.2.

This is an approach which has been successfully applied at companies such as IBM. Here teams of employees associated with organisational processes investigate means of making these more efficient and customer-friendly. Team meetings normally begin by establishing customer and supplier requirements and expectations. A typical group would then define the processes used by the group to meet customers' expectations by:

- listing the team's inputs;
- listing the team's outputs;
- listing the activities undertaken by the team;
- preparing simple block flow charts for each process.

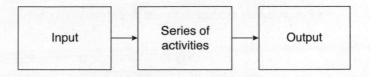

Figure 6.2 Example of a process

The definition stage takes several work sessions. As the charts are drawn it is helpful to list problems that come to mind that may offer opportunities for improvement. Some of these problems can be solved with immediate group action and the team must prioritise and select opportunities for improvement. Next, the team select the projects that can be accomplished by the group and also identify those that require management action or interaction with other function groups.

Once a team undertake an improvement process they are also responsible for measuring whether it is fulfilling the objectives of continuous improvement. For example, a customer's request for product literature may be passed from the telephonist to the sales office to the technical support department to the post-room. It is possible to identify how long each sequence of events takes, who is involved and whether the process can be shortened (see Figure 6.3). In this way, staff can be involved in alleviating 'bureaucratic bottlenecks'.

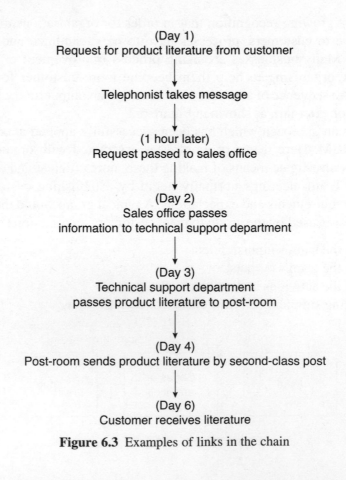

Figure 6.3 Examples of links in the chain

Start with a blank piece of paper

A more radical technique is for employees to envisage the best methods of providing a service to the customer 'in an ideal world'. Employees are asked to identify who is responsible for each event and to assess the service currently delivered by the organisation against the ideal service delivery. In this way, employees can highlight the inefficiencies and redesign how a service should be delivered. This could mean a dramatic departure from how things have been done in the past.

At Safeway supermarket chain, decisive steps were taken to involve employees in making it a more customer-focused player in the retail food sector. As part of this drive, around 6,500 management positions were reassessed and a new process-driven way of doing business introduced. Cross-team communication was encouraged. A conference for the top 120 people in the organisation heralded the new way of working. This included looking at internal service and the idea that everyone is a customer.

Service improvement teams

When people work together to solve common problems a greater degree of understanding can be encouraged.

Service improvement teams are often made up of people from a variety of different functions. They try to identify problem areas and put forward and implement ideas for improvement using problem-solving techniques.

Problem-solving techniques

Cause-and-effect or fishbone diagrams – sometimes known as Ishigawa diagrams, after the Japanese professor who devised them – are often used to identify the causes of a problem. They encourage study of every element or cause of a problem and depict the problem graphically in the form of a skeleton of a fish, with each bone representing causes of the problem and its head the effect. In this way participants are able to see a whole problem rather than just its elements and understand the relationships and parts of the problem. The order in which different aspects of the problem should be addressed can be also prioritised.

Figure 6.4 is an illustration of a fishbone diagram which looks at the problem of poor communication within an organisation.

Other techniques which can be used in problem-solving include problem checklists, the Pareto (80/20 principle), and multiple-cause diagrams.

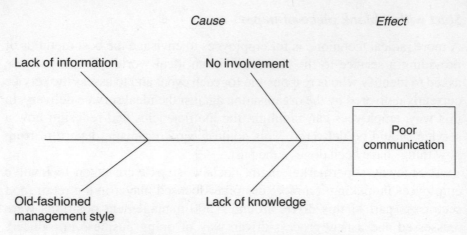

Figure 6.4 Example of a cause-and-effect diagram

Problem checklists allow participants to approach a problem in a systematic fashion. A typical checklist includes questions such as:

- What is the current problem?
- Why does this problem occur?
- What is the history of the problem?
- What is the ideal solution?
- What power have you to act?
- What action can you take now and in the future?

Participants work through the list in a logical fashion to identify possible solutions to problems.

Pareto analysis can be used to establish the pattern between a number of items and their contribution to the extent of a problem, and is particularly useful when analysing numerical findings. Pareto, who was an Italian economist, realised that 80 per cent of the Italian nation's wealth was owned by 20 per cent of the population. The same proportions apply in many other cases. This 80/20 rule (or in some cases 70/30 or 60/40) helps improvement team members concentrate on the principal causes of a problem.

Multiple-cause diagrams are a useful means of representing a problem graphically and showing all its causes and their inter-relationships. Figure 6.5 shows a multiple-cause diagram for a hypothetical problem of poor telephone response.

Other techniques available from the TQM stable include scatter diagrams to identify and increase relationships, control diagrams to control variation, and histograms to identify and measure variation.

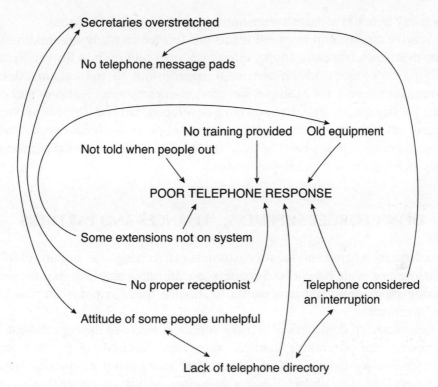

Figure 6.5 Multiple-cause diagram

Normally when a problem has been analysed in this way, further information is required and team members need to gather information which is then interpreted to arrive at a solution. Solutions are often more readily accepted by management when the idea is compatible with company objectives, so it is important that these are made known to the participants of improvement groups prior to them making a presentation to senior management.

At National Westminster Bank, Quality Service Action Teams were established to solve problems and implement solutions at a local level. Steering groups at regional level ensured support and direction. A six-stage process of problem solving was developed as follows:

1. Select the problem.
2. Identify the causes.
3. Investigate the problem.
4. Develop solutions.
5. Determine the action plan.
6. Presentation to management.

As many as 6,500 solutions were implemented from 3,500 teams.

Service quality improvement teams are formed in many organisations. However, each company adopts different names and utilises the problem-solving techniques which are most appropriate to the organisation. American Express, for example, ran service improvement teams as part of their service quality initiative and have developed 'Do and Review' service improvement teams to review department work methods and work-flow procedures by actually helping to do the work. Corrective action plans are developed, discussed and implemented.

DON'T FORGET SUPPLIERS, ALLIANCES AND PARTNERS

The drive for a better service for customers often changes an organisation's relationships with suppliers. Suppliers are an important link in a service quality programme and it is useful to include them in plans for service improvement.

One means of doing this is to make suppliers aware of the organisation's customer care programme and to exact high standards of product and service quality from them in return. The monitoring of quality from suppliers should be undertaken in a participative fashion rather than as an audit. This latter route often leads to defects being hidden, rather than a process of dialogue and cooperation taking place to ensure continuous improvement.

Some organisations include their suppliers in service quality improvement teams to investigate ways of jointly making improvements to processes and practices.

When John Egan took over as chairman of Jaguar Motors, he found that praise for the XJ6 series was overwhelmed by a reputation for unreliability and poor quality. By systematically questioning Jaguar owners, analysing warranty claims and other studies, he found that 150 recurring faults existed. The startling finding was that 60 per cent of the faults originated with bought-in components. Egan insisted that suppliers improved their standards. Testing systems were approved, joint studies initiated and quality audits introduced. All suppliers had to sign an agreement accepting responsibility for warranty costs arising out of their failure.

Likewise, as many organisations create partnerships and alliances, it is important that each understands the other's needs and requirements, plus the values which underpin the service offered.

STANDARDS AND CHARTERS

An important factor in the consistency of service delivery is the establishment of standards of service.

However, the standardisation of service may create some dissent among employees, as exhortations to constantly wish the customer 'A nice day', for example, can be seen to be American indoctrination. It is therefore necessary to strike a balance between delivery of *personal* service and the formulation of standards which can be guaranteed to be delivered on a consistent basis to the customer, and to convince employees that performance cannot be measured without standards.

All standards of service should be realistic, achievable and measurable. Members of staff must be involved in the setting of service standards which they know they can apply on a regular basis.

'Hard' as well as 'soft' standards may be set. Hard standards are quantifiable, for example to process 95 per cent of applications within 24 hours. Soft standards are qualitative, for example to be courteous and polite to customers. Standards may also be set on both a local as well as a national basis. World-class contact centres are changing from their past fixation on hard measures of agent productivity; eg number of cases answered, call duration; to measures on call *quality*: eg the empathy shown, the call resolution, as measured by customers' perceptions.

The Citizens' Charter aims to improve the accountability of public services by making sure that everyone is told what kind of service they can expect to receive and making sure that people know what to do if something goes wrong. Organisations such as the Post Office already have a Code of Practice which sets out standards of service, the complaints procedure, guidance and advice.

As a result of privatisation, the utilities also set out guarantees to their customers. For example, Thames Water guarantees to provide specific measurable standards of service in its day-to-day dealings with customers. If it fails, customers may rightfully claim payment. For the keeping of appointments, Thames Water's standard is, 'We will keep all appointments on the day notified to you, or otherwise give you at least 24 hours notice of cancellation. If we fail to do this, you will be entitled to payment of £5.'

Involvement in standard setting

To engender commitment to standards, it is important that members of staff are given the opportunity to set their own standards – clearly these must be in line with customers' expectations.

It is better to start with fewer standards and to ensure that these can be achieved rather than to set targets which are unrealistic.

One means of engendering commitment to service standards is to encourage managers to develop standards which can be set together with their teams and to jointly agree targets for attaining each standard, eg, 8 times out of 10 or 9 times out of 10.

'To answer the phone within three rings' is, for example, a standard which can be achieved by most people 9 times out of 10. There may be occasions, however, when someone is not at their desk and 1 out of 10 times this may not be possible. However, we urge caution in the setting of standards as these should be focused on what is important to the customer. It is no use, for example, answering the phone within three rings if the person taking the call is off-hand or has no product knowledge.

Here is an example of standards developed for a hotel reception:

1. Each guest must be acknowledged immediately upon arrival at the front desk and served on a first come first served basis.
2. All registration transactions must include:

   A welcoming smile
   Eye-to-eye contact
   Response to guest arrival, eg 'Good morning' or 'Good afternoon'
   The use of the guest's name at least once
   Confirmation of room type and length of stay
   Confirmation of method of payment and offer of express checkout, if applicable
   Handing over of key and key-card with rate clearly shown, and directions to room
   No room number should be mentioned for security reasons
   Offer of assistance with luggage
   An appropriate conversation close, eg 'I hope you will enjoy your stay'.

3. Guest registration should be an unbroken sequence. Should an unavoidable interruption occur, an apology must be offered to the guest.
4. Every effort must be made to accommodate individual guests immediately. A guest with a confirmed reservation should not be required to

---

Our standards

Telephone:
- To answer all calls within three rings.
- To answer with, 'Good morning/afternoon', name of department and who you are.
- Take a contact name and use the name in the conversation.
- Always say 'Thank you'.
- Return telephone messages within 24 hours.
- Always take your calls when in the office.

Correspondence:
- Reply to all correspondence within 24 hours.
- Circulate mail on a daily basis.
- Ensure typed correspondence is neat and free from errors at all times.

Meetings:
- Be on time for all meetings and phone ahead if there is any delay.
- Hold a team meeting each week.

---

wait if his/her arrival is after checkout time. If this is the case, then the guest must:

> be given an apology and, if feasible, be offered coffee, tea or a drink
> be informed of the time when his/her room will be ready
> be offered storage facility for luggage
> never be sent to a room which is not ready for letting.

Standards, therefore, should form the basis of the service delivery customers can expect from an organisation.

Standards may be set for both the external and internal customer. Here are some examples of internal standards set by an organisation's customer support department The department provides back-up support to other parts of the organisation.

Service standards can be compiled for each of the main points of contact with customers (for example telephone, correspondence, meetings, etc) and a checklist outlining the agreed standards can be prepared for all members of each team.

Standards must be part of the day-to-day running of a team and become the 'norms' of behaviour, thus ensuring consistency. The McDonald's ethic of customer service, for example, was formulated by its founder, Ray Kroc, and is sustained via a set of service standards which ensure that whether in Moscow or Maidenhead there is a consistent approach to delivering service to the customer.

Regularly reviewing standards against performance is important. This can be achieved by monitoring customer satisfaction levels against specific performance standards. Transport company The Lane Group, have set key performance indicators driven by its customer needs. These include:

- helpfulness of driver;
- appearance;
- on time delivery.

It is also useful for a self-monitoring process to take place via personal assessment. Manager and their teams can separately record how well they believe they individually and the rest of the team are achieving each standard. This can be discussed at a team meeting where both customer feedback and the self-assessment of standards can be reviewed. As the team achieves its standards, it is possible to add additional pointers to the checklist. In this way, service standards can be defined for each aspect of the business.

A standards-setting process

As an illustration, a national chain of retail outlets wished to set standards to ensure consistency of service across all its outlets as the first stage of a customer care programme (Figure 6.6).

Senior management met at a seminar to agree the purpose and aims of the customer care programme. At this seminar a theme for the programme was also developed and agreed.

Next, a team of service leaders, who had been seconded from various parts of the business, visited each branch in the country to explain the background and objectives of the customer service programme. At the same time a video and newsletter was sent out from the CEO outlining the basic purpose and aims of the programme.

Prior to the beginning of the programme both customer research and an internal staff attitude survey had been undertaken. Part of the findings of this research identified that as the organisation was geographically widely spread, service standards varied between regions and branches. It was agreed that to ensure consistency of service throughout the country, a core set of service standards should be developed. These could then be supplemented with service standards specific to individual locations.

To arrive at a set of core standards a questionnaire was sent to all individuals in a sample of typical outlets across the country, and to head office departments, which were representative of the network in terms of geographical split, size and sales performance. Individuals were asked to

Figure 6.6 Example of the standards-setting process

complete a questionnaire regarding the standards of service which they believed customers expected and outlining those standards which they were currently attaining. The questionnaires were completed anonymously. Managers then nominated one representative from each location to collate the questionnaires and to represent their branch or function at a workshop on standards of service.

At the standards of service workshop, representatives from each of the pilot locations discussed the result of the customer surveys and customer expectations. A core set of service standards was agreed which could be applied across the country, based on both employee reaction and feedback from customer research.

As a result of this exercise it became clear that managers needed specific support in implementing and maintaining the core standards and in the process of managing the setting of service standards in each location.

It was considered particularly important that managers themselves introduced the standards to their teams, so a two-day management seminar was held at which they were not only given practical guidance in setting standards, but also in the practical aspects of overcoming problems which occur in implementing and maintaining standards. The development of service action plans also helped managers to record and develop a strategy to introduce performance measures.

Subsequently, communication material was developed for managers to use with their staff to introduce the service standards and also as a means of monitoring performance. After an initial period the attainment of the service standards was also built into an incentive scheme based on feedback from customer research.

Following the successful pilot of the scheme the standards-setting process was then rolled out across the branch network and as a result a set of national as well as local standards was achieved.

When Granada took over Forte in 1996, it commissioned employee and customer attitude surveys to help understand perception. The results revealed inconsistencies in standards of service across the Forte hotel brands. One of the first steps in the 'commitment to excellence' programme, which aimed to focus more on the customer, was staff involvement in a standards-setting exercise for each of the brands. This led to a customer care training programme, in which employees learnt more about how to meet the required standards.

When the biggest lift company in the UK, Otis, developed a change programme to become more customer focused, it invested in training for all its 1,000 employees. The training set out new customer commitments linked to Otis's values: reliability, responsiveness and customer communication as well as new service behaviour and attitudes (assurance, customer care and internal communication).

SERVICE-LEVEL AGREEMENTS

In organisations such as IBM, Amoco, Chevron International, Sony and Powergen, internal customers are charged for services which are provided to them by other parts of the organisation.

In these companies, as in many parts of the NHS, service-level agreements have been established. These set out the services to be provided by the internal supplier, and the agreed quantity and quality.

Where service-level agreements are developed, the process should include:

- Defining who is the customer and who is the supplier and their respective roles.
- Setting out a description of the service and how this will be delivered in terms of quality, quantity and time.
- Defining a formula and procedure for determining the pricing structure for the service.
- Outlining the duration of the agreement and terms for amendment and termination.
- Defining how service quality will be monitored.
- Defining what involvement is expected of the customer.

SUGGESTION SCHEMES

Another means of encouraging internal service quality improvements is the use of suggestion schemes. Such schemes have existed in the UK for many years; the earliest known in this country was introduced by the Royal Navy in a Scottish shipyard in 1869.

Suggestion schemes can be run alongside customer service initiatives and are a useful method of bringing about service improvements. The United Kingdom Association of Suggestion Schemes, formed in 1987, believes that well-run suggestion schemes can not only pay for themselves, but also provide an excellent financial return. Some organisations achieve a payback of 15 to 1. Non-financial benefits include improved teamwork and a sense of ownership.

Suggestion schemes encourage lateral thinking and normally involve ideas for improvements in service quality, reductions in waste, increases in productivity and cost savings.

American Express ran a suggestion scheme called 'Dare to Succeed'. This was run by the Managing Director and the Executive Committee. Prizes won included certificates of appreciation awarded by the President in New York (the winners stayed one week there) and weekend holidays and financial awards.

East Midlands Electricity ran a 'Eureka' suggestion scheme at the suggestion of a total quality action team. It was highly publicised via the company newspaper, posters and local briefing seminars.

It is difficult to develop a successful employee suggestion scheme if a climate for dialogue between managers and staff is not generally encouraged. Also, there is a danger that when some of the suggestions made by staff are passed to management for consideration, ownership of the ideas can 'get lost in the system'.

Ideas for improvement need to be readily acknowledged in a speedy and personal manner. Often if senior managers administer the scheme they find difficulty in giving it the time and attention it requires. To overcome this, in some organisations a full-time administrator is employed to oversee suggestion schemes, at least for their initial start-up period. Other organisations set up staff committees to develop the scheme and evaluate suggestions. This can, however, involve a lengthy process if the committee becomes too large or does not consist of the appropriate members. Supermarket chain ASDA ran a suggestion scheme called 'Tell Archie'. Suggestions were sent by employees directly to Archie Norman, the CEO. The scheme generated 40,000 suggestions in five years.

Norman's strategy was for employees in stores to drive service improvement, as whether they were cleaners or checkout operators, they were closest to the customer.

Whatever the system adopted for administering the scheme, it is important that an easy method of sending in the suggestions is devised, preferably not through line management – employees can sometimes feel inhibited by their direct manager or supervisor to whom they may have made a similar suggestion in the past which has gone unheeded. All suggestions should be acknowledged quickly, and a timescale for a response given to the employee who has made the suggestion. Employees often become disillusioned with the scheme if no information is given to them on the outcome of their suggestions.

The rules applicable to the scheme and award levels for suggestions also need to be well publicised and seen to be fair by all those concerned. Ideas which are rejected need to be accompanied with a clear explanation of the reasons and a note of thanks for the employee's suggestion, otherwise employees can become quickly demotivated.

Fast rewards and the recognition of suggestions are critical to the success of a suggestion scheme. Good communication and marketing of the scheme are also important to keep it in the forefront of the employees' minds. One organisation, for example, not only communicates its suggestion schemes via posters, suggestion boxes and newsletters, but also prints reminders of the scheme on the napkins in the canteen, thus ensuring that the scheme is constantly visible.

EMPLOYEE CARE

As the drive for service excellence extends throughout organisations, the need for companies to commit themselves to high levels of staff care has become more apparent. As Mr Marriott, founder of the Marriott Hotel chain, has been quoted as saying, 'How can we, in a service industry, make customers happy with unhappy staff?' Marriott's philosophy is, 'Take care of your employees and they will take care of your customers.'

Organisations such as Thomas Cook take responsibility for employees' health, safety and welfare by organising facilities such as gyms, swimming pools, creches and private health care. Hi-fi retailer, Richer Sounds, puts 1 per cent of its profits into a hardship fund to provide grants or interest-free loans for staff to use.

Enhancing the environment

The environment in which employees work also shapes the quality of the service provided to customers. If a member of staff works in a draughty, ill-lit environment where information is not readily to hand or where equipment is below standard, service delivery can be affected. Call-centre environments, for example, can be viewed as 'satanic mills', and this, coupled with the intensity of the work itself, can lead to high levels of attrition.

Providing additional car parking space and more storage facilities, and improving meals in staff restaurants, can often influence an employee's attitude towards his or her employer. A lack of hierarchy can also have an influence. When Archie Norman joined ASDA, it was an organisation ridden with hierarchy. The then-CEO had to circulate a memo saying, 'My name is Archie' to prevent everyone from calling him by his surname. Other organisations such as Virgin Atlantic and Tesco have deliberately fostered environments in which there are fewer layers between the 'front line' and the directors. In a job vacancy advert, Tesco proclaimed, 'Our culture is free of bureaucracy, hierarchy and red tape . . . we encourage you to think outside the box, accept accountability and bring new, fresh, original thinking.'

As part of a service improvement quality drive in one building society department, staff members were involved in the process of identifying service improvements, which were recorded on a service action plan. From 80 suggestions for improvements, approximately half related to the environment in which the employees worked. The introduction of such items as green plants, a relaxation area, improved refreshment facilities and desk lights, although not directly linked to customer care, had a great impact on morale and motivation within the department. Importantly, it showed the staff that their managers were willing to listen to their suggestions and started a process of two-way dialogue.

When staff at Equitable Life were encouraged to organise their own work rosters and hot-desking procedures, their ideas included setting up 'Well done' boards to recognise achievement, 'fun squads' to organise social events and 'mufti days' during which employees could wear casual dress if they made a donation to charity.

SUMMARY

Everyone throughout an organisation is someone's customer and regularly provides a service to other people in the company.

Understanding internal customer needs is a key step in improving internal service quality.

There are various methods of engendering an understanding of internal customer needs, including conducting attitude surveys, holding workshops, setting up steering groups and encouraging service champions.

Process improvement is gaining in popularity as a method of providing a more flexible and customer-focused service and of breaking down departmental barriers.

Service improvement teams can use a wide variety of techniques to identify causes of problems and implement improvements.

Service standards and service-level agreements help specify what is expected of all sections and departments.

Suggestion schemes can run alongside service quality programmes.

Employee care is important in creating the right atmosphere for employees to care for their customers.

ACTION CHECKLIST

Ideas which can be implemented as a result of this chapter are to:

1. Encourage everyone to identify their internal customers.

2. Hold workshops and training sessions to discuss problem areas and how to solve these.

3. Train managers and team leaders in how to facilitate standard-setting in their teams.

4. Conduct an attitude survey to establish internal customer needs.

5. Set up a cross-functional service improvement steering group.

6. Establish service champions throughout the organisation.

7. Develop service standards for the internal customer.

8. Develop an action plan for service improvements in each department, and regularly review and update them.

9. Provide training in process improvement.

10. Set up service improvement teams.

11. Provide training in problem-solving techniques.

12. Develop service level agreements for internal suppliers and customers.

13. Establish and eliminate bureaucratic bottlenecks.

14. Set up an employee suggestion scheme.

15. Review your employee care and take steps to improve the way you look after your employees.

16. Constantly measure your performance against the standards set.

17. Measure the levels of hierarchy between the top and the bottom of the organisation and assess whether or not they are really necessary.

7

Training and Development for Customer Service

Training and development is an essential cornerstone in promoting a customer service philosophy. This chapter explores the need to include everyone throughout the organisation in training and development to enhance knowledge, skills and attitudes towards customer service. It outlines the different approaches to training and development that can be adopted, beginning by listening to customers. It also provides practical example of types of training which are appropriate for managers and staff. Finally, it reinforces the need for customer service to be a key recruitment criteria and for it to be built into the induction process.

THE GROWING IMPORTANCE OF TRAINING AND DEVELOPMENT IN CUSTOMER SERVICE

When customer service training was in its infancy in the UK, the focus tended to be on 'catch all' training for front-line staff which took place in an almost evangelical style. A recent Industrial Society survey found that today firms are putting more emphasis on training and development as they focus more on the customer and encourage employees to become empowered. The report showed that leadership, quality and teamwork are the top three priorities for management training; teamwork, quality and customer care were seen as the top three priorities for staff training.

Experience shows that training and development not only helps organisations be more flexible, proactive and customer focused in the face of fierce competition, but it is also a prime motivational tool. The emphasis on customer service training has changed, therefore, to a philosophy which recognises that to alter the culture of an organisation to one which is customer focused, training and development needs to be offered to all layers of management and staff.

IDENTIFYING TRAINING AND DEVELOPMENT OBJECTIVES

Listen to customers

Best-practice organisations use the information which customers provide to draw up training and development objectives for their organisations and to ensure they keep a clear focus on the business. As we have discussed in earlier chapters, customer service is what the customer says it is. Only by asking customers their opinion can a business gain a true perspective on what matters to customers and how well it is performing, and thereby identify areas for improvement.

The customer service department of pharmaceutical giant Glaxo SmithKline used this form of gap analysis to identify areas where it could proactively improve its service and add value to the customer. For example, the survey identified the expected response times to queries and the customers' level of satisfaction with the current response. As a result of the survey, the members of the customer service department were able to set service standards and identify training and development needs so that they could better meet customers' expectations.

Quantitative surveys are now common place in best-practice organisations, sometimes backed up by mystery shoppers to check that service delivery is consistent. One large high street fashion retailer introduced a new refund policy to better meet customer expectations. It provided a training package for all members of staff and their managers. Once the training had been introduced, a quantitative survey was undertaken followed by a mystery shop to each store to monitor whether the policy was being implemented. The results identified further areas of training need.

Customer focus groups and interviews are other methods that organisations use to get a more 'subjective' feel for customer expectation. The calling back of customers on a sample basis is another technique, used for example by Southern Electric to validate its service delivery. Research conducted among customers of Marriott International suggested that a guest's overall perception of a hotel's service is based disproportionately on the performance of front-line staff. In an effort to improve guests' perceptions, a training programme called 'front desk' was introduced. Aimed at front-line staff, the training was delivered by managers in modular format. In every hotel where training took place, there was a 1 per cent increase in customer satisfaction.

Listening to customers, therefore, helps prioritise the areas most in need of development. Key success criteria can then be agreed.

In setting training and development objectives and deciding on the methods to be adopted, it must be remembered that training and development will be more accepted when the trainee is motivated to learn and in addition, when management wants the learning to take place. Therefore it is important to create the right environment for learning to take place – training should be enjoyable and not be seen as a chore.

The objectives of the training and development must be clearly explained and agreed by both the trainer/manager and the trainee. A clear set of objectives will allow the training and development to be validated after it has taken place and performance to be reviewed systematically as part of an overall programme of customer satisfaction. This training cycle is illustrated in Figure 7.1.

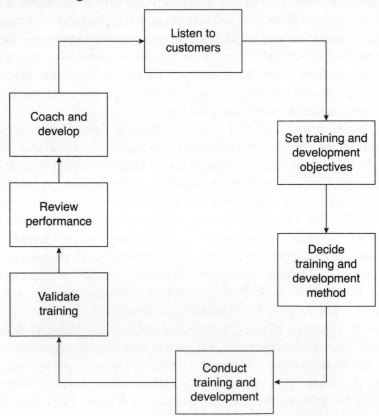

Figure 7.1 Training cycle

Training and development methods

In selecting the most appropriate training and development techniques for the target audience, there is a need to recognise that different people have different learning styles and that the training and development methods adopted must be most suitable for the learning style of the individual participants.

Before choosing a method, consideration needs to be given to:

- the learning to take place;
- trainees' preferred learning style;
- past experiences of training and development;
- time available for training;
- cost;
- work environment;
- degree of involvement required.

A lecture or prescribed reading, for example, involves a high degree of trainer/manager involvement, but little trainee participation. Discovery learning or work experience involves the trainee/manager setting a task, then a high degree of participation from the trainees themselves. The range of training methods is shown in Figure 7.2. In most companies the method selected for training and development in customer service is one which encourages participation, dialogue and debate.

Builders' merchants Wickes developed a modular computer-based training package aimed at improving employees' customer service. This was seen to be an effective option in a busy retail environment. Managers reinforced the training with one-to-one coaching, and recognition of increased skills and knowledge was provided via certificates and badges and a pay increase as each module was passed.

The Medical Information Department of Glaxo SmithKline undertook a programme of customer service training. Preceded by a customer satisfaction survey, the course was intended to give team members greater skills and knowledge of how to deal with customers. The programme was also aimed at generating greater awareness of customer requirements and a proactive approach to exceeding these.

Given the pressures of work and time constraints of a busy department, it was decided to run modular training sessions each week over a nine-week period. All department members met at 8 am for a two-hour session which was supplemented by 'home work' assignments each week. These were undertaken on topics related to the training and tackled on an individual and a group basis. The programme included areas such as:

Method	*Medium*	*Level of Involvement*
Telling and showing	Lecture	Trainer involvement high/
	Prescribed reading	Trainee involvement low
	Demonstration	↑
	Video	
	Programmed learning	
Knowledge	Group instruction	
	Workshop	
	Discussion	
Discussion and	Case study	
experience	Exercise	
	Role playing	
	Business games	
	Simulation	
Skill and understanding	Individual coaching	
	Mentoring	
	Computer-based training	
	Open learning	
	NVQs	↓
	Work experience	Trainer involvement low/
	The real thing	Trainee involvement high

Figure 7.2 Range of training methods

- Creating a departmental customer service vision.
- Benchmarking customer service.
- Setting customer service team objectives.
- Customer handling skills.
- Dealing with difficult customers.
- Adding value to customers.
- Identifying business opportunities.
- Written communication skills.
- Teamwork and customer service.

Discussions were highly interactive and participative and led by the team coach and departmental manager. Each team member kept a learning log of the programme. Halfway through the modules and also at the end of the programme, participants each presented their key learning points to the rest of the team. They also identified ways in which the programme could be continued through ongoing coaching and support.

The evaluation of the programme showed that the participative approach had helped not only develop the skills and knowledge of team members and their attitude towards the customer but had also created a greater sense of team spirit – in spite of the early mornings!

As emphasised earlier, training should begin with senior management and include everyone throughout the organisation:

1. Senior management.
2. Line management.
3. Supervisors/team leaders.
4. Front-line and support staff.

A plan for training and development should be drawn up to meet the needs of each level.

At Barclaycard, all 7,000 staff participated in service quality training that ranged for a whole week for management to four hours for more junior staff.

TRAINING AND DEVELOPMENT FOR MANAGERS

Clear indications of managerial support and involvement are key to making changes in customer service happen. The best training in the world will fail without the managers' praise, encouragement and good communication. Organisations such as BUPA, who instituted a change programme to help them continue to be customer focused in their highly competitive market, learnt from past experience that success depends on:

● Involvement which is actively encouraged.
● Visible and involved top management support.
● A clearly defined and communicated process and rationale for change, set in the context of a vision for the business.
● Demonstrable changes and improvements.

As front-line support staff have often the greatest exposure to customers, it is usually they who are the initial target for customer service training. However, training customer service at staff level is most effective when managers themselves have been involved in the development of the programme, actively participate in this and are seen to change their behaviour in response to training which they have undertaken, *prior* to members of staff being involved in a customer service programme.

To create a culture of customer service and empowerment, managers at the Benefits Agency attended specially designed training workshops. Prior to this they had each written a personal development plan based on a 360 degree appraisal process of feedback. The workshops themselves were run to discuss the multi-rate feedback and to help managers identify areas for behavioural change. These were followed up with a six-monthly progress review to help managers in the process of individual improvement.

Managers at NAAFI attended a development programme designed to help them and their teams to focus on the customer. Topics covered included managing change, listening, informing and coaching.

Management training and development needs to reinforce the fact that role modelling is key. Nothing kills the positive effects of training as much as contradictory behaviour from managers; words and deeds need to match. Supermarket chain, ASDA, insists on managers 'leading from the front', starting with the style and actions of its senior managers.

Typical training and development requirements of managers in customer service environments include: leadership, communication, coaching and facilitation, presentation skills, and teamworking.

Coaching

In unbureaucratic and customer-focused organisations managers need to move from the 'tell' style towards 'ask'. Coaching has come to be recognised as a valuable means of providing encouragement and support to employees as they take on additional responsibilities. Organisations such as Nuclear Electric have recognised the important role of managers in coaching employees to make the organisation more open and flexible. Senior managers have attended a 'people skills' programme covering coaching, open communications and people development.

Our experience demonstrates that managers do need training and support in this important area prior to a customer service initiative: this is a key step in bringing about a customer service culture which is often neglected in preference to beginning a training and development programme focused on front-line staff.

MANAGERS AS TRAINERS

Managers need to be actively involved in customer service and much effective training today is delivered with the involvement of managers themselves. At restaurant chain Pizza Hut, for example, 350 managers were trained in the delivery of a programme covering customer service, complaint handling, dealing with families, telephone skills, menu knowledge and health and safety. Likewise, managers at TNT delivered a

13-week programme designed to promote improvements in customer service.

When Forte sent all 47,000 temporary and permanent employees through 'Commitment to Excellence' programmes, it trained line managers to deliver the 20 hours' training which took place over two weeks. The programme resulted in a more open, empowering culture. In one year following the programme, complaints fell by one third while customer compliments rose by 28 per cent.

There are many advantages in utilising managers as trainers. First, the training itself can be carried out at times which are convenient to the workplace, rather than having to fit it into a central schedule. Second, in conducting training of staff, the manager or supervisor has a greater understanding of service standards and is able to more adequately maintain and review these. Third, training by managers encourages a two-way dialogue and allows an atmosphere of discussion and problem-solving to be encouraged.

It is short-sighted to expect managers to deliver training messages without being given training in presentation skills or training techniques or of having an opportunity to practise. One method is for managers to participate in the same training and development in which their staff will subsequently participate.

An effective trainer will establish previous knowledge before training begins. Someone with little or no knowledge of a procedure or task is likely to require more explanation, instruction and practice and a higher level of coaching than a person who has some knowledge but needs to develop his or her decision-making and thinking abilities.

A manager must fully explain the aim of the training and the content. He or she needs to communicate clearly and in a logical sequence when training. Starting with known and easy facts before going on to more unknown and difficult areas also aids comprehension. As we learn most through sight, demonstration is important in training. We also remember most of what we say as we do; therefore practice is important for the trainee, as is regular monitoring and feedback of results.

According to the Industrial Audiovisual Association, we learn most through:

Taste	3 per cent
Touch	6 per cent
Smell	3 per cent
Hearing	13 per cent
Sight	75 per cent

We remember:

10 per cent of what we read
20 per cent of what we hear
30 per cent of what we see
50 per cent of what we see and hear
80 per cent of what we say
90 per cent of what we say as we do.

Where a manager has a large department to coach and train, it may be possible to enlist the help of team leaders in the training process. Another helpful tool is development of a coaching plan where managers can set out specific training and development objectives for each individual and plan their timing and how these will be achieved. The plan can be used to monitor progress and as a means of review with trainees.

CUSTOMER SERVICE TRAINING FOR FRONT-LINE AND SUPPORT STAFF

Ten years ago, particular emphasis was placed on 'evangelical' type training which involved bringing together large numbers of staff and instilling a high degree of excitement and enthusiasm via a sophisticated and polished presentation. Organisations such as British Airways, American Express and Thistle Hotels used this approach and the reported benefits were that everyone in the organisation was involved for a relatively short period of time in the same shared experience.

The disadvantage of this type of staff training is that it relies heavily upon the manager or team leader endorsing the learning process once the participants have returned to the workplace. It also works on the basis of a 'one-off hit'.

In our experience the range and types of training needed to meet customer requirements have expanded enormously in recognition of the greater understanding of the many facets of servicing customer needs. In today's environment, training for front-line and support staff needs to cover such aspects as knowledge, skills, customer-focused attitudes, teamwork, empowerment, process improvement and problem-solving. At Surrey County Council staff have the opportunity of taking an N/SVQ in customer service. The Council is also a member of the Institute of Customer Service.

Customer service training should not be restricted purely to front-line staff. Many of the elements described below are equally applicable to staff in head office or support functions. To create a truly customer-focused organisation, *everyone* in the organisation should take part in customer service training.

Knowledge

To answer customer queries efficiently and effectively, front-line and support staff need to know procedures, have product knowledge and regular updates. Telephone banking service First Direct designed two schemes to improve staff's knowledge of the entire business: first, a communications programme where different parts of the business exchanged news of activities, and second, problem-solving with cross-functional teams. These schemes have helped improve both front-line and support staff understanding of the organisation and its customers. Other companies such as Texaco have developed a communications charter which promises employees regular updates of information on both products and organisational changes.

One investment bank recently held a series of product knowledge sessions for support staff where managers from each division presented an overview of their working day, together with information on the market-place. These proved very popular and helped increase support staff's knowledge of the organisation.

Front-line and support staff also need to be knowledgeable about service standards, and training plays an important part here. Every Little Chef restaurant, for example, displays its service standards as a commitment to customer satisfaction and this sets an agenda for development of staff to continually meet these standards.

In the United States Wal-mart recognises that not every individual learns in the same way. It has developed a variety of training methods including weekly TV broadcasts to appeal to different learning styles.

Skills training

Typically, skills training in customer service includes such aspects as:

- Listening and questioning skills.
- Assertive communication.
- Dealing with difficult customers.
- Written communication skills.
- Teamwork.

- Complaint handling.
- Managing pressure and stress.
- Problem-solving in teams.

At the RAC, patrolmen have undergone training in listening skills (active listening) which is seen as an essential skill for all personnel, particularly roadside patrols and rescue service operators who man the telephones. This is supplemented by further customer service training.

At Addenbrookes Hospital a customer care training programme was set up to countermand the increase in patient complaints. This focused on internal and external customer service and covered such aspects as assertiveness, stress management, confidentiality, disability, handling complaints and difficult people.

Companies are now much more precise about defining competences in customer service. For example, supermarket chain Tesco encourages staff to take NVQ Level 3 in customer service. This assesses individuals' competences in 16 components which include retaining reliable customer service, communicating with customers, developing working relationships, solving problems, and initiating and evaluating change to improve service. Tesco believes that this encourages staff to take a proactive approach to customer service.

National Vocational Qualifications are qualifications that recognise a person's ability to do a job. To show their competence in customer service skills staff need to provide evidence. This means that to achieve NVQs candidates do not have to do anything outside their job – in fact it means that they are encouraged to do their job to an even higher standard. The standards which have been developed by the customer service lead body and sponsored by the Employment Department are shown in Figure 7.3.

- organise, deliver and maintain reliable customer service;
- improve the customer relationship;
- work with others to improve customer service;
- monitor and solve customer service problems;
- promote continuous improvement.

Optional units:

- develop own and other's customer service skills;
- lead the work of teams and individuals to improve customer service.

Figure 7.3 NVQ in customer service, Level 3

One of the problems with skills training is that it needs practice. This is often difficult to simulate in a training environment. For example, role playing handling an angry customer with one's colleagues may not replicate true life. Increasingly, it is recognised that a course is not enough – feedback and coaching on the job are important for training to 'stick'. Companies such as the mail order clothing company, Landsend, use some customer calls as a means to coach staff with real data.

Customer-focused attitudes

Training can only influence attitudes towards the customer if it is part of an overall approach to development of customer responsiveness. Harvester Restaurants lays stress in its induction programme, which all new staff attend, on what they will do to personally fulfil the organisation's vision. Staff have first been taken through the mission and culture of the organisation and are invited to make a commitment to it. This commitment is then reviewed in working teams.

Although training can go some way to influencing attitudes, the greatest influence will be on the job, and again the role of the manager and the environment within which the individual works greatly influence the individual's attitude and performance. Encouraging employees to act as customers, and to perceive the organisation from the customers' point of view goes some way towards influencing attitudes. In an attempt to improve business relationships with small business customers, an 'understanding small businesses' course has been designed by Barclays. Here, managers learn from small businesses who have applied for a loan as well as preparing and presenting a fictitious small-business plan.

At Miami restaurant Chow Now, staff are each given $50 on a regular basis to experience other competitive restaurants and report on their service. The move towards introducing benchmarking as a means of creating competitive advantage also has a knock-on effect in making people realise that they may not always be the best.

In best-practice organisations such as British Telecom, employees are encouraged to undertake benchmarking studies to help gain a wider perspective of their company.

Intranet

Organisations such as financial services company, Nationwide, are making increasing use of the intranet for learning and development. Nationwide reports that as a consequence staff efficiency has improved as employees no longer have to phone round the organisation to check correct procedures. Web-based corporate universities are also increasing in popularity.

Teamwork

Organisations are recognising the power of teamwork to improve customer service. In order to engender greater cooperation and empowerment, team-building training and events are useful mechanisms.

One IT company designed a programme to train team members in communication and problem-solving skills and an understanding of the concept of teamwork. This was the foundation for a move towards greater emphasis on the customer and empowerment. It also dramatically lifted morale and productivity.

Team get-togethers and outings are also a powerful way of bonding teams. Training in problem-solving techniques as a team may also prove helpful (see Chapter 6).

Empowerment and multi-skilling

As we discussed in Chapter 5, there is a growing trend towards devolving responsibility for decision-making to employees in the belief that this will improve customer service. With this comes the need to train, develop and coach employees to help them take on additional responsibility.

The AA is typical of an organisation that has gone down the route of multi-skilling to provide a flexible response to customers. Initial investment in training has been repaid many times as problems are solved more readily and the quality of customer response has improved. Axa Sun Life reorganised its customer service department into 27 teams and multi-skilled them so that for the first time front-line staff were empowered to act as 'case managers' and process entire applications, rather than working on elements of an application in a production line. Each team was assigned a training officer and technical and behavioural competences have been established to guide staff in their new role.

At Nissan, team leaders have been trained to take responsibility for staff selection, training, communication and capitalising on ideas.

Process improvement and problem-solving

If the processes within an organisation are inefficient, bureaucratic and unfriendly to the customer, then no amount of skill will help. To overcome problems such as these, companies are training staff in continuous improvement skills – for example recognising the causes of problems and identifying straightforward ways of solving them. The Rover Group put all of its 30,000 employees through training in the philosophy and skills of total quality in order to refocus the organisation. Other organisations establish cross-functional teams to discuss improvements to service quality. They are normally empowered to implement these improvements. Such teams prove useful in breaking down departmental barriers and in recognising the needs of the internal as well as the external customer.

THE LEARNING ORGANISATION

The recognition of the link between individual employee's performance and organisational performance has led many businesses to promote the concept of personal development and access to learning for all. Ford, for example, allocates £100 per employee, per year, to pursue any kind of learning of the individual's choice. Peugeot dealer, Appleyard's of Chesterfield, aims to be the best Peugeot dealer in the UK. It is aiming to do this by raising the level of quality it provides via customer service and multi-skilling training for its workforce. The emphasis is on letting staff decide what to study and giving them open access to a learning and education centre. Each employee has a budget of £100 a year which is matched by the local Training and Enterprise Council. Topics which individuals have chosen to study include IT, maths, English, French, leisure activities and singing. Appleyard sees the outcomes in improved interpersonal skills, higher levels of staff morale and motivation and a greater flexibility to learn and adapt.

Other organisations make available to employees learning centres which contain self-study material such as free language and computer courses and Internet access. Unipart opened its own university to educate employees in the principles of lean production, continuous improvement and quality. Training is led by managers, supervisors and some production workers and the increased emphasis on education means that the number of days each employee attends training has risen from 2 to 10 a year.

Creating a learning environment is a proven means of encouraging employees' responsiveness to change.

Knowledge management

Learning organisations discourage people from being protective of the knowledge, instead urging them to use it for the good of the company. 3M sets up knowledge fairs to promote knowledge transfer. Harry Ramsden's fish and chip restaurant chain shared knowledge among all of its branches regarding the best way to achieve the perfect batter.

If a valued employee leaves the company, the organisation can lose knowledge of the best practice in a specific area; the 'tacit' knowledge that the individual had in his or her head. Many organisations are now using technology to help individuals to share the knowledge they have about customers, and are reinforcing this by making knowledge management a part of performance review criteria.

BUILD CUSTOMER SERVICE INTO ALL TRAINING AND DEVELOPMENT ACTIVITIES

Recruitment

The United States only consistently profitable airline, Southwest Airlines, has been known to turn down a brilliant pilot because he or she was rude to a receptionist. Its motto is summed up by the phrase, 'you can train skills, you cannot train attitude'.

Best practice organisations build customer service as an essential element in their recruitment criteria. Effective employee retention begins with the interviewing, screening and hiring process. As courier company DHL points out, 'We are looking for staff who can act as representatives of the company.' At dry cleaning and laundry company, Clean Dudes in the USA, top managers use their business cards to recruit front-line people. When they personally encounter other service providers who go out of their way to help, they hand the service provider a card which says, 'I was impressed with your service. If you are ever looking for a job please call me.' This, they believe, has reduced the cost of recruitment and created a greater customer focus within the organisation. Others encourage staff to recommend like-minded friends to join the company.

To succeed at customer service it goes without saying that you must recruit the right people. Studies of organisations which excel at providing customer service reveal that they invest heavily in recruitment and selection processes. Organisations such as First Direct and TGI Friday have set up an intensive system for selection including producing customer-oriented candidate profiles which include such aspects as:

- attitude towards customer service and people;
- knowledge;
- skill;
- experience;
- flexibility;
- communication skills;
- resourcefulness;
- intelligence;
- personality;
- appearance.

TGI Friday has developed a set of criteria for all new recruits which includes image and skills. They are looking for recruits who have salesmanship and previous job knowledge, as well as aptitude and character. Each department in the restaurant creates a profile of the characteristics and skills of the team members it requires. Common to each department is the need to employ people who are team- and people-oriented, communicate well, are intelligent and can act as leaders and, vitally, can 'get up and go'.

On average only 5 per cent of people who apply get through the vigorous recruitment process which includes group exercises, interviews and psychometric testing in service orientation, people skills and emotional consistency. A profile of each candidate is compared against top performers in the company. A final interview is then held with the general manager of the restaurant. The TGI management team who are involved in the recruitment process have been thoroughly trained in interview and selection skills.

Other organisations, such as Holiday Inns – a part of the Bass Group in the UK – 'audition' for food and beverage staff in order to identify candidates with the right attitude. In call centre and other service environments, tests and simulations, as well as psychometric testing, help to screen suitable candidates. Audi has developed a recruitment process available to all of its dealerships which matches candidates' attitudes and behaviour to those of its top performers. This includes two sets of structured telephone interviews before a final face-to-face meeting. Other organisations, such as Pret à Manger, invite potential recruits to do a day's work. They are judged for employment by the rest of the staff.

Induction

Induction is a critical period when employees' attitudes towards the customer are often formed. Horst Schulze, CEO of Ritz-Carlton Hotels, explains that 'An employee is never more focused, malleable and teachable than [on] the first day on the job.'

It is vital, therefore, to ensure that customer service is given proper emphasis to new recruits and that training in customer service is given as a key part of the induction package. At DHL every new recruit for whatever part of the organisation, including external agencies who provide a service to the company, spends a five-day induction period with a courier. First Direct does not allow new recruits to staff the telephone on their own until a three-month training period has been completed. Southern Electric puts employees through a 10-week programme, covering service ethos before progressing on to job-specific skills. Week-by-week experience is tested and, after this, built up by working with a mentor.

Cross Channel Catering, the company which runs the on-board service for Eurostar passenger trains, ensured that all new recruits undertook a four-week customer service induction before they began work. The first week included an introduction to the company and the environment. This was followed by two weeks of health and safety and tunnel safety. In the final week staff acted as customers on an on-board mock-up, where they were served as customers by other members of staff. These sessions were videoed and feedback given.

Even temporary staff require training in customer service if they are to come into contact with your customers, as they still represent the organisation in customers' eyes. Manpower instigated a scheme for all temporary staff who are on their books to help improve quality and customer care. Based on eight videos, temporary staff studied in work groups over a course of three to four months to improve their skills in listening, problem-solving, telephone techniques and quality.

Customer service training is equally important for part-time staff. As demand from customers for flexibility increases, many retailers have responded by taking on additional part-time staff, thereby offering longer opening hours. This can cause headaches to employers, because the part-time nature of the work means there is not the time available for training and development. Organisations such as BHS send all staff on customer care training, including part-timers, as they recognise that the customer does not know (or often care) whether the person is working full- or part-time – he or she still requires the same standard of excellent service. This means that training methods have to be more flexible and often training modules are delivered on a self-study basis with coaching from the manager.

Companies which treat their new staff in the way they wish them in turn to treat their customers, set a positive example from day one.

Managers need to view induction as a powerful means of demonstrating their own personal commitment to quality. Giving time to new recruits to provide, in person, an overview of the service philosophy, the vision and values of the organisation and providing anecdotal examples of how these values translate into behaviour, is an emphatic means of reinforcing a service strategy. Where senior managers cannot see new members of staff in person, a video of their message can be produced.

At Britannia Airways, the UK's second largest airline, training for new recruits is aimed at developing attitude and teamwork. In the airline's experience the calibre of the trainers themselves is crucial in this period. Induction trainers are selected from front-line staff and are first trained by a small number of full-time training staff who also prepare all the course contents. The training school is responsible for all promotion, refresher and other training courses and sees induction as playing a key part in motivating staff in customer care.

In other organisations new recruits are taken as observers to quality circles and service improvement team meetings to ensure that they have a full understanding of the service philosophy and how it applies to the business.

Competences

One way many organisations reinforce the need for customer service as a key behaviour for success is to include this in competency frameworks. These frameworks specify the standard of behaviour which is required to perform successfully in any given job. Thomas Cook, for example, has developed a whole section on empowerment in its competency framework to encourage enthusiasm and flexibility.

At NatWest Bank customer service is a key competency in many people's job. The underlying behaviours which make up the customer service competence are described as 'To deal with customers in a way which delivers a high quality service: accurately identify and meet customer needs in a cost-effective way'.

Competences are also linked with the appraisal system where, for example, people may be rated on how well they:

- find out what customers want;
- talk to customers to discuss problems;
- listen to customers' complaints and comment sympathetically;
- resolve customers' problems;
- plan their work and the work of staff to respond to customer needs;
- change what they are doing at short notice to deal with customers' needs;
- make others aware of the importance of satisfying customer needs.

It is, of course, possible to link the attainment of competences to training and development programmes.

In order to ensure that quality is ingrained into company culture, British Telecom decided to sponsor a project to identify and train managers whose attitude and skills would act as a positive role model for the total quality principle.

Behaviours were identified by managers and staff which, it was believed, echoed quality principles and company values. This helped the process of identification with the ownership of these behaviours, mainly because they were in a language that the managers could recognise and identify from their own experience. The identified behaviours were that a manager:

1. Gets full use out of staff, knows their capabilities, encourages, considers their feelings and aspirations.
2. Has strength of purpose, is willing to deal with important issues head-on, no matter how tough.
3. Does the job for the company and the customer, puts in 110 per cent, sees self as part of the team.
4. Is open and honest, approachable and dependable, a good listener, and displays an interest in other points of view.
5. Will take action – 'let's go for it'.
6. Will discuss decisions and listens to arguments. Disseminates all relevant information.
7. Inspires confidence, and is to be trusted – decisions have been reached and thought through.
8. Delegates – demonstrates trust and encourages ownership.
9. Asks for people's ideas – is prepared to be persuaded by logical, relevant discussion.
10. Cares about people and their problems – is interested on a personal level.

11. Gives realistic objectives, has clear criteria and ground rules.
12. Knows what's going on, has a bigger picture, looks at problems globally, and can communicate the company view.

From identification of the behaviours, it was then possible to analyse them in order to make explicit those skills that would increase the likelihood of them being modelled throughout the management group. Also, to ensure and reinforce consistency with quality principles, a grid was designed to highlight the lines between the behaviours, skills, quality principles and company values. This was used as the basis of training design.

Forty-five managers in a discrete regional unit responsible for the maintenance, installation and repair of a local telephone network were trained. This activity centred on a two-day workshop involving groups of 15 people, and a one-day follow-up event six months later encompassing the whole group. A questionnaire, designed to measure attitudes to quality management, was administered to the group and also to a similar group of managers acting as a control. Statistical analysis compared these groups and the changes within each group separately.

The results showed strong evidence that the form of training given produced a significantly more positive attitude to quality among the trainees than the control group. Evaluation of the training via follow-up interviews and observations showed positive changes in skill levels, awareness and style.

It was recognised, however, that much of the positive behaviour change would be short term unless it was incorporated into a long-term structure. A follow-up one-day event was therefore designed to make the most of the supportive environment and the operational value already generated by bringing all management together to structure their ideas for improvement through product teams. At the follow-up event an important principle consistent with 'the quality philosophy' was demonstrated. The ideas for improvement came from the bottom up. They were received and prioritised by senior management. Immediate feedback was given on the rationale behind the eventual choice of projects. Where practical, managers elected themselves to the projects in which they wanted to participate. The enthusiasm and commitment to this process was evident in the consistently positive reaction from the participating managers during and immediately after the event. A positive attitude to quality was therefore enhanced as training was designed and implemented to make the link between the customer and the organisation.

Performance review

Customer focus should play an important part in an employee's performance review. For example, all employees at FedEx are annually appraised for their:

- customer orientation;
- enthusiasm;
- ability to fit into a team;
- loyalty;
- flexibility;
- technical expertise.

This helps to reinforce the importance of customer-focused behaviour.

Personal development plans

Personal development plans (PDPs) help individuals to spell out their development goals and work out how to achieve them. At British Aerospace, for example, all 46,000 staff have a PDP. At Audi, everyone takes part in a personal development cycle of 12 weeks, which is overseen by a line manager and is part of each individual's ongoing personal development.

REVIEW AND REFRESH TRAINING AND DEVELOPMENT

Research by the Institute of Personnel Development shows that the most successful performing companies have proper systems of performance management, employ managers who coach and mentor, and provide training on an ongoing basis. This means that training constantly needs to be refreshed and renewed.

Training and personnel departments will find it beneficial to develop their own standards and to regularly measure their own performance through techniques such as questionnaires, personal visits, telephone surveys and customer focus groups. Additionally, a planned programme of refresher training, reminders, training checklists and guidelines needs to be considered to ensure the consistency of the training method.

Organisations should not forget the effect of training and development on motivation. As Tom Farmer, Chairman and CEO of Kwik-Fit states:

In difficult times training is even more important because it is a tremendous motivational factor. It keeps morale high, it is a good way of communicating and it boosts confidence because it proves you are still investing in people.

SUMMARY

Training and development in customer service is a key method of bringing about change.

The best training and development is that which is based on customer feedback.

Expect training to include all members of staff and managers. Training for managers should include leadership, coaching and facilitation, communication and presentation skills. Customer service training for front-line and support staff should include a mixture of skills, knowledge, teamwork, process improvement and empowerment.

Customer focus needs to be an important criteria in recruitment and induction. It can also be linked to competency frameworks.

Customer service training benefits from constant renewal and refreshment. It should be an integral part of the performance review process and included in people's PDPs.

ACTION CHECKLIST

The action which can be taken after reading this chapter includes:

1. Listening to customers to identify training and development needs.

2. Comparing skills, knowledge and attitudes in your organisation to those of competitors.

3. Providing training at all levels of the organisation.

4. Regularly updating product and technical training.

5. Training managers and team leaders to become coaches.

6. Providing training for customers and suppliers where it enhances the organisation's relationship with them.

7. Holding discussion-based workshops and events to enhance people's knowledge of the organisation.

8. Integrating customer service into induction training.

9. Setting customer service criteria for all recruitment.

---

10.   Outlining the organisation's service philosophy in recruitment material.

11.   Reviewing current training methods to ensure they are appropriate and tailored to the organisation.

12.   Ensuring that training videos and training programmes are available in the workplace via the intranet.

13.   Investigating external sources of training materials.

14.   Encouraging the training department to measure their customers' perceptions of their performance.

15.   Establishing a customer service training school within the organisation.

16.   Integrating customer service into a competency framework.

17.   Using managers and internal staff members as trainers and presenters.

18.   Integrating customer service into all management training.

19.   Providing training in leadership and coaching for managers.

20.   Investigating open learning and modular training which can be used in the workplace.

21.   Providing personal development learning programmes for all employees.

22.   Ensuring that each employee has a PDP.

23.   Including customer orientation as an important appraisal criteria.

8

Communications

Service quality cannot happen without communication. Communication is the life-blood of developing and sustaining a service initiative. Studies show that employers are increasingly recognising the value of communication in engendering a customer focus.

In this chapter we investigate how a service philosophy can become part of the culture of an organisation via constant and consistent communication. Integrating a service message into *all* organisational activities in both external and internal communication ensures that a service philosophy becomes part of everyday life.

We also investigate the need to develop a communication plan to ensure that the most appropriate medium is chosen to convey the message to the target audience, so that actions follow words.

DISSEMINATING THE MESSAGE

An important principle of a service quality philosophy is open and two-way communication. The development of communication media to convey the service philosophy is a vital means of creating an awareness of the investment that an organisation is making in service.

There are many methods of communication, and organisations must be wary of not losing the message in the medium.

Surveys show that team briefing is the most common form of employee communication. Verbal communication is immediate and allows participation and interest, but calls for careful preparation and good presentation. Communication skills, such as listening and questioning, are important to encourage two-way dialogue. The disadvantages of verbal communication can be that the message may not be retained by the listener or that the message is not received in a uniform manner.

The Automobile Association has found, for example, that keeping team briefing concise and relevant is critical to its success. It also advocates making at least 50 per cent of the content local issues to generate greater interest and involvement.

Although written communication should ensure consistency of message in a timely manner, the written word is often open to misinterpretation.

Visual media such as videos are powerful methods of conveying a message as people learn most through sight. Most vital of all, the power of behaviour is often overlooked by management in organisations (see Figure 8.1).

Managers should be aware of the advantages and disadvantages of each medium before developing a communication plan which matches the media with the message. The AA uses a variety of media to communicate with its staff, including regular monthly mailshots targeted at patrols, a quarterly audio tape for field staff, a monthly magazine, videos, and an answerphone where staff can phone to leave comments and questions and are guaranteed an answer within 24 hours. Its communication objectives are to:

- implement a framework for communication for its diverse and remote workforce;
- create a climate where trust is re-established and where open communication is the norm;
- inform, motivate and create a platform for dialogue, aimed at improving quality and reducing cost.

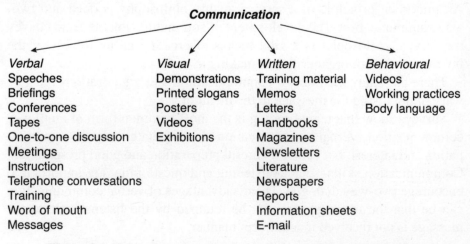

Figure 8.1 Some examples of verbal and non-verbal communication

Regular and thorough communication is difficult in a call-centre environment with shift work, part-timers and heavy call volume. Southern Electric communicates on several levels: daily team-talks to review results and targets, monthly team briefs and weekly one-to-ones.

DEVELOPING A COMMUNICATIONS STRATEGY

At the beginning of a customer service strategy, a communication strategy also needs to be developed to ensure the consistency of message to all stakeholders (see Figure 8.2). Lloyds TSB Bank has developed a communications charter and communications standards to ensure a consistent approach.

In addition, it is useful to debate and agree a set of communication objectives in the light of each target audience. Then, a plan of action can be developed for how the service philosophy can be disseminated throughout the organisation on a long-term basis and, importantly, how feedback can be generated to ensure that the communication is two-way.

In developing a communication plan, factors to be considered include:

- How does the communication strategy fit into the overall service programme?

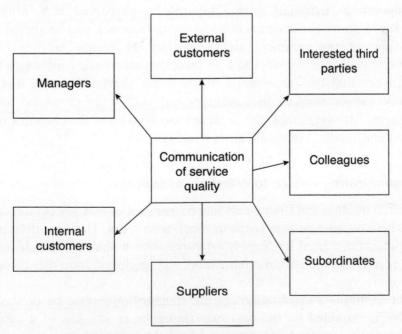

Figure 8.2 Communication with stakeholders

- What are the objectives of communication?
- What are the precise messages to be delivered?
- Who are the target audiences and where are they located?
- What is the current level of understanding of the audience?
- What is the culture in which they work?
- What communication channels are currently being used to communicate to this audience and how effective are they?
- What is the budget for communication overall?
- How should this budget be split?
- How can feedback be generated?

Management needs to consider all these factors before any form of communication design or development is undertaken. The reason for asking these sort of questions is that it is easy to begin a programme of communication using sophisticated corporate messages which raise the expectations of employees and customers, only to flounder after several months when promises are not met or the messages fade away – if indeed the communication continues at all.

Once the organisation has made an investment in communicating its message, management should ensure that it is consistent (as long as this is appropriate), otherwise there is a real risk of demotivating employees and disappointing customers with what may be perceived as a 'nine-day wonder'. Likewise, managers need to invite feedback and be prepared to *listen* and act upon comments and suggestions for change.

One organisation we worked with recently sent so many messages to its employees that the importance of customer service became lost. An attitude survey showed that members of staff were confused by the messages. Managers took the feedback on board and developed a much clearer and concise communication strategy.

Communicating service to external customers

Research by Bain and Co. reveals that 67 per cent of existing customers go elsewhere because no one keeps in touch with them. This is substantiated by studies conducted by Nortel Networks, which showed that customers who received frequent communication and feedback from the company were more loyal.

The customer's expectations of the standard of service he or she will receive is moulded by the past experience he or she has of a supplier and also the standards of service which are communicated via other organisations in press and radio, television, advertising, via word-of-mouth and the Internet.

An organisation should carefully consider how its service quality is communicated to its customers so that it does not 'over-promise and under-deliver'. Many retail outlets, banks and financial institutions place mission statements, customer charters or customer policies in their outlets extolling 'the customer as king'. It is disconcerting to the customer, therefore, if the service he or she receives in that particular outlet does not match the standards of service that have been promised. A useful practice is to read customer-communication material or visit your organisation's Web site to discover what customers are being told.

Charters and service guarantees

Many businesses create customer charters or service guarantees which they advertise to their customers. Alliance & Leicester, for example, has set service standards such as, 'all correspondence will be actioned with 48 hours of your enquiry' and 'we will send out policy documents within 48 hours'.

Some organisations are more cautious in publishing their standards by defining tighter measures. Sureway Parking, for example, states that: 'At our parking shop we aim to deal with 95% of personal customers within 10 minutes of arrival' and '95% of postal applications will be dealt with within one day'.

At BT, guarantees include one month's free line rental for each day it is late in keeping an appointment and £25 per line to business customers. Although service charters and guarantees can help build customer relationships, our experience is that unless employees are involved in their development and believe they can keep the promises, charters and guarantees are not properly implemented. Where promises set out in charters and guarantees are met, this sends powerful messages to customers (see Figure 8.3). For example, hotel training centre, Lancaster House, has seen a 25 per cent increase in business since advertising a money-back guarantee. Hampton Inns, a hotel chain in Memphis, Tennessee, found that when it offered a money-back service guarantee, the programme cost them $1.1 million in one year. However, the repeat and new business in the year totalled $11 million and there were big increases in staff morale.

Some organisations go further by publishing service improvement plans. These recognise there are problems with services and state what the

- You should be given a personal, rather than a block, appointment at a hospital out-patient clinic and be seen within half an hour of the arranged time.

- Emergency (999 call) ambulances should arrive within 14 minutes if you live in an urban area, or 19 minutes in a rural area.

- You have the right to see your medical records in most cases.

- If your operation is cancelled on the day you arrive at hospital, you should be admitted within one month of the cancellation.

- All health workers should show consideration towards your privacy, dignity and religious and cultural beliefs.

Figure 8.3 Extract from the Patients' Charter

organisation will do to put them right. West Middlesex Hospital NHS Trust, for example, published a leaflet for patients setting out the improvements it would make to services in the coming year. These included improving the treatment of people with low back pain and employing more surgeons to shorten the waiting time for patients with gastric problems.

Tone of message

Organisations can show that they care for their customers by conveying a message in a helpful and caring tone. British Airways used customers' endorsements (verbatim comments from the visitors' book) to publicise its Heathrow and Gatwick arrival lounges.

A customer questionnaire, photographs of staff together with their names and job titles, an award plaque on a branch wall – all convey that a particular outlet is interested in not only caring for its external customers, but recognising its internal customers too.

Holiday Inns ran a press advert that stated:

17% of the travellers will forget something anyway

No matter how you pack, there is often that small but essential item that gets left behind, like a toothbrush, a comb or a razor. That's why at Holiday Inns we provide those items we know our guests must often forget. We call it our 'Forget something' programme. It is just a small example of our big commitment to service so next time you travel why not give us a call and we'll take a load off your mind?

Other organisations ensure that their communication material is easy to follow, well laid out and written in easy to understand terms. Virgin Direct, the financial services company, is a good example of an organisation that produces clear communication material.

Communication of service quality to the internal customer

Just as the message given to external customers and the tone in which it is conveyed is important in reinforcing the importance of quality service, how this message is presented within an organisation often fashions employees' attitudes towards a service philosophy.

Employees should be the prime target audience of an organisation's communication plan. Undertaking an employee audit will provide managers with a better perception of how well communication policies are succeeding and help identify areas for improvement.

Managers at one company discovered that almost 50 per cent of people disagreed with the statement, 'I can express my opinion without worrying about getting into trouble', which was included as part of an employee attitude survey. As a result, a communications Quality Action Team was formed whose task was to change employees' poor perceptions. A customer charter for communications was developed. This included such items as:

- holding regular participative meetings of work groups (minimum standard: one per month with communications as a permanent agenda item);
- updated organisational charts/telephone directories and key departmental contact persons/points will be accessible to all (minimum standard: updated quarterly).

The result was that a far more open and responsive style of communication has been developed throughout the organisation.

Transport company The Lane Group, runs regular roadshows in depots around the country to spread a service culture. They have a 99 per cent attendance rate and are an invaluable way of communicating customer focus.

Awareness, comprehension, conviction, action

At the initial stage of a service quality programme, communication with employees should be aimed at creating awareness and comprehension of the need to change, to thus convince employees that they must take action which mirrors the desired vision and values of the organisation. Managers have a key role to play in the communication process.

The turnaround at computer company, Compaq, was spearheaded by a worldwide management communication group. The CEO met 150 to 200 managers from all over the world every week to explain to them in very clear terms what was happening and why.

SELL DON'T TELL

People's attitudes to service quality within an organisation can be influenced by the way in which the message is conveyed (Figure 8.4).

We have spoken earlier of the need to develop a mission and set of values which is evident to all employees and other stakeholders. We also outlined in Chapter 2 methods of involving all employees in the development of this mission. Service missions and visions are often communicated to employees via written statements. These statements must be seen to emanate from senior management. A personal letter from the chief executive to all employees explaining the importance of service philosophy, for example, endorses senior management's commitment to the concept, but is not sufficient in itself. To encourage awareness and comprehension, discussion and debate must take place. Managers need to explain a service philosophy in person via presentations and participatory sessions and make time for two-way conversations. At financial services organisation Egg, directors run quarterly communication sessions at all sites. They also hold staff breakfast communication sessions and are available to contact through the Internet.

At software company SCO, managers sat down with each member of staff to discuss the organisation's vision and values. Each employee was given a booklet which summarised these. At a later date workshops were held to review how well the organisation was keeping to the values.

Face-to-face is best

The experience of many organisations undertaking service initiatives demonstrates that verbal communication which promotes discussion, rather than a one-way imparting of messages, is the most effective means of communication. Team briefings and meetings, therefore, form an important part of the communication of customer service, as do training and staff events where an *interchange* of views is encouraged.

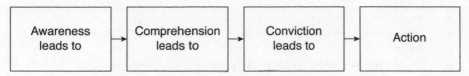

Figure 8.4 The process of selling an idea or concept

There is a trend away from the 'sheep-dip' type of roadshows, often used by companies where large groups of staff gathered to hear presentations on customer service, towards more two-way dialogue.

Nationwide Building Society ran a series of 'Talkback' sessions where groups of employees attended forums with senior managers to ask questions and put forward ideas. This encouraged greater dialogue and two-way communication. Importantly the agenda was set by the employees, not the managers.

Managers at Marriott Hotels in the United States hold 15-minute reviews before every shift for customer-contact staff. The reviews focus each day on one of the 20 basics of service that the hotel has identified and committed to as standards – from appearance to handling customer concerns.

Involve employees in developing internal standards

As the importance of internal service quality is recognised, many organisations involve employees in the development of internal standards and charters which are then communicated to employees within the business. Here is an extract from HMV's internal standards for helping customers.

HMV CUSTOMER SERVICE STANDARDS

HELPING CUSTOMERS

Customers will always feel they receive polite, helpful, friendly and efficient service in HMV Stores.

In all our contacts with customers we will:

- *give customers priority over other tasks;*
- *make eye contact and greet each customer;*
- *focus attention on the customer, and be polite, friendly and interested throughout;*

- *respect individual customer tastes and preferences;*
- *apologise for any delay in giving service and advise of actions we are taking to help;*
- *thank each customer, and end the contact in an appropriate way.*

HELPING CUSTOMERS AT THE TILL

Customers will always feel they are given polite, efficient and friendly service at the till.

We will:

- *never leave a customer waiting unattended at a till;*
- *ensure that customers do not feel they have been delayed unnecessarily;*
- *handle the transaction at a speed appropriate to the individual customer;*
- *point out offers, campaigns and other useful information where appropriate;*
- *only interrupt a member of staff who is serving a customer when it is to offer help;*
- *treat products and payment with care, and hand goods to the customer.*

Whitbread Inns identified the need to develop standards for every area of their pub operation. Three staff working parties were formed to agree best practice and develop a set of standards which were meaningful to staff and avoided the 'have a nice day' syndrome. These were then communicated to employees as part of an interactive training programme. (See Chapter 6, on the internal customer.)

Videos

Some companies use corporate videos in which the chief executive plays a leading role in explaining the need for enhanced customer service. This cannot replace personal contact but the advantage of the visual medium is that pictures and sounds can quickly and effectively put across key customer service messages in a memorable way.

To say for example, that 'it is important that we differentiate from the competition which poses a threat to our survival and service; this is the means which we have adopted to implement this strategy' is a strong, straightforward message. To produce a video which actually shows the threat of the competition has far more impact and the subsequent retention of this message will be higher. FedEx, for example, provided a video following the journey of a parcel through the organisation. This brought to light areas where improvements could be made. FedEx also has a quarterly news update chaired by the CEO which is broadcast on its own satellite network.

News programme-type videos are used by many organisations to update employees on the progress of service strategies.

BMW takes the importance of visual communication seriously, and believes that immediate communication to a dispersed workforce can benefit the business. It has invested in a private satellite network across 160 sites where every week dealership staff gather round their TV sets to watch a topical 20- to 30-minute broadcast, produced overnight and beamed by satellite directly to them.

Ford Motor Company also broadcasts a fortnightly news programme to cafeterias and rest rooms at 23 of its plants. It is reported to find this method a useful way of transmitting corporate messages, rather than the days or even weeks it can take for news bulletins to be circulated throughout the company.

Intranets

Intranets also provide an opportunity to share knowledge and the best practices in customer service. Egg has developed an intranet site with examples of positive behaviour which supports the organisation's values.

When pharmaceutical giants Astra and Zeneca merged, they found that the introduction of the intranet helped provide one-step access to future plans and developments. In Denmark, for example, the company has an e-asthma site. Here customers, doctors and researchers exchange ideas.

REINFORCING THE MESSAGE

The development of material which imparts key messages as part of employees' working lives is also a useful means of reminding members of staff about customer care. When a logo or slogan is developed for a customer service strategy this can successfully be applied to such items as:

> screensavers;
> letterheads;
> message pads;
> pens;
> mugs;
> tee shirts; and
> key rings.

These can be used in the employees' workplace and act as a useful reminder. They can also be used as prizes for suggestions of service improvements.

Training material

Training material which is consistent with the customer care message can also be produced to reinforce the quality message.

House of Fraser produced a video to review the progress of its service quality programme. It was to be the central part of a training session to be run for groups of staff by the manager of each store. The video presentation box, managers' desk-top presenters, training guide and staff certificates were specially designed using the company's service quality logo and sent to each store in a high-quality presentation package.

A further impactful idea is to produce a special welcome pack for all employees attending customer care training courses which is personalised to each participant and contains a letter of encouragement from the chief executive, together with training material and other information on the service quality initiative.

Notice boards and posters

It is also useful to provide notice boards, conveniently located around the company, where information relating to customer service and customer service activities can be displayed, either as separate boards or as part of overall staff notices. It is our belief that special notice boards for customer service create more impact. Location is important. At Body Shop, for example, posters are often pinned on the toilet doors as this is one location it knows all employees will visit!

Many posters are also available reminding employees of the importance of service quality. These posters serve only as reminders to members of staff of the service philosophy and must be seen as an 'add-on' – they are not the key to effect changes of attitude, only reinforcers.

Likewise, organisations often place notices in reception areas declaring their commitment to customers. Unless the behaviour of the receptionist or those employees who come into contact with visitors to the company uphold the beliefs outlined in such statements, the notices are often empty promises.

The impression received by visitors to the company often forms their opinion of the company as a whole. Often visitors to large organisations are met by unfriendly employees working in anonymous offices. At the DIY retailers B&Q's head office in Southampton, this impression is completely different as each department is clearly signposted and a description of the department's function is hung over each section of the department for all to see.

Staff directories

Improvements in internal service quality can also be brought about by employees understanding who does what. Organisational charts which are regularly updated can ensure that employees have a better understanding of the different roles and functions of the company and how each individual fits into the whole. Pictorial charts with diagrams and photographs beside them also help to break down communication barriers. These, of course, must be kept up to date. Likewise, telephone, intranet and Internet directories and directories of services which are current and regularly updated help improve communications.

Newsletters and newspapers

Many organisations integrate a section on customer service into existing newspapers and bulletins, but it is often useful to develop a special newspaper or newsletter to communicate the progress of customer service initiatives in which the activities of the employees, together with achievements to date, can be communicated. Barclaycard, for example, developed a quality newspaper as part of its quality initiative. This proved a useful means of recognising achievements.

Service newspapers can also be used to invite feedback and monitor the progress of service improvements. Readers can be invited to send in examples of good service and new ideas. The London Borough of Sutton, for example, publicised success stories as part of its service quality initiative to demonstrate positive examples of standards of service to all employees. At manufacturer of home improvement group, Cego, a special newspaper called *Quest* publicised achievements and progress in service quality.

Management should also take advantage of photo opportunities to advertise the success of service improvements. The intranet is also a useful medium for sharing ideas.

Competitions and suggestion schemes are also a successful means of communicating service initiatives and results can be published in newsletters. One company, for example, ran a competition where members of staff were asked to identify what aspect of service was most in need of improvement, from a customer's point of view. The results, which were published in the newspaper, also provided useful feedback to managers on staff's perceptions of the areas of the business most in need of change.

Feedback

As communication is a two-way process and requires both a receiver and a transmitter, management must remember to invite feedback on all communication activities. This can be done in both an informal and formal fashion, inviting comments on a one-to-one basis, holding discussion groups on the effectiveness of communication media and via formal questionnaires.

An ongoing process

Effective communication is an ongoing process. The temptation is to put a lot of effort into communicating service quality at the introduction of a service strategy and then to let it fade as time goes on. Just like training, communication needs to be constantly renewed or refreshed.

Axa Sun Life has developed a communication initiative called 'The Galaxy Programme'. Six times a year external speakers are invited to give presentations on relevant business topics to employees. The top 10 managers hold lunch meetings with groups of 15 to 30 employees six times a year in order to listen to ideas. Senior managers also undertake a regular programme of branch visits. A conference is held for the top 300 managers every 18 months. Responsibility for communication has been devolved to nominated people in each of the company's 20 business units. Communications has also been built into the company's wider competency framework.

By undertaking a variety of initiatives, Axa Sun Life hopes to improve the communications process within the company.

TIPS ON EFFECTIVE INTERNAL COMMUNICATION

Too little communication can lead to staff demotivation. Too many messages can lead to confusion.

Alan Mitchell, a journalist working for Marketing Business,[16] has 10 tips for effective internal communication:

1. Lead from the top. If the chief executive and the board are not committed it's unlikely to succeed.

2. Conduct an audit. Like all good marketing, understand what the target market needs and thinks.

3. Communication is two-way. Listening is harder than talking. Proving you have listened is even harder.

4. Don't get mesmerised by media. Internal communications is not the same as the production of an employee magazine or video. Choice of communication channel should be determined by the message and the circumstances.

5. Face-to-face is best. Employees usually want to hear the news from their own managers and supervisors.

6. Have something to say. If the board is not clear about where the business is going, why, and what employees' role in this future is going to be, it has little of substance to communicate.

7. Constantly measure how well the messages are being received, and how the process of communications is viewed by staff.

8. Honesty is the best policy. Employees usually don't trust glossy razzmatazz or Good News Charlies.

9. If your external and internal messages don't coincide and reinforce each other, you've got a problem. If they do, you may have a competitive edge.

10. Communication is an integral part of the management process. It is not an afterthought.

A COMMUNICATIONS CASE STUDY

An example of an organisation which has successfully used a variety of media to bring about a change in culture and which has also successfully used feedback, is ICI Paints and its 'Focus on the Customer' programme.

ICI Paints' broad objectives were to bring about a service-orientated culture in a manufacturing and science-based industry, to ensure that employees understand and subscribe to the concept of the 'internal customer', and to recognise that the quality of service that reaches the customer begins with the quality of service that people inside the company give each other.

Market research was carried out among customers to compare ICI Paints' performance, products and services against those of competitors.

Among employees it helped define where opportunities for improvement existed and gave everyone a chance to say what frustrated them about the organisation, or hindered them from doing a better job. This was preceded by a personally addressed letter from the Principal Executive Officer to every employee.

The research was repeated at the end of the first year to measure progress.

In the UK, where the programme started, the target audience was about 3,500 employees (from weekly-paid to senior management) across the head office, two major production plants and a network of distribution depots. The programme has been adapted for wider use in Europe.

Ownership of the programme

To bring about the required culture change it was necessary for employees to feel they owned the 'Focus' programme. The strategy was to:

- Create a desire for change by undermining complacency.
- Give people a common vision of a customer-focused organisation and encourage them to achieve it.
- Provide a 'forum' to enable people at all levels to plan together and put forward ideas to improve the business.
- Help people identify the needs of their customers and direct their efforts to meet these.

The 'Focus on the Customer' programme used a variety of communications techniques. However, ICI Paints was careful not to invite employee cynicism by obvious extravagance and 'glitz'.

The 'Focus' process for change involved training, preparation, teamwork, speed of response and competitiveness. The initial employee research had highlighted that inefficiency arose from lack of understanding of how the business operates (for instance departments placing unreasonable demands on one another). The survey also surfaced the need for better handover from one department to another. This led to the creation of a visual device based on a relay team: 'Baton Change'.

The first year's budget for communicating the programme was £200,000, the second year's £360,000.

The launch

The market research findings were instrumental in convincing employees at all levels of the need for 'Focus on the Customer'. This confidential research was presented to employees with no holding back.

Before the launch, briefings for the board and senior management were held to gain their commitment.

The launch event was a major roadshow presentation made at all locations over four weeks. All employees attended within their departmental groups. Presentations were given by a board member, together with their own senior manager, making use of videos, vox pops, interviews and a range of audio-visual techniques. The messages were:

- The dynamic nature of the world paints business.
- The threat from major international competitors in the UK and world-wide.
- The need for competitiveness.

Employee and customer research was presented in terms of an overview of ICI Paints' performance and then employees heard detailed research messages specific to their own departments. (This second element was confidential to their presentation.)

After each presentation employees were given a booklet summarising the key messages and actions and had an opportunity to question their managers.

The programme

The programme itself consisted of the following parts:

Management lectures on quality service strategy, to add credibility and build commitment. Internationally acclaimed management 'guru' and author Tom Peters lectured to an audience of some 300 managers and a video was made for wider distribution.

Focus groups were a practical response to the market research in which employees said they wanted to contribute problem-solving ideas and have a say in how the business operates. Employees were involved in small-group discussions on ways of improving service to both external and internal customers. They established action 'Hit Lists' within each department, or 'Baton Change' issues which crossed department boundaries. Special focus packs were prepared containing desktop presenters and literature for focus groups together with a short video reminder of the launch presentation and survey results.

Recognition gifts: exclusive quality silk ties for men and scarves for women were designed, for presentation to 'champions' of business improvement ideas identified by the 'Focus' groups. This was separate from any financial incentives through the employee suggestion scheme.

Employee newspaper: each month this featured reports on initiatives and successes within the programme. It also featured customers' views of ICI Paints' service, written by an independent business writer. An 'If I were Chief Executive' competition invited employees to imagine themselves in the top job and put forward ideas on how they would change things, with travel prizes for best suggestions.

Notice boards: the importance of notice boards was indicated by a survey into communications. To make more effective use of them, the notice boards were changed to give them categories: 'Focus on the Customer', Company News, Vacancies, Social and Recreation, Employee Representation. A system was established for updating content and 'housekeeping'. Special News Bulletins and 'Focus' update papers were produced for notice boards.

Posters: a series of posters was produced with 'Focus on the Customer' messages for general use. Poster 'blanks' with a colour logo were produced to enable specific departmental 'Focus' messages to be over-printed.

Merchandising: notepaper, Post-it pads and pens were provided, branded with the logo, to keep employees constantly reminded.

Educational booklets: these were targeted at specific groups to explain in everyday language concepts such as data integrity, and setting and measuring performance levels.

ICI Paints in focus

In the second year, a major event was run to inform employees how the business operates, with emphasis on interdependence of departments, and to provide fresh impetus to the programme. A theatre and exhibition were housed in a giant marquee on site car parks. Presentations in the theatre included: what had been achieved under the 'Focus' programme; targets for the future; measuring success; a review of business performance; and playback of second-year market research among employees and customers.

The exhibition used over 200 exhibition panels, AV displays, and interactive computers to give an overview of the world business, show how business areas and functions interrelate to deliver quality service to the customer, and to explain the financial facts of life.

Market research at the event showed an overwhelmingly favourable response from more than 90 per cent of employees.

The theatre and exhibition were also used for presentations to suppliers on their role in ICI Paints quality initiative.

A series of business awareness videos was launched at the event. These are now released at regular intervals to build an understanding of the business and how it works.

Measurement

Three hundred Focus Groups were voluntarily established by employees with more than 80 per cent of employees taking part.

More than 1,500 business and service projects emerged from these groups and more than a third have been completed so far.

Translated into financial terms, the estimated spin-off through improved efficiencies from just the first 100 ideas was about £500,000 in the first year, and this was exceeded by savings in year two. The full financial impact will be felt over a longer period.

The enormous potential power of the workforce has been channelled by ensuring that everyone can have a say in removing frustrations associated with their jobs and improving efficiency. More awareness of interdependence of departments in the quality chain is overcoming barriers.

Employee research revealed a positive attitude, with 80 per cent saying they would like to continue or increase their involvement. Employees also mentioned a big improvement in communication between work groups.

ICI Paints stresses that the programme is not about short-term returns. Nevertheless, after one year, more than 40 per cent of customers researched noticed a significant improvement in levels of service.

SUMMARY

Good communication is central to a service quality programme.

Careful consideration needs to be given to the vehicles used for communicating a consistent service quality message and a strategy should be developed to address this.

Detailed attention should be given to how a service philosophy is communicated to all stakeholders. Employees especially should be the key target audience for service messages and a variety of techniques should be adopted to disseminate information and encourage feedback.

ACTION CHECKLIST

Practical action which can be taken in your organisation to ensure two-way communication includes:

1. Reviewing your current communication strategy. Gaining feedback from employees, customers and other interested parties on the effectiveness of your current communications.

2. Devising a communications plan which encourages two-way dialogue.

3. Stressing the importance of visual and behavioural communication.

4. Sending managers and team leaders on presentation skills courses.

5. Reviewing written communication with customers to ensure a friendly and straightforward style.

6. Holding regular team briefings with your staff – encouraging them to run part of the meeting.

7. Developing a poster campaign to remind employees of the programme.

8. Inviting guest speakers from inside and outside the organisation to talk on topics of relevance to service quality.

9. Providing videos on service quality initiatives, business information and news topics.

10. Disseminating information on competitors.

11. Publishing customer letters and comments.

12. Devising a customer service newspaper.

13. Holding company-wide service events to encourage a review of progress and two-way discussion.

14. Developing reminder material such as notepaper, telephone pads, etc.

15. Providing a handbook for all employees on the principles of a service quality initiative.

16. Providing service quality notice boards.

17. Holding cross-functional conferences.

18. Setting aside regular time each week for informal discussion with the team.

19. Holding competitions on relevant service topics.

20. Devising a slogan and logo for a customer service programme.

21. Producing special training material and literature in keeping with the programme.

22. Installing videos throughout the company so that news programmes can be transmitted; alternatively investigating satellite TV and videoconferencing.

23. Reviewing your communication material through the eyes of the customer.

24. Using the intranet to communicate service messages to employees and to share knowledge of the best practices.

25. Providing Internet access for customers.

9

Recognition and Reward

This chapter considers the vital process of motivating the team, managing performance and recognising and rewarding excellent service.

MOTIVATION

In energising the team to deliver superior customer service, managers have a difficult but crucial role to play. They must be seen to be personally committed to customer service, to practise what they preach. They need to create an environment where processes are customer-driven and where standards are set to deliver a consistent level of service. They need to train and develop their staff and involve everyone in focusing on the customer. They must encourage excellence without peering over people's shoulders, build motivation and commitment, and measure, review and reward performance. Furthermore, they often have to manage performance in an environment where staff numbers may have been reduced and more is expected from those who remain.

Signs of demotivation

We have probably all experienced service delivered from poorly motivated staff. Signs of lack of motivation include apathy, indifference, lack of ownership of problems, poor performance and poor time-keeping, uncooperative attitude and unwillingness to change.

Imagine you are the manager of a busy customer service department. How do you ensure that customers receive a consistently high reward of service?

Different strokes for different folks

In the same way as managers encourage their staff to treat customers as individuals, effective managers remember to be flexible in the style and approach they use with each of their staff. Some research suggests that extroverts respond better to praise and public recognition and introverts are more influenced by censure and prefer private praise.

It is often the extrinsic, 'hard' factors which organisations focus on when it comes to deciding how to motivate and reward their staff, using incentives such as improved working conditions or improved status. Intrinsic factors such as sense of purpose, feeling of achievement, advancement, recognition, responsibility and reviewing feedback in a job are often overlooked as they belong to the 'touchy, feely' school of management which is less easy to control.

Interestingly, research shows that demotivated employees are most concerned about 'soft issues' when they are in the workplace. When they become so demotivated that they decide to change jobs, it is the 'hard' factors which they cite as reason for leaving.

Surveys

Involving your employees in the design of reward incentives ensures greater ownership for the scheme. The first step is to ask employees what motivates them and why. This can be done either on an individual or team basis in attitude surveys, focus groups or cross-functional task groups. The task of every effective manager is to understand what motivates his or her team. Head office staff at ASDA, for example, identified that a meaningful reward for good service would be reserved parking at the front of the building. This was because there were limited parking spaces at head office. As a result, the 'Golden Care' award was developed.

PERFORMANCE MANAGEMENT

Good performance over time will only come from well-motivated staff.

Performance management is an approach which allows managers to impact their goals and responsibilities in serving the customer internally and externally.

It involves a cycle of clarifying business goals and customer needs and then agreeing individual objectives and standards of performance. With coaching, development and rewards, improved performance is possible from employees who know:

● what is expected of them;

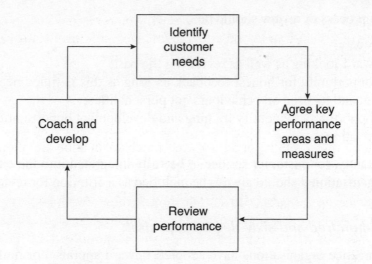

Figure 9.1 The performance management cycle

- how they are doing;
- what they need to do next;
- what help they will receive.

Increasingly, best-practice organisations begin the performance management cycle, shown in Figure 9.1, by identifying the needs of their external and internal customers.

At one electricity company, for example, a performance-related pay scheme was developed which involved each team identifying their customers and specifying their needs as well as agreeing how customers would measure their effectiveness. From this process, five to eight key performance areas were agreed per team and individuals in the team set their own objectives in relation to the team's key performance areas.

Many organisations such as NatWest build customer service into the competency framework and performance review systems. In this way the importance of customer service can be reinforced.

Review

Once key result areas and measures of success have been set, it is not sufficient to review them once a year. Reviews should take place on a rolling basis with new key result areas and further measures being set on the way. Many organisations now review performance on a six-monthly cycle as well as holding regular informal discussions.

The process of review should be:

- two-way;
- forward-looking as well as reviewing the past;
- an opportunity for honest feedback as long as this is timed near to the event and focused on behaviours not personalities;
- an opportunity to identify training and development opportunities;
- motivational.

Importantly, for customer service to be fully integrated into the culture of the organisation it should always be included as a criterion for review.

Three-hundred-and-sixty-degree appraisal

Best-practice organisations have adopted upward appraisal or multi-rater, 360-degree appraisal as a means of encouraging greater customer focus.

Research carried out by the London Business School reveals that traditional appraisal systems serve only to encourage un-empowered behaviour. Upward appraisal and 360-degree appraisal (the first where feedback is supplied from a manager's staff, the second from a variety of sources including peers, managers, staff and customers) now account for approximately 15 per cent of all appraisals undertaken.

Organisations such as Post Office Ltd has found that upward appraisals encourage teamwork and supportive behaviour.

Managers at BT undertook multi-rater appraisal as part of a programme called 'Leading through Teamwork' and since the mid-1990s, 360-degree appraisal has been compulsory for all top managers.

The advantage of multi-rater appraisal is that:

- it provides more explicit understanding of customer needs;
- it provides specific targets for employee development which can be measured;
- it creates mutual cooperation between supplier and customer.

The disadvantages can be that:

- feedback for different groups can be confusing or conflicting;
- the administration process can be lengthy or time-consuming;
- the process requires the commitment of senior management, extensive training and testing.

FedEx is an example of another company that uses upward appraisal to set training and development targets for its top 75 managers in the UK. Every employee completes a questionnaire on the performance of his or her manager. The forms are analysed and returned to the managers. Good and average performing managers then arrange feedback sessions with their staff to see how they can improve their performance. Poor performing managers meet to plan improvements with the personnel department and are then re-surveyed six months later. The MD of Mortgage Express displays the results of 360-degree feedback in his office for all to see.

Coaching and development

Reviewing performance will not bring about customer-focused behaviours unless the actions that have been agreed to be taken *are* taken. This will often involve the manager in coaching his or her staff to reach their goals.

Coaching is not telling. It involves helping and supporting the members of staff to reach the goals that *they* set for themselves. The manager has a role to play in helping each member of staff to:

- set his or her own goals;
- see where he or she is now;
- review the options of how to get there;
- decide on the option which is right for him or her.

The skills of the coach include:

- empathy;
- a genuine desire to help the individual;
- active listening;
- questioning;
- understanding of the options available;
- being non-judgmental.

DEVELOPING A REWARD AND RECOGNITION SCHEME

Effective customer-oriented performance needs to be recognised and rewarded. The compensation and benefits an organisation provides its employees should reflect the importance given to customer-oriented behaviours.

What gets rewarded gets attention

The old adage, 'what gets measured gets done' can also be interpreted as, 'what gets rewarded gets attention'. Once you have established the motivational factors within your organisation, the next step is to select incentives which help achieve greater customer satisfaction – satisfy the company as well as employees.

- Who   –   individual, team or company.
- What   –   money or a token.
- Where   –   which locality.
- When   –   monthly, quarterly, or annually.
- Why   –   what behaviour you are supporting.

Many businesses adopt reward schemes in addition to performance management techniques which run alongside existing compensation and benefits packages to encourage excellent service.

Whenever an organisation develops a reward scheme for customer service a number of factors should be considered:

- What is the objective of the reward scheme and who is it intended to reward?
- Will the reward cover all the organisation?
- Who should make the reward? Customer, staff, management or colleagues?
- Do the rewards fit in with the values of the organisation?
- Are they to be based on recognition; token or monetary benefits?
- What is the budget for the reward and who will be responsible for allocating the reward?
- Is the reward fair to everyone?
- How long will the reward scheme operate?
- Will the scheme set a precedent and therefore be difficult to replace?
- How frequently will the excellent customer service be rewarded?
- How will the reward be communicated?

Payment for achievement of customer service objectives can have a powerful impact on getting target tasks achieved. Companies like IBM and Xerox link pay for some employees to levels of customer satisfaction. At Richer Sounds every time a customer ticks 'excellent' in a feedback form the sales assistant involved gets an extra £3. They receive £100 if all four areas tested in a mystery shopper exercise are correct. At Pret à Manger sandwich stores, if a member of staff scores 90 per cent or above in a mystery visit, he or she is entitled to a 50p-per-hour bonus for the rest of the week. Outstanding service is immediately rewarded with a £50 bonus.

Whenever a reward scheme is being devised, care needs to be taken that other, non-targeted areas do not suffer and that competition between groups or employees does not become destructive. For example, a large retailer introduced a scheme for all its front-line staff. This caused resentment among head office and support staff who were not included in the programme.

Team or individual

Managers who devise customer service reward schemes should consider carefully whether to award teams or individuals. Rewarding teams encourages collaboration and achievement of team goals, but it can discourage individual effort.

Although it is estimated that only a small proportion of organisations rewards on a team basis, there is a trend towards including an element of reward based on team performance in individual's pay as the emphasis on teamwork grows. At Sun Express, a subsidiary of Sun Microsystems in the United States, the telesales centre has a pay structure in which 70 per cent of the reps' commission is based on individual sales achievement, 20 per cent on a team sales target and the last 10 per cent on achieving further team objectives.

Beefeater restaurants' customer service programme focuses on teamwork as a means to achieve customer satisfaction. It has devised an incentive scheme called 'Gold' to encourage all its outlets to deliver excellent customer service. Once a unit reaches its customer target, all members of the team are eligible for prizes, chosen from a catalogue selection.

Individual customer service awards for outstanding performance can lead to definite improvements if the culture is right. However, such schemes need to have clear and fair selection criteria if they are not to demotivate lots of others who wonder why they have not been chosen.

At courier company TNT, individuals can be nominated by their colleagues or manager for 'going the extra mile.'

At TGI Fridays, members of staff who go beyond the call of duty are awarded a WOW badge.

Rewards can be made when teams reach improvement targets or for specific achievements such as speed of telephone response, or friendliness and courtesy with customers. Such rewards can be made to both teams and individuals. Importantly, they must be seen by those involved to be relevant and fair.

Selecting the appropriate criteria

Make certain that the target level of customer service is not attained at the expense of other aspects of the service. For example, the improvement of overall telephone response is a more customer-oriented achievement than the speed of answering the phone. In the latter case the customer's call may be answered quickly, but the customer may be kept holding on the phone and may not be transferred efficiently.

Avis includes in its customer satisfaction measurement both 'hard' measures of customer satisfaction such as speed of telephone response and 'soft' measures such as enthusiasm.

Whatever the criteria for the award they must be seen to be a credible base for decisions. Citroen, for example, consulted both its employees and its customers in order to establish the criteria for a 'customer-driven award scheme' for forecourt staff and their managers. Customers were asked to score forecourt staff against a range of criteria. All completed survey forms were entered into a prize draw for a Xantia car. The team that scored the most points from the feedback won prizes.

When to use rewards

Research shows that reward is best given when it is SMART:

- **S**imple, sincere
- **M**eaningful
- **A**ppropriate
- **R**elevant
- **T**imely

An example of a SMART reward was a call-centre manager who recognised one of her team leader's efforts by unexpectedly washing the team leader's dirty car. A simple gesture, but meaningful to the recipient and appropriate, as the team leader did not like attention or fuss.

The spectrum of rewards

Recognition plays an important part in raising the status of service quality throughout an organisation, and the manager or team leader plays a key role in acknowledging good performance.

Recognition is often a reward to employees, and this is often an incentive in itself for an employee to perform well. When deciding on a recognition

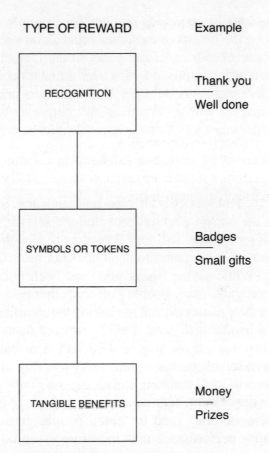

TYPE OF REWARD   Example

RECOGNITION

Thank you
Well done

SYMBOLS OR TOKENS

Badges
Small gifts

TANGIBLE BENEFITS

Money
Prizes

Figure 9.2 The spectrum of rewards

scheme for an organisation, a tailored approach is the most successful. Different approaches and emphases are needed for different types of business activity, the characteristics of the people within a service organisation, economic factors and other individual variables.

The nature of the business will determine the nature of the rewards and recognition scheme. At one end of the scale a 'well done' given publicly or in private is sufficient recognition for many people. At the counter at the local McDonald's, stars on a badge are seen as an adequate incentive. At the other end of the continuum the achievement of a single customer order may win several thousand pounds for the individual.

Within a customer service environment there are three types of incentive – recognition, symbols and tangible benefits, as shown in Figure 9.2. In wishing to recognise achievement managers need to consider which type of reward is most appropriate to the organisation.

An environmentally conscious retailer, for example, ran an incentive scheme based on the results of customer satisfaction surveys, and offered store managers weekends at leisure parks in the United States as prizes. Senior managers were surprised to discover a low level of enthusiasm for the scheme. Store managers were not motivated by a prize which was not seen to be compatible with the organisation's corporate 'values' and which only rewarded the managers for their branch's efforts, not their team.

Recognition

Recognising excellent service is an important motivator. Saying 'well done' gives value to the person who has provided the service. The most appropriate means of recognition will vary according to who the member of staff is and the nature of the organisation and does not necessarily have to be a concrete thing. While saying 'thank you' and 'well done' is sufficient to motivate and recognise many people's efforts, other people may feel motivated by seeing their names in print or shaking the chairman's hand. In other organisations a handwritten note, a public vote of thanks, a longer lunch break or an extra day's leave may be sufficient. Tim Waterstone, CEO of Waterstones booksellers, makes a point every morning of writing six postcards to members of staff, thanking and recognising their efforts.

Often employees comment on the negative aspects of organisational life and many managers may tend to 'catch people getting it wrong'. To recognise quality performance it is therefore essential that efforts that directly support specific service goals are recognised, particularly those that set good examples for others. Recognition should preferably be given for exceptional service rather than routine tasks.

Management must remember to recognise performance as soon after the event as possible. In this way, the manager reinforces the organisation's commitment to service quality as well as recognising the individual's contribution to service standards. Recognition should itself provide a fillip to the employee's performance.

Recognition does not merely need to come from managers or supervisors, however. Customer letters, comments and feedback are useful forms of recognition, as is peer group recognition. Opticians Vision Express, for example, regularly displays customer letters of recognition in its head office reception.

Exceptional performance may be recognised via awards which single out a 'job well done' or 'exceptional service to the internal customer', as well as managers or supervisors who 'manage people well'.

When Xerox won the first-ever European award for achievement in total quality, senior management decided that no one should work on their birthday that year as a token of appreciation.

Publicity is vital to the success of a recognition scheme. Kwit-Fit, for example, publicises service successes and failures to everyone on a monthly basis. Other organisations regularly include public 'well dones' to employees providing good service, with examples of their achievements in house magazines. Hotels and restaurants display photographs of 'employee of the month'. Other organisations use examples of exceptional customer service as part of their promotional literature.

Symbols and tokens

In many companies the recognition of service achievement goes hand-in-hand with symbols of achievement, be it a change in title, a certificate or a public written statement. The symbol of achievement may be very small – a bunch of flowers, a special card, a name badge – but whatever the symbol it must provide an accolade for the receiver.

At the AA, one patrolman is nominated each year as 'Patrolman of the Year'. The winner receives a two-week holiday and has a special logo emblazoned on his vehicle.

Some companies develop their own symbols of recognition. At my own company, for example, The Stairway Consultancy, a special set of steps has been commissioned which sits on the desk of those individuals who have received positive feedback, based on customer and peer group comments. The gesture is small and fun, but significant to the recipient.

Midland Bank managers can treat their staff to anything from a box of chocolates to £800 worth of travel vouchers.

At hi-fi retailers Richer Sounds, an ABCD badge (a gold aeroplane) is issued to all employees who go 'Above the Call of Duty' and deliver excellent service. This is awarded together with a personal 'thank you' letter from Julian Richer. ABCD achievers are also advertised in catalogues to customers.

Recognising the attainment of skill and competency levels after training courses by the issue of certificates, plaques or badges is another effective means of motivation.

Tangible rewards

Many companies link the attainment of customer satisfaction to the provision of cash awards, merchandise, holidays and other tangible rewards. Although these have been shown to work, research shows that they often only have a short-term effect on motivation. Incentives can often be creative and include such prizes as mystery weekends, film production courses and treasure hunts in chauffeur-driven vintage cars.

The Woolwich Building Society, for example, ran a 'Tribute Scheme' as part of its customer care programme in which staff who achieved high standards were given rewards with a range of gifts and activities.

At Pizza Hut, a £1 million reward scheme was developed for 8,000 employees, linking bonus payments with successful achievement of service standards, judged by mystery shoppers, achieving sales target levels and successful performance in a new training programme. At Moat House Hotel Group, general managers are given bonuses for service performance as well as profit performance. Moat House has found that its most profitable hotels produce above-average service performance. At Birmingham Midshires Building Society, an annual bonus for all employees is linked to customer-satisfaction measures.

Criteria for awards

Criteria for rewards can depend on customer, management and peer group nominations. In many retail outlets customers are asked to nominate individual staff for awards. Selfridges, for example, ran a 'Rewards for Excellence' scheme where customers were asked to nominate members of staff who provided excellent service. Supermarket chain, Safeway, ran a service award scheme which encouraged customers to nominate anyone in the store 'for making a difference'. Many organisations, such as Pizza Hut UK, use a combination of customer surveys and mystery-shopper reports as the basis for recognition. Significantly Pizza Hut recognises not just the top performers, but also the branches which make best improvements over time.

At Tandon Computers two different reward systems have been used. Many individuals, especially non-direct sales employees, have management-by-objective payments that are directly related to a specific customer or group of customers achieving their goals. Managers receive a 'measurement bonus' designed to reflect their success in attaining and increasing the level of satisfaction based on such criteria as repeat business with existing customers, loss of customer accounts, and survey results. Other reward schemes are in place, some of which include the individual's family.

In English Lake Hotels, staff nominate each other for individual awards. At the London Borough of Sutton, an ACE (Award for Customer to

Excellence) scheme means individuals can be nominated by their peers for awards. At Condant UK, a 'caught in the act' scheme allows employees to nominate colleagues for awards and spot prizes of sweets, teddy bears and tee-shirts. In other organisations, particularly those which are geographically spread or where there are many functions, award schemes have been developed based on the results of customer surveys and input from managers.

A management input is normally felt to be an important element of an award scheme since, although the scheme should not be based on management judgement alone, managers are able to take into account special circumstances (for example unforeseen absenteeism, renovation, special service efforts, etc) which can affect performance.

One restaurant chain, for example, has developed an award scheme based on feedback from customer questionnaires, mystery visits and phone calls, plus management reports. Awards are made on a regional basis. Feedback is converted into marks out of a hundred and each individual branch receives details of their results, together with a league table of other branches in the region. The award takes place once a quarter and the winning branch, and the branch which have made the greatest improvement over the last quarter, receive commemorative plaques. Members of staff from the winning branches each receive a special badge and a prize is also given to the team. The regional finalists enter an annual national award.

The scheme is perceived to have many benefits because, in addition to being a motivational tool, it recognises those branches which have made efforts to improve and also allows managers and employees in the branches to see which outlets provide the best service on both a regional and national basis and to analyse the reasons for this achievement.

European Quality Award and the balanced scorecard

Many organisations adopt a quality framework to assess their progress towards service quality. The European Foundation for Quality Management (EFQM) model and the balanced scorecard (see Chapter 2) provide a measure of progress in developing service quality.

The Benefits Agency has developed a Quality Framework of its own, based on the EFQM model. The framework is broken down into four areas:

- customer service;
- caring for staff;

- bias for action;
- value for money.

The framework was designed to give individual units the freedom to assess their progress towards service excellence and concentrate on areas for improvements. Each unit assesses its performance against these criteria and Quality Awards are made after external validation.

Partnership rewards

More often than not, reward and recognition programmes are focused on employees. Innovative companies recognise that suppliers and third parties connected with the business are equally as likely to benefit from incentive schemes as employees. This is particularly important as the trend towards out-sourcing increases. Incentive schemes do not have to be money based. The training and development department of one major bank invites its suppliers on a six-monthly basis to a special evening. It chooses two suppliers it sees as having provided outstanding service over the past six months to make a presentation of their work to the rest of the suppliers plus a group of managers from the business. The evening includes a briefing from the training and development director on future strategy and concludes with a dinner. The effect is not only recognition for the suppliers but increased commitment to the client.

Flexible benefits

Flexible benefits are also an increasingly important way of recognising an employee's worth. In recognition of the need to give employees greater choice, PricewaterhouseCooper developed a flexible benefits plan giving employees options to chose holiday, car, childcare vouchers, retail vouchers, travel, medical and dental insurance, permanent health insurance, critical illness, personal accident insurance, life assurance, pensions and cash.

REVIEW AND RENEW

There comes a time with all incentive programmes when they cease to motivate and energise employees. It is important to recognise that 12 months down the line what may have originally been a powerful scheme may have lost its bite. One building society ran a reward scheme linked to its customer satisfaction programme. Branches competed against each other to gain points based on feedback from customer questionnaires, customer focus groups and mystery shoppers. Six months into the programme the building society surveyed its staff to gain their reaction to the scheme. As a result it supplemented the programme with internal awards for excellent service, and a percentage of points was allocated on a regional basis by area managers who could take into account individual branch circumstances. In the following year it again reviewed the scheme and added, at the staff's suggestion, awards for those branches which had made the best progress plus an annual competition for regional finalists which was created in an 'It's a Knockout' style.

SUMMARY

The recognition and communication of examples of service excellence are essential elements in creating commitment to a service quality philosophy.

Best practice organisations build effective performance management systems which often include customer service competences and upward or 360-degree appraisal. Coaching plays an essential part in performance management.

The type and basis of a reward scheme need to be given careful consideration to ensure that it achieves a motivational effect and that it fits in with the values of the organisation.

Rewards can be based on customer, peer group, management and external feedback.

Managers in particular should be encouraged to 'catch people getting it right' as token and monetary award schemes can often be no substitute for saying 'well done' for a good job.

ACTION CHECKLIST

Practical exercises you can undertake after reading this chapter are to:

1. Survey your staff to establish what motivates them at work.

2. Provide training to managers in creating a motivating climate.

3. Help managers to give positive feedback by showing them what it feels like to receive positive feedback – compliment your staff the next time they provide a good service.

4. Use the EQFM award criteria as a checklist for the health of your service quality programme – what score would your company obtain?

5. Establish a league table of service performance, based on customer feedback. Reward people who make the best improvements over time.

6. Ensure career progression within your organisation is linked to the provision of good service.

7. Investigate a bonus scheme for senior management based on customer satisfaction indicators.

8. Feed back customer comments and compliments, and ensure that a note of any relating to individuals is made on the relevant employee's records.

9. Investigate awards for individuals and teams who provide good service based on recognition, token or monetary benefits.

10. Instigate a 'job well done award' for individual employees.

11. Issue certificates of achievement or similar token awards when employees attain defined training and skills levels.

12. Instigate an award for good service to the internal customer.

13. Develop a bonus scheme for support staff, based on front-line staff achievement.

14. Develop a 'people management' award for managers and ask staff to make nominations.

15. Ensure team as well as individual service excellence is recognised.

16. Adopt a system of 360-degree appraisal for your management team.

17. Publicise examples of good service in staff magazines, customer literature and on the Internet.

18. Develop a fun symbol of success which is linked to the name or values of your company.

19. Give departmental managers a cream bun allowance.

20. Provide training in performance management.

21. Include customer service as a key aspect in appraisal.

22. Develop customer service competences in your staff.

23. Use the EFQM or the balanced-scorecard approach as a departmental or company-wide measurement scheme.

Sustaining a Customer Focus

Jan Carlson of Scandinavian Airlines is quoted as saying: 'Excellent service is about being 1 per cent better at 100 things, not 100 per cent better at one thing.'

A step-by-step approach to service improvement aids the integration of a service ethic into an organisation's culture. This involves cultural change, which many experts estimate can take between two and five years to achieve.

In this chapter the barriers to implementing a long-term service quality programme within an organisation are discussed and a range of ideas put forward on how to sustain a customer focus.

PROBLEMS IN SUSTAINING THE FOCUS

For service champions who take quality to their hearts customer service can become a way of life. It can change not only the way that they conduct their business life but also how they approach their relationships outside work, encouraging openness, fairness and empowerment.

Nevertheless, other people within an organisation committed to quality may not show the same transformation. Every company trying to engender a service ethic encounters problems in implementation. These problems normally occur after the launch of the initiative, when the first enthusiasm has died down (Figure 10.1).

Although difficulties are specific to each organisation, in general the reasons for lack of ongoing support of service strategies can be summarised as follows:

1. Senior managers do not endorse customer service with ongoing commitment – in the face of more pressing business problems, many senior managers abdicate the task of spearheading the customer care strategy to their subordinates and pay lip-service to customer satisfaction.

Figure 10.1 Customer care plateau

2. Lack of a defined customer service strategy – service quality programmes happen on a piecemeal basis and are not explicitly linked to organisational performance.
3. Service quality fails to be integrated into company culture and all aspects of the management of the business – the management style within the company is so ingrained that the service quality philosophy fails to break the organisation's paradigm and old habits continue.
4. The concept is introduced with too much razzmatazz and is seen as 'flavour of the month', so scepticism exists among staff – members of staff are still resistant to the programme; they are not fully convinced of the need to change and do not 'own' the programme.
5. Managers' behaviours fail to demonstrate a customer focus – they send the message, 'Do what I say, not what I do.'
6. The organisation does not listen to its customers – it has its own agenda and perceptions of what is important and these do not match the customer's view.
7. Internal customer relationships have not been fostered – the 'them and us' barriers still exist and efforts made to overcome these have failed.
8. Customer service has not been fully integrated into the training and development process – training in customer service may be seen as an abstract concept or a one-off event. There is no attempt to integrate service into recruitment and induction, competences and performance review. Alternatively, the service quality programme may be seen to be led by one department and not fully integrated into all parts of the business.

9. Improvement teams have not produced results – the teams have spent too much time discussing minor details without achieving tangible results.
10. Poor communications and no link with rewards – the results of service initiatives have not been fed back to employees and there has been failure to recognise achievement.
11. Managers have not viewed improvements in customer satisfaction as part of a culture-change process, consequently expectations are of short-term gains and these have not been forthcoming.

Every company will experience these and other problems in implementing and sustaining a customer focus. Philip Crosby, the quality guru, says:

> Quality has much in common with sex. Everyone is for it. (Under certain conditions, of course.) Everyone feels they understand it. (Even though they wouldn't want to explain it.) Everyone thinks execution is only a matter of following natural inclinations. (After all, we do get along somehow.) And, of course, most people feel that all problems in these areas are caused by other people. (If only they would take time to do things right.)

Although this analogy initially causes amusement, its underlying message is true.

To be successful a service quality programme needs to lead to demonstrable changes *in behaviour* and to be seen as a regular part of all employees' jobs, not a novelty – you don't have to be sick to get better.

There are no set rules on the most appropriate means of overcoming difficulties in engendering a service culture – each organisation needs to develop its own strategy for maintaining the initiative.

Supermarket retailer Tesco's continued focus on the customer has paid great dividends. In 2001 Tesco's sales reached £20 billion. Tesco.com is the world's biggest online retailer with sales of £300 million a year and breaking even.

Tesco's success story is even more remarkable given that it came from a culture of 'pile it high, sell it cheap'. By benchmarking the then market leader, Sainsburys, in the late 1980s and early 1990s, underlying profits moved from £30 million in 1977 to £544 million in 1992. Yet in the early 1990s the company begin to realise that customers were disaffected.

Tesco developed a five-step plan to achieve a customer focus:

- Core purpose
- Marketing

- Market research
- Innovate and invest
- Look after staff.

A huge research study of 250,000 customers helped re-focus Tesco in fulfilling customer needs, not chasing the competition. The Tesco Clubcard, introduced in 1995, now has 14 million members. Continuous listening to customers has allowed Tesco to prioritise service improvements such as shortening checkout queues, family parking, wider store entrances, 24 hour opening. At the same time Tesco set about building simpler, better work processes and developing balanced scorecards ('Steering Wheels') to measure success.

Tesco developed a change programme called 'Futures' to help create a greater customer orientation in its employees. This included the introduction of 360 degree feedback for all directors and managers. Store workers were encouraged to come up with innovations in work design and customer service, many of which, such as employing runners to deliver food to shelf stockers, have resulted in increased customer retention.

DEVELOPING A MAINTENANCE STRATEGY

Just as it is important to develop a plan and strategy for the implementation of a service philosophy, the development of a maintenance strategy is vital to ensure the programme is continuous.

It is useful to discuss and agree a maintenance strategy at the beginning of a programme to ensure its survival and to anticipate pitfalls as it progresses. A plan to keep the programme alive needs to be developed and reviewed on an ongoing basis.

In preparing a strategy, senior managers need to avoid overstating the benefits of a service philosophy as this can lead to disillusionment and unrealistic expectations. Likewise, managers need to avoid giving the impression that service quality is a finite task and that service initiatives will bring about instant solutions. IBM in Japan, for example, has been developing its quality programme for the past 20 years and improvements are ongoing and incremental.

The maintenance strategy should also ensure that understanding is generated of the need for ongoing management commitment and the customer renewal and refreshment of genuine initiatives.

Lasting commitment

Organisations must constantly review their progress to build on their strengths and overcome weaknesses, rather than abandon a programme and adopt another strategy which may in turn become 'flavour of the month'.

REVIEWING PROGRESS

At regular periods it is essential to review the progress of a quality initiative (Figure 10.2). Measurement of customer satisfaction and employee opinion should provide the starting point for a review. Questions to ask include:

- How far are we achieving our original objectives?
- How does the performance to date measure against the agreed key success criteria?
- What are the successes of the programme – both tangible and intangible?
- How can the organisation build on these successes?
- What are the disappointments?
- What have been the major barriers in preventing the organisation reaching its goals?

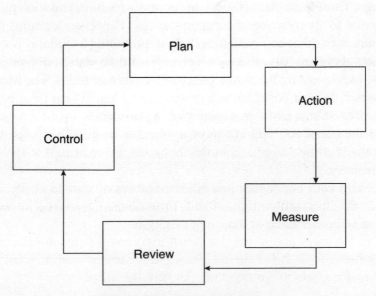

Figure 10.2 Cycle of activity

- Have our customers' expectations of service quality changed?
- How do our company's service standards now compare with the competition?
- In which areas does significant improvement to service quality still need to be made?
- What are the major priorities, and in which order should they be addressed?

As many people should be involved in the review process as possible – employees, customers and suppliers.

In reviewing achievements to date and developing a maintenance strategy to overcome disappointments, particular attention should be given to the following elements:

- Strategic clarity.
- Developing the role of managers.
- Ongoing monitoring.
- Empowerment, involvement and communication.
- The internal customer.
- Training.
- Motivation and reward.
- Reinforcement.

Consistency and attention to detail are key to reinforcing a service quality message. There is no blanket secret to success – each organisation must tailor its service to its own specific circumstances. However, learning from the experiences of other companies can help in providing a stimulus for change.

Below there are lists of ideas which organisations have adopted in developing plans to ensure the maintenance of a customer focus. The lists are not exhaustive, but are based upon a selection of ideas which have been tried and seen to be successful in a variety of organisations.

Use the ideas you feel are most applicable to your business, together with other actions suggested in this book, to arrive at a plan for ongoing improvement.

Speak to your colleagues and other members of staff to identify further ways of developing a customer focus. Provide team leaders with an outline of these and other ideas as a prompt to action.

Strategic clarity

Management can show their commitment to the customer on an ongoing basis by visibly demonstrating the importance of the service message in a number of ways:

- Review the progress of your service quality initiative at every level, develop a maintenance strategy which encourages continuous improvement.
- Ensure that the objectives of the programme are clear to everyone throughout the organisation. Remind everyone of what these objectives are.
- Regularly review service performance against key success factors.
- Feed back the progress of the customer service initiative at regular intervals to all employees.
- Regularly share business information with employees – financial performance, customer feedback and performance against competitors.
- Make information on what is happening in the service world available to employees.
- Review the organisation's mission and vision – is it still appropriate?
- Spend time and money in training and development for all members of staff.
- Spend more time *listening* to staff's ideas – and act upon them.
- Be available to welcome new employees – impress on them the importance of service quality.
- Spend more time with customers, welcome and act on their feedback.
- Publish examples of good service, be honest about poor performance.
- Instigate a programme of ongoing measurement.
- Publish a corporate quality service action plan and regularly review this.
- Eliminate the special status of any one group within the organisation.
- Publish a communications charter.
- Hold more effective meetings, make sure they start on time and keep to the point.
- Ensure that all work is error free.
- Instigate a company-wide programme of care for the local community.
- Enhance the environment – both the premises external customers use and those of internal customers.
- Ensure that health and safety standards are met within your organisation.
- Review the infrastructure of the organisation to ensure a leaner, simpler, direct customer focus.

- Identify with members of staff – wear their uniform, eat with them at break times.
- Review the cost of service quality and prioritise areas for improvement.
- Talk at external and internal conferences and customer events about the organisation's service quality initiatives.
- Integrate customer service into all job descriptions.
- Develop a competency framework and include customer service as a key element.
- Make service quality an important part of the performance review system, and the remuneration package.
- Regularly visit employees in all parts of the organisation – make some of these visits unannounced. Spend more time listening than talking.
- Attend other group's team meetings – invite outsiders to your own.
- Publish employee suggestions for sustaining a customer focus. Provide employees with ideas to stimulate further improvements.
- Hold cross-functional workshops to review progress and come up with new ideas for improving service quality.
- Review and improve your processes.
- Report on the progress of the customer care initiative to all stakeholders.
- Use outside experts to help review your organisation's progress.
- Benchmark your customer service.
- Compare notes on progress with other organisations undertaking similar programmes.
- Include reports on service improvements in all team briefing material.
- Attend customer focus groups.
- Encourage senior management to join a quality improvement group.
- Conduct an internal audit of employees' perceptions of the programme.
- Celebrate success.
- Continuously plan, action, measure and review.

The developing role of managers

Line managers have an important role to play in coaching and developing their staff to deliver excellent service. This can be achieved by:

- Sharing ideas and information with staff and colleagues.
- Including service criteria in the recruitment and selection processes.
- Involving customers in the selection of new recruits.
- Developing and reviewing departmental action plans.
- Linking customer satisfaction to performance reviews.

- Setting up and encouraging problem-solving teams.
- Sharing progress and ideas on service improvements with customers.
- Adopting a customer.
- Making time to be with staff.
- Measuring supplier performance.
- Undertaking 360-degree appraisal.
- Publicly recognising the service excellence.
- Contacting the DTI for promotional literature and videos on quality.
- Issuing questionnaires on the quality of the service the department or function provides.
- Encouraging visits to customers among staff.
- Becoming mystery shoppers.
- Attending external conferences on service quality.
- Providing feedback from customers to staff.
- Reporting regularly on departmental or team progress.
- Facilitating training sessions in customer service.
- Agreeing specific goals and performance standards with staff.
- Encouraging creativity and new ideas.
- Facilitating the setting and revision of standards.
- Ensuring regular contact between front-line and support staff.
- Recognising the cost of quality, conformance and non-conformance.
- Holding informal discussions with staff on the importance of service quality and welcoming and acting on their feedback.
- Setting up a management quality action team, with managers seconded on a rotational basis from all parts of the business.
- Manning the organisation's customer service and complaints department with managers, rather than members of staff.
- Developing a customer service training package for line managers to use in coaching their staff.

Ongoing monitoring

The ongoing monitoring of customer satisfaction is an important element in sustaining a service initiative. Action which can be taken includes:

- Using CRM techniques to identify most profitable target customers.
- Using CRM techniques to tailor your offered services.
- Measuring customer satisfaction on a regular basis.
- Conducting an annual audit of customer satisfaction.
- Sending questionnaires to internal as well as external customers.

- Undertaking telephone and Internet surveys.
- Visiting customers on a regular basis.
- Providing a freephone telephone line for customers to phone in with their comments.
- Doing the same for staff.
- Holding focus groups and user panels with customers.
- Conducting attitude surveys among staff.
- Improving the time it takes to conduct and feed back results of surveys.
- Telephoning competitors.
- Asking customers to identify those areas most in need of improvement and actioning these improvements.
- Reviewing the effectiveness of measurement systems on an ongoing basis.
- Plotting customer satisfaction and importance factors on an ongoing basis.
- Feeding back results to all employees.
- Conducting an internal audit on employee care.
- Publishing a league table of results of customer satisfaction surveys.
- Linking measurement to reward systems.
- Making awards for the most significant service improvement.
- Reviewing how results of customer surveys are presented.
- Taking action as a result of customer feedback.
- Involving employees in this action.
- Recognising successes.

Empowerment, involvement and communication

Empowering employees to take greater control and decision-making in their jobs is a powerful way of becoming more customer focused. Involving all employees in service improvements encourages ownership. Communication of the progress of a customer service campaign also allows positive examples to be set for employees. Communication of service promises to external customers allows an organisation to differentiate itself from the competition.

Ideas which can be adopted to maintain involvement and consistency in communication include:

- Conducting an audit of all employees to identify the degree of decision-making they currently have.

- Setting a framework for empowerment and agreeing the level and degree of authority you wish employees to adopt.
- Providing training to managers in coaching and facilitation skills.
- Not being quick to chastise employees when they make mistakes – use these as a learning opportunity.
- Providing encouragement and support to employees to take on new responsibilities.
- Publicising examples of successful empowerment.
- Encouraging each manager to ask his or her team what additional responsibilities they can take on and how their manager can help them in this.
- Holding 'a day in the life of' event, to encourage understanding of everyone's roles.
- Developing a quality newsletter for employees.
- Encouraging customer visits by all staff.
- Holding an exhibition of the functions of the different departments within an organisation.
- Placing reminder posters around the organisation.
- Developing a logo for a service programme and applying this to a variety of material on a consistent basis.
- Publishing the results of service improvements on a regular basis.
- Developing a suggestion scheme.
- Producing photographs of key people in each team/department and publishing these for all employees.
- Encouraging job swaps and secondments.
- Running a name campaign to encourage everyone to give their name when dealing with customers.
- Holding a competition to see how many customers employees know by name both inside and outside the organisation.
- Holding a national conference for service improvement team members to review progress and share ideas.
- Establishing a directory of who does what within the organisation, by function as well as department.
- Encouraging front-line staff to 'look their best' for customers by placing a reminder slogan on mirrors and doors of cloakrooms.
- Providing videos with examples of good practice from different parts of the organisation.
- Encouraging employees to develop a 'good service' diary.
- Reminding employees on all pay-slips that the customer pays the salary.
- Encouraging participation in service quality teams.
- Rotating the members of service quality teams.

- Holding conferences and roadshows to communicate and review progress.
- Holding a 'never say no' day where employees are encouraged to take a positive attitude to customers.
- Providing signs and name plaques for all members of the organisation.
- Encouraging new recruits to sit in on service improvement meetings.
- Developing cross-functional teams to solve problems.
- Encouraging support staff to adopt a sales person and vice versa.
- Holding a 'zero defects' day.
- Sending letters of encouragement to all employees from senior management.
- Encouraging employees to present the successes of service initiatives to their peers.
- Regularly asking staff their perceptions of customer expectations and providing information on what these actually are.
- Setting up a network of 'service leaders' throughout the organisation.
- Asking team members to appraise their standard-keeping.
- Communicating the organisation's customer care policy to external customers via posters, leaflets, plaques and other communication material.
- Ensuring that all communication material is written in simple, user-friendly language.
- Instigating a programme of community care such as helping the elderly, sponsoring local charities, etc.
- Asking employees to keep a log of service improvements and reviewing this.
- Reinforcing the importance of service in the organisation's annual report.
- Holding customer evenings and events.
- Reinforcing the importance of employees through including staff in advertisements.
- Publishing departmental/team newsletters on service quality.
- Providing welcoming signs in reception areas.
- Involving team members in formal reviews of the service quality.

Training and development

To be effective customer service training must be constantly renewed and refreshed. Action that can be taken to ensure this includes:

- Providing training and development for all levels of the organisation from senior management downwards.
- Conducting a training needs analysis at regular intervals to identify new areas of training needs.
- Reviewing the effectiveness of the training provided and developing plans for the future.
- Keeping trainers regularly informed of the progress of customer service initiative.
- Integrating customer service training into induction.
- Providing training in TQM techniques.
- Including customers in service training.
- Ensuring customer service training includes skills, knowledge, attitude development, empowerment and process improvement.
- Offering a programme of self-development to all employees.
- Offering opportunities to take an NVQ in customer service.
- Including part-timers in training programmes.
- Keeping a record of all employee training.
- Providing certificates when training has taken place.
- Integrating customer service into a competency framework.
- Developing a recruitment and selection process which highlights customer-mindedness.
- Ensuring all employees have sufficient product training.
- Providing specialist speakers on specific topic areas and on developments in new products and services.
- Providing training in leadership to managers.
- Developing a programme of coaching and facilitation for managers.
- Including practical work-related activities in all training programmes.
- Being creative in training – looking for new ways of providing stimulation such as the use of music, acting and drawing.
- Ensuring all employees receive interpersonal training as well as technical training.
- Sending employees on external as well as internal training courses to benefit from other companies' experiences.
- Encouraging managers to provide on-the-job training.
- Coaching managers in training techniques.
- Using innovative training techniques such as open and distance learning and activity-based learning.
- Integrating learning into the work place via work-based activities.
- Using tape-recordings and videos of employees and competitors providing customer service to stimulate discussion.

- Encouraging the use of competitive products by employees.
- Providing team-building events and training for work teams.

Motivation and reward

Incentives and rewards are frequently used to encourage motivation and recognise good service performance, thus maintaining a service ethic. Actions which organisations can adopt to encourage high performance include:

- Integrating customer service as a key component of appraisals.
- Instigating a programme of staff care.'
- Encouraging upward or 360 degree appraisal.
- Rewarding complaint-free departments.
- Devising non-monetary awards such as plaques and badges.
- Developing bonus schemes linked to attainment of quality service.
- Holding formal presentations and thank yous for service heroes.
- Developing prize schemes based on feedback from customers.
- Instigating good manager awards based on staff feedback.
- Instigating internal customer service awards for the quality of service provided internally.
- Recognising the efforts of service teams rather than individuals.
- Conducting surveys among employees to develop a suitable motivational scheme.
- Holding company-wide competitions to encourage service improvements.
- Regularly reviewing and publishing the results of motivation schemes.
- Training all managers in performance review techniques.
- Encouraging regular feedback and review sessions between managers and their staff.

REINFORCEMENT

Organisations must constantly reinforce the message that service quality improvements are continuous and that the organisation has made a lasting commitment to the customer.

All indications point towards continued growth in the importance of the customer, not only in the UK and Europe but on a worldwide basis. Those businesses which strive for greater empowerment, teamwork, involvement and participation from their employees in service improvements and ensure effective leadership of their organisations can be expected to maintain a competitive advantage.

SUMMARY

This chapter outlines typical problems encountered in sustaining a customer focus and provides suggestions for maintaining a service philosophy. I hope that you can use many of the suggestions to help your organisation continue to focus on the customer.

Use the ideas in this chapter to aid an honest discussion at all levels of the organisation on the progress to date of your initiatives. Debate which of these suggestions, or others you may come up with, can be applied in your organisation.

To summarise the contents of this book in a few words: all business depends on customers, and the quality of service provided to customers says more about your products and your organisation than any words, written or spoken. Customer orientation must become a way of life. Commitment to customer satisfaction ends only when your business ends.

I wish you good luck with your quest for service excellence, and leave the last words to Professor Theodore Levitt:

> A customer is an asset that's usually more precious than the tangible assets on the balance sheet.
> You can usually buy balance sheet assets – there are lots of willing sellers.
> You cannot so easily buy customers.

Additional Sources of Information

PUBLICATIONS

There are numerous publications on customer-care-related topics. Here is a selection of some of the better ones:

Albrecht, Karl (1990) *Service Within*, Dow Jones-Irwin.

Chang, Richard Y and Kelly, P Keith (1995) *Satisfying Internal Customers First! A practical guide to improving internal and external customer satisfaction*, Kogan Page.

Christopher, Martin (1992) *The Customer Service Planner*, Butterworth Heinemann.

Clutterbuck, David (1995) *The Power of Empowerment*, Kogan Page.

Freemantle, David (1998) *What Customers Like About You: Adding emotional value*, Nicholas Brearley.

Heskett, James *et al* (1997) *The Service Profit Chain*, Free Press.

Hill, Nigel (1998) *The Handbook of Customer Service Measurement*, Gower.

Martin, William B (1993) *Quality Customer Service*, Crisp Publications.

McKean, John (1999) *The Information Masters: Secrets of the customer race*, John Wiley & Son.

Murley, Peter (1997) *Gower Handbook of Customer Service*, Gower Publishing.

Peters, Glen (1994) *Benchmarking Customer Service*, Pitman Publishing.

Reichheld, Frederick F (1996) *The Loyalty Effect: The hidden force behind growth, profits, and lasting value*, Harvard Business School Press.

Richer, Julian (1996) *The Richer Way*, Emap Business Communications.

Seybold, Patricia (1998) *Customers.com*, Times Books.

Sterne, Jim (1996) *Customer Service on the Internet*, John Wiley & Sons.

Williams, Tom (1996) *Dealing With Complaints*, Gower Publishing.

TRAINING MATERIAL

There are many items of training material and videos available on customer care and service quality. Companies such as Video Arts and Melrose, both based in London, provide training material and videos to rent or to purchase.

FOR MORE INFORMATION

Information on customer focus can also be obtained by contacting organisations such as:

European Foundation for Quality Management
www.efqm.org

e-customerserviceworld.co.uk
info@quest-media.com

Customer Management magazine
www.info@quest-media.com

The Stairway Consultancy
www.thestairway.co.uk

References

1. 'When Missionary Zeal Falls Flat' by Philip Sadler, *Director*, July 1993.
2. 'The Pioneers who Put People First' by Rob MacLachan, *People Management*, 10 August 1995.
3. 'Case Studies in Organisational Excellence', published by IFS, October 1993.
4. 'Case Studies in Organisational Excellence', published by IFS, October 1993.
5. 'The Pioneers who Put People First' by Rob MacLachan, *People Management*, 10 August 1995.
6. 'Legends in Their Own Time' by Ian Fraser, *Marketing Business*, December/January 1995/6.
7. 'Mr Motivator' by Julian Richer, *Director*, January 1996.
8. 'Hi-de-hi Hopes of Family Fun' by Rowena Rees, *Sunday Times*, 11 June 1995.
9. Based on paper given at the Effective Complaint Management seminar, April 1995.
10. Based on paper given at the Measuring and Monitoring Customer Satisfaction seminar, January 1995.
11. 'Making a Meal of Learning' by David Littlefield, *Personnel Management Plus*, October 1994.
12. Based on paper given at the MRS customer care seminar, October 1991.
13. For more information see 'Customer Focus for Successful Business Strategy at Eurodollar' by John Leigh, *Managing Service Quality*, number 4, 1995.
14. 'The Value of Strong Opinion' by Anet Arkin, *Personnel Management Plus*, September 1994.
15. 'Peak Performance' by Lisa Donaldson, *Personnel Today*, 9 February 1993.
16. 'The Message Not the Media' by Alan Mitchell, *Marketing Business*, November 1994.
17. With thanks to Kim Parish, Scottish and Newcastle Retail.
18. With thanks to Kim Parish, Scottish and Newcastle Retail.

Index